Building Classroom Discipline

fifth edition

Building Classroom Discipline

C. M. Charles
San Diego State University

Collaboration by
Gail W. Senter
Karen Blaine Barr

 **Longman** *Publishers USA*

Building Classroom Discipline, Fifth Edition

Longman, 10 Bank Street, White Plains, N.Y. 10606

Associated companies:
Longman Group Ltd., London
Longman Cheshire Pty., Melbourne
Longman Paul Pty., Auckland
Copp Clark Longman Ltd., Toronto

Photo Credits
p. 9: The University Archives, Wayne State University
p. 27: Courtesy of Harvard University
p. 43: The University Archives, Wayne State University
p. 61: AP/Wide World Photos
p. 83: Courtesy of the Alfred Adler Institute of Chicago
p. 105: Courtesy of Lee Canter & Associates
p. 127: AP/Wide World Photos
p. 145: Courtesy of William Glasser Inc.
p. 163: Courtesy of Effectiveness Training International
p. 183: Courtesy of Dr. Richard Curwin & Dr. Allen Mendler, Discipline Associates

Associate editor: Travis Lester
Production editor: Ann P. Kearns
Editorial Assistant: Matthew Baker
Text design adaptation and cover design: Delgado Design, Inc.
Production supervisor: Richard C. Bretan
Compositor: R/TSI

Library of Congress Cataloging-in-Publication Data

Charles, C. M.
    Building classroom discipline / C.M. Charles : collaboration by
Gail W. Senter, Karen Blaine Barr. — 5th ed.
        p.   cm.
    Includes bibliographical references and index.
    ISBN 0-8013-1507-7
    1. School discipline.   2. Classroom management.   I. Senter, Gail
W. II. Barr, Karen Blaine.   III. Title.
LB3012.C46   1996
371.5—dc20   95-14822
                                                         CIP

2 3 4 5 6 7 8 9 10-MA-9998979695

Contents

CHAPTER 4   **THE GINOTT MODEL: DISCIPLINE THROUGH CONGRUENT COMMUNICATION   61**

PART II.   THE APPLICATION MODELS   81

CHAPTER 5   **THE DREIKURS MODEL: DISCIPLINE THROUGH DEMOCRATIC TEACHING AND CONFRONTING MISTAKEN GOALS   83**

CHAPTER 9   THE GORDON MODEL: DISCIPLINE THROUGH DEVELOPING SELF-CONTROL   163

CHAPTER 10   THE CURWIN AND MENDLER MODEL: DISCIPLINE THROUGH DIGNITY AND HOPE   183

CHAPTER 13　**EXEMPLARS: PERSONAL SYSTEMS OF DISCIPLINE**　**237**

Preface

Teachers are keenly concerned with maintaining pleasant, well-mannered behavior in their classrooms, and there are times when they must use some form of discipline in order for class time to remain interesting and productive. *Building Classroom Discipline*, Fifth Edition, presents the suggestions of leading authorities for reducing the types of student misbehavior that stifle learning and produce stress for both teachers and students.

Building Classroom Discipline is appropriate for pre-service courses in discipline and classroom management, learning and instruction, methods of teaching, and educational psychology. It is equally appropriate for teachers already in service who are experiencing difficulty with classroom discipline. Instructors in school district training programs and teacher institutes will also find the book useful.

In keeping with previous editions, *Building Classroom Discipline*, Fifth Edition, takes an eminently practical approach to classroom discipline. Comprehensive enough to serve as a single or primary text, yet compact enough for use with other texts, it describes for analysis models of discipline developed by some of the most influential educational thinkers of the past half century. Information about each model is augmented with material on related topics, such as organizing classrooms to reduce misbehavior and tailoring systems of discipline to teacher preferences, the realities of school, and the special needs of students. Application exercises are included to help users refine their discipline skills.

NEW TO THIS EDITION

The fifth edition features several important additions and modifications. For example:

- *Two new models of discipline* have been added to the original core of eight: that of Thomas Gordon, which emphasizes the development of student self-control, and that of Richard Curwin and Allen Mendler, which stresses student dignity and the restoration of hope. Gordon's model epitomizes present efforts to help students accept greater responsibility for their own behavior. Curwin and Mendler's model is especially valuable to teachers of students whose behavior is chronically disruptive.

- *The Canter model* has been thoroughly revised in consultation with the author to reflect the newer philosophy and procedures stressed in Canter's Assertive Discipline.

- *The Dreikurs model* has been updated through inclusion of Linda Albert's expansions on Dreikurs's original work.

- *The Glasser model* has been updated to reflect Glasser's increased emphasis on control theory in matters of education and discipline.

- *Classification of models.* In this edition, the 10 models have been separated into two groups: (1) foundation models that, although very innovative and influential when introduced, are insufficiently complete to serve as overall discipline systems in modern classrooms and (2) application models that are balanced, complete, and suitable for use in today's classrooms.

- *Additional exemplary systems of discipline* have been included in Chapter 13. These exemplars are systems of discipline contributed by teachers. They reflect those teachers' preferences and show the attention given to student needs.

- *Two appendixes and a bibliography* have been added. Appendix I includes classroom scenarios to be used for behavior analysis, practice, and application of new learnings; Appendix II includes a comprehensive list of the approximately 300 discipline concepts that receive attention in the text; and the Bibliography includes a comprehensive list of approximately 150 references and recommended readings.

- *Chapter format.* Chapters 1 through 10 now present the various discipline models within a consistent format. The models include biographical information about the models' originators, their contributions to discipline, their central focuses, their principal concepts and teachings, analyses of the models, ideas for initiating the models, and additional comments.

- *New exercises* have been added following each foundation and application model to help users understand and apply the information presented in each chapter. Concept Cases, which call for application of different model techniques to the same instances of misbehavior, continue to appear in many chapters, facilitating readers' understanding and permitting comparisons with various authorities' approaches.

ACKNOWLEDGMENTS

The author gratefully acknowledges the valuable contributions to this edition made by the following people:

Teachers

Roy Allen

Constance Bauer

Linda Blacklock

Tom Bolz

Michael Brus

Gail Charles

Ruth Charles

Diana Cordero

Keith Correll

Barbara Gallegos

Kris Halverson

Leslie Hays

Elaine Maltz

Colleen Meagher

Nancy Natale

Linda Pohlenz

David Sisk

Deborah Sund

Mike Straus

Deborah Trivoli

Virginia Villalpando

Critical Reviewers

Linda Albert, Cooperative Discipline Institute

Dale Allee, Southwest Missouri State University

Lee Canter, Lee Canter & Associates, Inc.

Richard Curwin, Discipline Associates

Philip DiMattia, Boston College

Karen M. Dutt, Indiana State University

Carolyn Eichenberger, St. Louis University

Thomas Gordon, Effectiveness Training International

Marci Greene, University of South Florida at Ft. Myers

C. Bobbi Hansen, University of San Diego

Thomas J. Lasley, The University of Dayton

Bernice Magnus-Brown, University of Maine

Janey L. Montgomery, University of Northern Iowa

Merrill M. Oaks, Washington State University

Mary C. Shake, University of Kentucky

JoAnne Smatlan, Seattle Pacific University

Kay Stickle, Ball State University

Sylvia Tinling, University of California, Riverside

Kathleen Whittier, State University of New York at Plattsburgh

Publication

Longman Editor Laura McKenna
Longman Associate Editor Travis Lester
Longman Production Editor Ann Kearns

Introduction

The scene is an inner-city school. Classroom 314 is quiet as students listen attentively to the teacher's questions about a recent lesson. Suddenly, eager hands begin to wave and bodies twist out of their seats amidst shouts of "ooh me," "I know," "ooh-oh." Quiet returns when one student is chosen to answer. As soon as she has responded, others begin to yell out refutations or additions and compete again for teacher recognition. As they participate wholeheartedly in class, several students are simultaneously but secretly passing notes and candy and signaling to each other in sign and face language.

When the questions end and seat work begins, some students offer to help others who are unsure of how to proceed.

But across the hall in room 315, chaos reigns. The room is noisy with the shouting, laughter, and movement of many children. Though most students are seated, many are walking or running aimlessly around the classroom. Some stop at others' desks, provoke them briefly, and move on. Several students who are lining up textbooks as "race courses" for toy cars laugh when the teacher demands their attention.

As the teacher struggles to ask a question over the noise, few if any students volunteer to answer. When one student does respond correctly, others yell out, "You think you're so smart." (Schwartz, 1981, p. 99)

By most teachers' standards, the discipline in Room 314 is good, while that in Room 315 is poor. But what is the difference? In both rooms, students are making noise and behaving in ways usually considered unacceptable. Yet the teacher in Room 314 is probably quite satisfied with the lesson, while the teacher in Room 315 is probably frustrated and laboring with stress. Why? Because in the teacher's eyes, students in Room 315 are misbehaving, while those in Room 314 are not.

BEHAVIOR AND MISBEHAVIOR

Behavior is whatever one does, whether good or bad, right or wrong, helpful or useless, productive or wasteful. *Misbehavior* is behavior that is considered inappropriate for the setting or situation in which it occurs. Generally speaking, classroom misbehavior is intentional, not inadvertent; students know they should not do it. An accidental hiccup during quiet work time is not misbehavior, but when feigned for the purpose of disrupting a lesson, the same behavior is justifiably disapproved.

Five Types of Misbehavior

Teachers contend with five broad types of misbehavior. In descending order of seriousness, as judged by social scientists, they are as follows:

1. Aggression: physical and verbal attacks by students on the teacher or other students
2. Immorality: acts such as cheating, lying, and stealing
3. Defiance of authority: refusal, sometimes hostile, to do as the teacher requests
4. Class disruptions: talking loudly, calling out, walking about the room, clowning, tossing objects, and the like
5. Goofing off: fooling around, not doing assigned tasks, dawdling, and daydreaming

Teachers concur with the levels of social seriousness indicated for the five categories of misbehavior. They especially dread having to deal with aggression, immorality, and defiance, but in practice they seldom have to do so. The misbehavior they usually contend with is less serious, such as goofing off and talking—innocuous behaviors that nevertheless waste much instructional time and interfere with learning. Lee Canter (Canter & Canter, 1992), whose Assertive Discipline is one of the most widely used discipline systems, was asked how he could justify sending a student to the office for misbehavior as benign as inappropriate laughter or talking without permission. He replied that it was precisely such behaviors, which no one considers serious, that drive teachers to distraction and ruin learning for everyone.

DISCIPLINE AND MISBEHAVIOR

The word *discipline* has several different definitions, but in this book it means what teachers do to help students behave acceptably in school. You can see that discipline is tied directly to misbehavior—where there is no misbehavior, no discipline is required.

Discipline is intended to suppress and redirect misbehavior. All teachers know that students sometimes behave with sweetness, kindness, gentility, consideration, helpfulness, and honesty. Their doing so makes teaching one of the most satisfying of all professions. But students also behave at times with hostility, abusiveness, disrespect, disinterest, and cruelty, all of which damage the environment for learning. Ideally, the goal of discipline is to reduce the need for teacher intervention over time by helping students learn to control their own behavior. When teachers apply various discipline techniques, they hope not only that misbehavior will cease but that students will internalize self-discipline and display it in the classroom and elsewhere.

IS DISCIPLINE A SERIOUS MATTER?

Every year since 1969, Phi Delta Kappa has sponsored a Gallup Poll of the public's attitudes toward education. One question on the survey asks: "What do you think are the biggest problems with which the public schools of this community must contend?" In most of those years, the public has listed discipline at or near the top of its concerns. In 1994 discipline tied for first place with a category called fighting/violence/gangs. In third place was lack of proper financial support, and in fourth place, drug abuse (Elam, Rose, & Gallup, 1994).

Of course, public opinion can be suspect because it is influenced by the sensational, such as physical attacks on teachers and severe vandalism of schools. In the case of discipline, however, little disagreement exists between educators and the public. Administrators perceive a widespread increase in school violence (Boothe et al., 1993), and most teachers maintain that student misbehavior interferes significantly with their teaching (Elam, 1989). The resultant frustration produces stress that affects some teachers as severely as does battle fatigue experienced by soldiers in combat, symptoms of which include lethargy, exhaustion, tension, depression, and high blood pressure.

The concern about discipline is not declining but is growing year by year. Numerous studies list discipline as a major problem with which teachers must contend and a significant factor in teachers' leaving the profession—it is responsible for 40 percent or more of departures during teachers' first three years ("Study backs," 1987; Curwin, 1992). Adding to the problem is the fact that experienced teachers try to transfer away from schools that have high levels of misbehavior, leaving those schools in the hands of teachers not yet skilled in discipline.

MODELS OF DISCIPLINE AND CLASSROOM PRACTICE

It has been less than 50 years since educators began giving serious attention to positive classroom discipline, that is, to discovering ways to promote good student behavior by means other than intimidation and punishment. Indeed, it has only been three decades since discipline rose to the top of teachers' concerns. But many ear-

Foundation Models of Classroom Discipline

Redl and Wattenberg 1951	Neo-Skinnerians c. 1960	Kounin 1971	Ginott 1971
Dealing with the group	Behavior shaping	Classroom management	Congruent communication
Student roles	Operant behavior	Withitness	Sane messages
Group dynamics	Reinforcement	Group alerting	Inviting cooperation
Influence techniques	Behavior modification	Delaying satiation	Correcting by directing

Application Models of Classroom Discipline

Dreikurs 1972	Canter 1976, 1992	Jones 1979, 1987
Democratic teaching	Assertively taking charge	Positive classroom discipline
Genuine goal of belonging	Rights in the classroom	Body language
Mistaken goals	Consequences	Incentive systems
Influence techniques	Teaching responsible behavior	Efficient help

Glasser 1969, 1985, 1992	Gordon 1974, 1989	Curwin and Mendler 1988, 1992
Discipline without coercion	Developing self-control	Discipline with dignity
Students' needs	Problem ownership	Behaviorally at risk
Quality	Behavior window	Restoring hope
Lead teachers	Active listening	Social contract

FIGURE I.1   Foundation and application models of classroom discipline

lier educators saw the problem emerging. In response, occasional scholars began seeking approaches that teachers could use to lessen the impact of misbehavior.

The first approach that was sufficiently organized and complete for classroom use was set forth in 1951 by Wayne State University professors Fritz Redl, a psychotherapist, and William Wattenberg, an educational psychologist. Their landmark work dealt with characteristics of group behavior and how individual behavior within groups could be understood and controlled. Around 1960 their model was joined by that of the Neo-Skinnerians—followers of B. F. Skinner's teachings on shaping desired behavior through reinforcement, a position referred to as behavior modification. Later, in 1971, Jacob Kounin's landmark studies on lesson management appeared, followed by Haim Ginott's 1972 commentaries on controlling misbehavior through humane treatment and congruent communication. Those four models, highly important but rarely used today in their entirety, are those referred to in Part I of this book as foundation models of discipline.

As concern about discipline continued to grow, other educators, psychologists, and psychiatrists undertook to develop still better approaches to school discipline. Among the best known and most useful of those wide-ranging approaches were the democratic teaching of Rudolf Dreikurs, which appeared in 1972; Assertive Discipline of Lee Canter, a preeminent model that has been continually revised since 1976; Fredric Jones's Classroom Management Training Program, in use since 1979; control theory of William Glasser, which in 1985 reflected a different approach from his landmark work in 1969 and which continues to be modified; Thomas Gordon's self-control approach, set forth in 1989 but based largely on his earlier Effectiveness Training work; and Richard Curwin and Allen Mendler's discipline with dignity, explained in their 1988 and 1992 publications. Those six models comprise what are referred to in Part II as application models of discipline.

The first 10 chapters in this book give attention to the foundation and application models. Figure I.1 indicates the central concepts of those models and shows the approximate dates when they impacted educational practice.

As you proceed to examine the 10 models, note how each introduces new concepts and techniques. Note also how elements of earlier models are incorporated into models developed subsequently. A wealth of information is contained in the models, but if it is to serve you best, you must organize that information in your own mind so that it meshes with your outlook and personality and, of course, with the realities of the students you teach. Part III includes three chapters to help you develop a personal system of discipline.

REFERENCES AND RECOMMENDED READINGS

Boothe, J., et al. (1993). The violence at your door. *Executive Educator, 15* (1), 16–22.

Canter, L., & Canter, M. (1992). *Assertive discipline: Positive behavior management for today's classroom* (2nd ed.). Santa Monica, CA: Lee Canter & Associates.

Curwin, R. (1992). *Rediscovering hope: Our greatest teaching strategy*. Bloomington, IN: National Educational Service.

Elam, S. (1989). The second Gallup/Phi Delta Kappa Poll of teachers' attitudes toward the public schools. *Phi Delta Kappan 70*(10), 785–798.

Elam, S., Rose, L., & Gallup A. (1994). The 26th annual Phi Delta Kappa/Gallup Poll of the public's attitudes toward the public schools. *Phi Delta Kappan, 76*(1), 41–56.

Hughes, H. (1994, February). *From fistfights to gunfights: Preparing teachers and administrators to cope with violence in school*. Paper presented at the annual meeting of the American Association of Colleges for Teacher Education, Chicago.

Landen, W. (1992). Violence and our schools: What can we do? *Updating School Board Policies, 23,* 1–5.

Rich, J. (1992). Predicting and controlling school violence. *Contemporary Education, 64*(1) 35–39.

Schwartz, F. (1981). Supporting or subverting learning: Peer group patterns in four tracked schools. *Anthropology and Education Quarterly, 12*(2), 99–120.

Study backs induction schools to help new teachers stay teachers. (1987). *ASCD Update, 29*(4), 1.

The Foundation Models

The models presented in Part I represent pioneering efforts in the movement toward better classroom discipline. While these models are not usually considered sufficient in themselves for complete systems of classroom control, they present many important concepts and have strongly influenced the models in use today. These important foundation models are the following:

1. The Redl and Wattenberg Model: Discipline through Dealing with the Group
2. The Neo-Skinnerian Model: Discipline through Shaping Desired Behavior
3. The Kounin Model: Discipline through Classroom Management
4. The Ginott Model: Discipline through Congruent Communication

CHAPTER 1

The Redl and Wattenberg Model

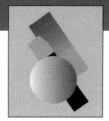

Discipline through Dealing with the Group

William Wattenberg

BIOGRAPHICAL SKETCHES OF REDL AND WATTENBERG

Fritz Redl, born in Austria, immigrated to the United States in 1936 and devoted his career to research, therapy, and teaching, principally as professor of behavioral science at Wayne State University. He was also recognized for contributions made while a member of the department of criminal justice at the State University of New York at Albany, where he worked with deviant juveniles. Redl's numerous writings in the field of education and psychology include *Mental Hygiene in Teaching* (1951, revised 1959), coauthored with William Wattenberg; *Controls from Within* (1952), coauthored with David Wineman; *Discipline for Today's Children* (1956), coauthored with George Sheviakov; and *When We Deal with Children* (1972).

Redl's collaborator, William Wattenberg, was born in 1911 and received his doctorate from Columbia University in 1936. He specialized in educational psychology and held professorships at Northwestern University, Chicago Teacher's College, and Wayne State University. Wattenberg's writings include the above-mentioned *Mental Hygiene in Teaching*, coauthored with Redl, as well as *The Adolescent Years* (1955) and *All Men Are Created Equal* (1967).

REDL AND WATTENBERG'S CONTRIBUTIONS TO DISCIPLINE

Redl and Wattenberg presented in their 1951 book, *Mental Hygiene in Teaching*, the first set of theory-based suggestions designed specifically to help teachers understand and deal with misbehavior in the classroom. Prior to Redl and Wattenberg's contributions, classroom discipline was envisioned as teachers' trying to impose their behavior requirements upon students. Although many teachers were certainly considerate and humane, the common practice was to apply discipline requirements autocratically and somewhat harshly.

Redl and Wattenberg's investigations led them to believe that a markedly different approach to discipline could maintain control and at the same time better help students develop their own self-discipline. Redl and Wattenberg were the first to describe how students behave differently in groups than as individuals and the first to identify social and psychological forces that affect classroom behavior. Based on their findings, their specific disciplinary techniques not only helped teachers maintain control but strengthened students' emotional growth and working relationships as well. Their contributions established a beginning point for newer views of discipline that were to come later and provided insights into behavior that teachers find useful today.

REDL AND WATTENBERG'S CENTRAL FOCUS

Redl and Wattenberg focused on group behavior, its manifestations, causes, and control. Their purpose was to help teachers understand and deal with group behavior in the classroom. They showed how group behavior differs from individual behavior, pinpointed some of the causes of those differences, and set forth specific techniques for helping teachers deal with the undesirable aspects of group behavior.

REDL AND WATTENBERG'S PRINCIPAL CONCEPTS AND TEACHINGS

Group behavior. People in groups behave differently than they do individually. Group expectations influence individual behavior, and individual behavior in turn affects the group.

Student roles. Within any group, various students adopt roles such as leaders, instigators, and fall guys. Teachers should be aware of the emergence of such roles and help limit the detrimental effects that some of them have.

Group dynamics. Forces generated by and within groups strongly affect behavior. If teachers are to deal effectively with group behavior, they must understand these forces, how they develop, and how they affect behavior in the classroom.

Teacher roles. Group behavior in the classroom is influenced by students' perceptions of the teacher. Students see teachers as filling many different roles. Teachers must be aware of those potential roles and what students expect of them.

Diagnostic thinking. In order to solve behavior problems correctly, teachers are encouraged to employ a diagnostic thinking process that involves (1) forming a first hunch, (2) gathering facts, (3) exploring hidden factors (background information), (4) taking action, and (5) remaining flexible.

Influence techniques. Teachers can correct student misbehavior and maintain class control by using influence techniques such as (1) supporting student self-control, (2) offering situational assistance, (3) appraising reality, and (4) invoking the pleasure-pain principle (reward and punishment).

Supporting student self-control. With this low-key influence technique, teachers address an emerging problem before it becomes serious. Teachers use eye contact, move closer to misbehaving students, provide encouragement, make use of humor, and in some cases simply ignore minor misbehavior.

Providing situational assistance. This influence technique is also low-key. When students have difficulty regaining self-control, teachers provide situational assistance by (1) helping students over a hurdle, (2) restructuring the time schedule, (3) establishing new routines, and (4) removing seductive objectives. Occasionally it might be necessary to (5) remove a student from the situation or even (6) physically restrain a student.

Appraising reality. This influence technique involves helping students understand the underlying causes of their own misbehavior and foresee the consequences if they continue. Teachers speak openly and frankly about the situation and reemphasize existing limits on behavior, but at the same time they offer encouragement. In more severe cases, this is done in individual conferences with students.

Invoking the pleasure-pain principle. This influence technique consists of rewarding good behavior and punishing bad behavior. Punishment should be used only as a last resort, however, because it is frequently counterproductive.

ANALYSIS OF THE REDL AND WATTENBERG MODEL

The Redl and Wattenberg model is explained through further examination of needs, roles, and behaviors in the classroom, group dynamics, psychological roles of teachers, diagnostic thinking, and influence techniques.

Student Roles and Behaviors in the Classroom

Redl and Wattenberg believe that if teachers can learn to identify the basic causes underlying behavior and conflict, they can correct most of those causes and thus maintain desirable classroom control. They suggest that outward behavior has roots in identifiable needs, and they recognize that students are continually torn between personal desires and the expectations of society.

Redl and Wattenberg emphasize that students behave differently in groups than when alone, and further, that teachers seldom deal with students on a purely individual basis, since the entire class is usually affected by the behavior of each member. This does not mean that teachers can never use insights into individual behavior but only that they must come to understand group behavior as well.

Redl and Wattenberg (1959) view the group as an organism. As they put it,

> A group creates conditions such that its members will behave in certain ways because they belong to it; at the same time, the manner in which the parts function affects the whole. (p. 267)

In other words, group expectations strongly influence individual behavior, and individual behavior in turn affects the group.

Redl and Wattenberg identify several *student roles* that are likely to be adopted when students function within groups. The roles serve to fill personal needs and are usually reinforced in some manner by other members of the group. The following are some of the roles that every teacher is likely to encounter.

Leaders.   A role as *leader* is available in almost every group. This role varies according to the group's purpose, makeup, and activities. Within the same group, different individuals may act as leaders in different activities. For example, a student who is a leader in physical education may fill a different role in music.

Group leaders tend to share certain qualities. They usually show above-average intelligence, responsibility, and social skills. They generally have a highly developed understanding of others, and they embody and reflect group ideals.

Teachers must be aware that the leaders they appoint are not necessarily the group's natural leaders. Such mismatches often lead to conflict within the group.

Clowns. *Clowns* are individuals who assume the role of entertainer in the group. Students sometimes adopt this role as a way to mask feelings of inferiority, thinking it best to make fun of situations and especially themselves before others do so. Clowning can be beneficial to both the teacher and the group, especially when the group is anxious or frustrated. At times, however, clowning hinders group progress, and group members may support the disruptive antics of the clown as a way of expressing hostility toward the teacher.

Fall Guys. A *fall guy* is an individual who takes blame and punishment in order to gain favor with the group. Fall guys give members of the group latitude to misbehave, since the group can set them up to suffer any penalties that might result. Teachers need to be aware of this kind of manipulation and be sure to focus their corrective actions on the instigators of misbehavior.

Instigators. *Instigators* are individuals who cause trouble but make it appear they are not involved. They often solve their inner conflicts by getting others to act them out. They may even feel that they are benefiting the victim in some way. Teachers need to look into recurring conflicts carefully to see if there is an unnoticed instigator. It may be necessary to point out this role to the group, as they are often unaware of it. The group may need help in recognizing and discouraging this role.

Group Dynamics

Previous paragraphs described some of the roles and role expectations that influence behavior. Membership in groups affects individuals in other ways, too. Groups create their own psychological forces that strongly influence individuals. These forces are called *group dynamics.*

Group dynamics help produce unwritten codes of classroom conduct. When these codes run counter to the teacher's expectations, conflict occurs. Because teachers are powerful, they seem to win out in conflicts with students. However, the group code usually prevails under the surface, contributing to lasting attitudes that may be the opposite of what the teacher desired.

The following are some of the dynamics that, according to Redl and Wattenberg, often lead to behavior problems in the classroom.

Contagious Behavior. Undesirable behavior becomes *contagious behavior* when it spreads quickly in the classroom, as occurs frequently. One student's misbehavior may be a good indication of what other students are also itching to do. Once the ice is broken, others may join the misbehavior, especially if the perpetrator has high status.

Therefore, before reacting to misbehavior, the teacher should evaluate the misbehavior's potential for spread. If the potential is high, the teacher should squelch the misbehavior at once. If the potential is low, it may be safe to ignore the behavior or use a low-pressure technique such as reminding students that more appropriate behavior is expected.

Teachers can reduce incipient contagion by attending to negative factors that foster it, such as poor seating arrangements, boredom, fatigue, lack of purpose in lessons, and poor student manners.

On the positive side, desirable behavior can also be contagious, though this effect is rarely so rampant as it is with misbehavior. Teachers can encourage positive behavior through approval, reinforcement, and giving status to those who display it.

Scapegoating.   *Scapegoating* is a phenomenon in which the group seeks to displace its hostility onto an unpopular individual or subgroup. The target person or subgroup is usually weak or outcast, unable to cope well with normal occurrences in the classroom. Scapegoating has undesirable consequences for everyone concerned, and teachers must be alert to stifle it whenever it occurs. When so doing, however, they should take care that their approach does not produce even more hostility toward the target.

Teachers' Pets.   When a group believes that a teacher is playing favorites, it reacts with jealousy and resentment. These emotions may be manifested as hostile behavior toward the favored individual or group, who are referred to as *teachers' pets*. Hostility may also be directed at the teacher. When it is necessary to give individual students extra help, teachers should make sure that their actions never suggest favoritism but are seen as impartial, necessary, and professional.

Reactions to Strangers.   It is common in most schools for strangers to enter the classroom occasionally. *Reactions to strangers* provide teachers with a key to group emotions. When a stranger enters the classroom, tension increases for teachers and students alike, and a marked change in student behavior usually occurs. If the stranger is a new student, the group code may become exaggerated to show the newcomer how to act. For example, if the group prizes cooperation, they might go to great lengths to be helpful to the newcomer and each other. On the other hand, the group may test the new student. They may withhold acceptance, vie for friendship, or even taunt the new student or each other.

If the stranger is an adult, the students may rally to support their teacher, provided the teacher is liked and respected. If they do not respect their teacher, the students may misbehave rudely and boisterously.

Teachers should note class reactions when a stranger enters the room. Extreme behaviors provide clues to underlying motivations and feelings that are operating within the group.

Group Disintegration.   Groups serve many purposes, and good group behavior is highly desirable. Teachers hope to establish groups that will prosper, grow in maturity, and help meet everyone's needs. Even the strongest groups, however, show strain as time passes. *Group disintegration* can occur when a group loses its cohesiveness.

Consider Mrs. Brown's discouragement when her group began to disintegrate. Early in the year her class worked strongly together, helpfully and cooperatively. But as the weeks passed, cohesion began to decline. Increasingly, students dawdled, looked out the window instead of paying attention, and talked during Mrs. Brown's lessons. Cliques developed, and jealousies surfaced. Mrs. Brown did not know how to get her students to work together as before, which left her frustrated and dismayed.

Teachers frequently encounter such situations and do not know how to correct them. Redl and Wattenberg suggest that when a formerly effective group begins to disintegrate, teachers should ask themselves the following questions:

1. Are class activities becoming boring to the students?
2. Is there too much emphasis on competition among groups?
3. Have unexpected changes occurred in leadership roles, environment, or schedules?
4. Are new class activities needed to stimulate and provoke thought?
5. Are students given ample opportunity to experience success, or are too many experiencing frustration and failure?
6. Has the classroom climate become threatening rather than supportive?

Conditions such as these can create emotional changes within the group, which can cause class members, especially the weaker ones, to feel insecure concerning their places and expected roles. An increase in deviant behavior is likely at such times, with a lessening of mutual support within the group.

Disintegration is not inevitable, however, nor necessarily permanent. New activities, new purposes, and new working relationships all can help provide a new sense of group cohesiveness.

Psychological Roles of Teachers

Group and individual classroom behavior is greatly influenced by how students perceive the teacher. Students assign many different *teacher roles* and expect teachers to present many different images. Sometimes teachers have little choice about those roles, but normally they have some control over which they will accept and how they will carry them out. These roles and images include the following:

Representatives of society. Teachers are seen to reflect values, moral attitudes, and thinking patterns typical of the community.

Judges. Teachers are supposed to judge students' behavior, character, work, and progress.

Sources of knowledge. Teachers are seen as the primary source of knowledge, a resource from which students can obtain information.

Helpers in learning. Teachers are expected to help students learn by giving directions, furnishing information, removing obstacles to learning, facilitating problem solving, and requiring that work be done.

Referees. Students expect teachers to arbitrate and make decisions when class disputes arise.

Detectives. Teachers are to oversee security in the classroom, discover wrong-doing, identify guilty students, and impose penalties.

Models. Teachers are to model the best in customs, manners, values, and beliefs, which students may or may not elect to imitate.

Caretakers. Teachers are to reduce anxiety by maintaining standards of behavior, regular schedules, and safe environments.

Ego supporters. Teachers are to support student egos by building student self-confidence and bettering student self-images.

Group leaders. Teachers are expected to lead the class in such a way that harmony and efficiency prevail.

Surrogate parents. Teachers are to be like parents in providing protection, approval, advice, correction, and affection.

Targets for hostility. When student hostility cannot be appropriately expressed to other adults, it can be displaced with relative safety onto teachers.

Friends and confidants. Teachers can be talked with and confided in.

Objects of affection. Teachers are to be ideal people, worthy of esteem, affection, and hero worship.

Control Techniques for Misbehavior

So far we have examined several of Redl and Wattenberg's teachings about how groups function, how they are affected by group dynamics, and how group behavior is influenced by the roles assumed by students and teachers. Now we move attention to how teachers are advised to control misbehavior. Redl and Wattenberg offer two groups of specific suggestions. The first has to do with diagnostic thinking in the classroom and the second with applying influence techniques. Let us see what is involved in each.

Diagnostic Thinking

Redl and Wattenberg suggest that teachers employ a procedure of *diagnostic thinking* when faced with incidents of student misbehavior. Their diagnostic thinking approach seems at first laborious, but with practice it can become second nature. The process includes forming a first hunch, gathering facts, exploring hidden factors, taking action, and remaining flexible.

Forming a first hunch. When a problem first becomes apparent, it is natural to form a preliminary hunch about its underlying cause. This hunch is not based so much on specific data as on a general feeling about the incident.

Gathering facts. Next, the teacher quickly reviews obvious facts. Are students inattentive? Is someone breaking a rule? Are students arguing angrily? Is someone crying?

Exploring hidden factors. Teachers should add to the obvious facts hidden factors of which they might be aware, such as background information on students involved and general knowledge of human psychological and moral development.

Taking action. Once teachers have quickly considered facts, background information, and possible motivations behind the misbehavior, they should take action to resolve the situation. Their first efforts may be successful; if not, they need to revise their appraisal of the situation and make new efforts to resolve it.

Remaining flexible. When teachers take action (or fail to take action) to resolve a conflict, they may, by their action or inaction, alter classroom dynamics, thus creating a situation that requires further attention. A single action is often not enough. Teachers may need to employ a series of steps that lead ultimately to a resolution of the situation, and they may have to change their minds or approaches while doing so.

Redl and Wattenberg offer an additional word of advice concerning diagnostic thinking in resolving problem situations: student feelings are very important. Teachers should therefore try to put themselves in the students' place, both those students who commit offenses and those who are victimized. By understanding the feelings of everyone involved, more suitable resolutions can usually be found.

Applying Influence Techniques

Redl and Wattenberg give considerable attention to the actions that teachers use when attempting to resolve problem behavior. They call these actions *influence techniques*.

Every teacher uses several different influence techniques to maintain class control. Some of those techniques may be embedded in the overall school discipline policy, and some may have been acquired over years of effective use. Some work well, some work in certain situations and not in others, and some almost never produce positive results.

What do teachers do when students misbehave? Redl and Wattenberg found that some shouted at students, some removed students from the class, some invoked punishment, and some simply ignored the misbehavior. Some of these actions were taken consistently, others inconsistently. In order that teachers might acquire a consistently effective procedure for dealing with misbehavior, Redl and Wattenberg urge that teachers ask themselves a rapid series of questions before taking action.

1. What is the motivation behind the misbehavior?
2. How is the class reacting?
3. Is the misbehavior related to interaction with me?
4. How will the student react when corrected?
5. How will the correction affect future behavior?

The answers to these questions help teachers select a corrective technique likely to produce positive results overall. Four categories of corrective techniques are (1) supporting self-control, (2) providing situational assistance, (3) appraising reality, and (4) invoking the pleasure-pain principle. These four categories are discussed in the following paragraphs. It should be remembered that for any of these techniques to be effective, students must know exactly what the issues are, know how they are expected to behave, and understand the consequences of breaking or following the rules.

1. Supporting Self-Control.   Most students, most of the time, want to behave correctly and thus enjoy the teacher's approval. Only occasionally do they misbehave simply because they want to be unpleasant. Therefore, when misbehavior does occur, teachers should first assume that the misbehavior is not ill-intentioned and that it may represent nothing more than a momentary lapse in student self-control, which can easily be corrected.

Techniques for *supporting self-control* are low-key. They are not forceful, aggressive, or punitive but aim at helping students help themselves. Such techniques are very useful. They often eliminate the need to confront students and dole out penalties, and they give students much needed opportunities to work on controlling their own behavior. But it should not be expected that supportive techniques can correct all misbehavior. They work only when misbehavior is mild or just beginning. If they don't get the message across, firmer, more direct techniques are required. Redl and Wattenberg describe five ways to support student self-control.

Sending Signals.   Teachers use *signals* that show students they know what is going on and that they do not approve. Examples are making eye contact, frowning, and shaking the head. These signals are most effective during the first indications of misbehavior.

Physical Proximity.   If students do not respond to signals, teachers can move into closer *physical proximity* of the offenders. By doing so, teachers communicate that they are aware of the misbehavior and want to help students regain control, which allows students to draw strength from the nearness of the teacher. It is usually enough simply to move closer to the offender, but sometimes a friendly touch on shoulder or head might be needed.

Showing Interest.   Even students who normally have good self-control may begin to misbehave when they lose interest in an assignment. Teachers can help by going to such students and showing *interest* in their work. A teacher might say, "I see you've completed the first five problems correctly. I bet you can finish all of them before the end of the period." This technique is only effective, of course, if the student feels able to do the assignment.

Humor.   Using *humor* is a pleasant way of making students aware of lapses in self-control. It is important that this humor be gentle and accompanied by a smile. An example might be "My, there is so much chattering, I thought for a minute I was in the cafeteria." Teachers must be careful that they do not use sarcasm or ridicule in their attempts at humor, for students usually interpret sarcasm as punishment, not support.

Ignoring.   Occasionally, simply *ignoring* misbehavior is appropriate, especially in classes that are normally well behaved. Ignoring sends a signal to other students that they should do the same; the misbehaving student therefore receives no reinforcing attention.

2. *Providing Situational Assistance.*

When misbehavior reaches the point that students cannot regain self-control, the teacher must step in with *situational assistance* to guide students back onto the proper course. Punitive measures are not needed. Instead, the teacher should provide only the assistance needed to help students regain control. In their second set of influence techniques, Redl and Wattenberg describe several things that teachers can do.

Provide Hurdle Help.   Suppose an algebra assignment has been made. Susana begins work as expected but soon realizes she does not understand the procedure involved. She begins to talk to another student. In this case, the teacher need only provide *hurdle help* to assist Susana in understanding what to do rather than attack her for talking instead of working.

Restructure or Reschedule.   Mr. James's sixth-grade students have returned to class after participating in a hotly contested game of volleyball. He knows it will be difficult for the students to get to work on their math lesson, so instead of the regular assignment, he improvises by using the game's scores to construct a number of computational problems.

Mr. James's appraisal of the situation suggested that overexcitement would almost certainly interfere with the regular lesson. He therefore restructured the lesson so he could use student interest to advantage. Other ways of *restructuring activities* involve giving a brief time for rest, changing the nature of the activities, or rescheduling the work for a more appropriate time.

Establish Routines.   Often students misbehave when they do not know exactly what they should be doing or when. Teachers can forestall such problems by *establishing routines* that make the curriculum more predictable. Routines are especially valuable in helping students get to work quickly and complete work expeditiously.

Remove Seductive Objects.   Attractive objects that students have in their possession—photographs, toys, and the like—can often overpower self-control. When that happens, *removing the seductive object* is all that is required. This is a temporary measure and should be explained as such to the student. The object is returned at the end of the period or day.

Remove the Student from the Situation.   When a student has lost self-control and is disturbing the rest of the class, the teacher needs to do something immediately so that the class can continue the lesson. A lengthy confrontation with the offending student will be a waste of class time, so simply *removing the student* from the situation is often the teacher's best alternative. For example, third grader Travis is upset and disrupts the lesson by continually blurting out negative comments. The teacher, in accordance with consequences anticipated by the class, tells Travis to take a seat at a table in the far corner of the room, saying, "When you decide you can help us, you may return to the group."

This should be done in a nonpunitive way. The teacher should emphasize that Travis is only exiled until he regains his self-control. It is important, too, that the incident be followed up with a private talk, in which the feelings of both student and teacher can be discussed.

Use Physical Restraint.   Very occasionally, students who lapse in self-control may become a danger to themselves or others. When this happens, the teacher may have to use *physical restraint*. Restraint should be used only in dire circumstances, and then with caution. Teachers may get injured themselves, and if a student is injured, the threat of a lawsuit is a distinct possibility. The guiding principle is that the teacher should always try to safeguard the student in a reasonable and prudent manner and get help as quickly as possible.

3. Appraising Reality.   By *reality appraisal* Redl and Wattenberg mean having students examine a behavior situation, noting its underlying causes, and foreseeing its probable consequences. This knowledge helps students develop their own values so they behave more appropriately in future situations.

For incidents that disturb the class, it is usually advisable to postpone reality appraisal discussions until a later time. Emotions may be running strong, and both teacher and students are apt to say things that make it doubly hard for parties to listen to each other. After emotions have cooled down, causes and feelings can be sorted out without lecturing or scolding. It is important that the teacher understand why students felt and behaved as they did, and it is equally important for students to understand the teacher's feelings and behaviors. When these matters are aired, it becomes easier to handle similar situations in the future.

Because student misbehavior often escalates for reasons that are not clear, Redl and Wattenberg suggest that teachers do the following to help illuminate and defuse situations involving misbehavior.

Clearly Make a Frank Appraisal.   Too often teachers overlook the simplest method for dealing with students, which is to make a *frank appraisal* by explaining exactly why behavior is inappropriate and to outline clear connections between conduct and consequences. Teachers should not underestimate students' ability to comprehend statements such as "Let's raise our hands, please. If everyone talks at once, no one gets heard" or "These assignments have to be completed. If you don't keep up with them, you aren't going to learn what you should." Students respect reasonable rules whose purposes they understand, and they appreciate teachers who insist that they learn.

Show Encouragement.   When using reality appraisal, teachers may seem to be critical of students. Few people respond well to criticism. Teachers therefore should express themselves in ways that show *ecouragement* rather than criticism. They should stress that students are capable of the best behavior, and they should urge students to do the best they can. In making frank appraisals, teachers must guard against humiliating students, attacking their personal values, or frustrating them with impossible expectations. The teacher's primary role is always to support and encourage, not to attack or blame.

Set Clear, Enforceable Limits.   Students often misbehave just to see how much they can get away with, which is their means of determining where the limits of permissible behavior actually lie. Teachers can prevent such misbehavior by *setting limits* that are clear and enforceable. They discuss with the class exactly what is expected and what constitutes acceptable and unacceptable behavior. They clearly explain the reasons for those limits and the rules associated with them. Students usually respond positively, appreciating the security provided by knowledge of limits and rules. Redl and Wattenberg caution teachers about making threats when explaining limits, contending that threats imply that the teacher expects the rules to be broken. Students should know in advance about consequences, but those consequences should be stated in a matter-of-fact manner, never as threats.

4. Invoking the Pleasure-Pain Principle.   When behavior problems persist despite a teacher's attempts to support student self-control, provide situational assistance, and appraise reality, it becomes necessary to move to the strongest influence technique in the Redl and Wattenberg model: invoking the *pleasure-pain principle*. In describing this principle, Redl and Wattenberg refer to rewards and punishments but give relatively little attention to the reward (pleasure) aspect, while having much to say about the punishment (pain) aspect.

With regard to pleasure, they limit their discussions to acknowledgments that praise, rewards, and teacher promises can influence behavior for the better, but they provide no specific suggestions as to how these elements can be used systematically.

With regard to pain, Redl and Wattenberg emphasize that pain, when used to control misbehavior, must not be harsh punishment but rather simply consequences that are somewhat unpleasant to the student. It is important to recognize the benign nature of the suggested unpleasant consequences.

Punishment.   Redl and Wattenberg say that *punishment* should consist of planned, unpleasant consequences, the purpose of which is to change behavior in positive directions. Punishment should not be physical, nor should it involve angry outbursts that indicate lack of self-control on the part of the teacher. Neither should it consist of actions taken to get back at misbehaving students or to "teach them a lesson." Instead, it should require students to make amends for breaking rules, to do correctly what was done incorrectly, or to forgo enjoyable activities in which they would otherwise participate.

Even when punishing in this manner, teachers should communicate the idea that they are not angry at the students but are truly trying to help. Students should see punishment as a natural and understandable consequence of unacceptable behavior. If students sense good intentions from the teacher, they will be at least partly upset with themselves for losing self-control and will not focus anger or hostility on the teacher.

Overall, punishment should be used only as a last resort when other approaches have failed. That is because there are many things that can go wrong when punishment is used, as follows:

1. Punishment takes the form of revenge or release from tension.
2. Punishment has detrimental effects on student self-concept and on relations with the teacher.
3. Over time, punishment reduces the likelihood that students will maintain self-control.
4. Students may endure punishment in order to elevate their status among peers.
5. Punishment presents an undesirable model for solving problems.

Threats versus Promises.   The pain component of Redl and Wattenberg's pleasure-pain principle should be communicated to students as promises. *Promises* are assurances that unpleasant consequences will be invoked when rules are broken. Promises can be made without negative connotations, and they do not promote undue fear or other negative reactions.

Threats, on the other hand, are emotional statements that make students anxious and fearful. They often interfere with learning and damage the classroom climate. Threats tend to be harsh and negative, taking the form of "If you don't . . . I will . . .!" Teachers who make dire threats almost never carry them out, and that is all too often their undoing; because of their inconsistency, teachers' ability to control misbehavior consequently erodes, as does their ability to relate positively with the class.

Instead of making threats, Redl and Wattenberg would have teachers explain to students the kinds of behaviors that are unacceptable and identify the consequences associated with those misbehaviors. Unlike threats, these calm assertions lend security to the classroom and help students maintain their own self-control.

ADDITIONAL REMINDERS FROM REDL

Redl, in his 1972 book *When We Deal with Children*, reminds teachers of several principles when misbehavior must be confronted:

1. Give students a say in setting standards and deciding consequences. Let them tell how they think you should handle situations that call for punishment.
2. Keep students' emotional health in mind at all times. Punished students must feel that the teacher likes them. *Always* talk to students about their feelings after the situation has calmed down.
3. Be helpful, not hurtful. Show students you want to support their best behavior.
4. Punishment does not work well. Use it as a last resort. Try other approaches first.

5. Don't be afraid to change your course of action if you get new insights into a situation.
6. Mistakes in discipline need not be considered disastrous unless they are repeated.
7. Be objective, maintain humor, and remember that we are all human.

COMMENTS ON THE REDL AND WATTENBERG MODEL

Redl and Wattenberg made three landmark contributions toward helping teachers work more effectively with students. First, they described how humans behave differently in groups than they do individually, thus helping teachers understand classroom behaviors that might otherwise seem perplexing. Second, they provided the first well-organized, systematic approach to improving student behavior in the classroom. Prior to their contributions, teachers relied mostly on aversive techniques that intimidated students and caused them to be fearful and experience other emotions counterproductive to long-term working relationships. And third, they devised for their system a procedure for diagnosing the causes of student misbehavior, in the belief that by dealing with causes, teachers could eliminate most misbehavior.

The Redl and Wattenberg model not only provided teachers a better way of dealing with classroom misbehavior but set the stage for other discipline models to come. In later models, you will see frequent inclusion of elements that Redl and Wattenberg championed, such as supporting student self-control, providing situational assistance, linking behavior to consistent consequences, and urging great caution in the use of punishment.

APPLICATION EXERCISES

REVIEW OF SELECTED TERMINOLOGY

The following terms are central to the Redl and Wattenberg model of discipline. Check yourself to make sure you can explain their meanings.

student roles	situational assistance
group dynamics	hurdle help
contagious behavior	restructuring activities
scapegoating	reality appraisal
teacher roles	setting limits
diagnostic thinking	pleasure-pain principle
influence techniques	punishment
supporting self-control	threats
signals	promises

CONCEPT CASES

For each of the discipline models explored in this book, four concept cases—nonworking Kristina, talkative Sara, show-off Joshua, and hostile Tom—are provided so that you may practice and compare each authority's advice on dealing with misbehavior.

Case 1: Kristina Will Not Work

There is a behavior common to all grade levels that continually frustrates teachers: One or more students do not willingly participate in classroom activities. The students are often neither disruptive nor confrontive; the problem is simply that they will not complete assignments or participate in classroom happenings.

Kristina, in Mr. Jake's class, behaves in that manner. She is docile, never disrupts, and does little socializing with other students. She rarely completes an assignment. She is simply there, putting forth almost no effort.

How would Redl and Wattenberg deal with Kristina?   Redl and Wattenberg would suggest that teachers take the following steps in attempting to improve Kristina's classroom behavior.

1. Use diagnostic thinking: develop a hunch; gather facts; try to discover hidden factors; apply a tentative solution; and try out another solution if the first does not work. That might lead to questions such as, Does Kristina have emotional problems? Are things terribly difficult for her at home? Does she try to escape into a fantasy life? Will a warm, caring approach help her?
2. Depending on the conclusions reached in diagnostic thinking, the teacher would try one or more solutions such as the following:
   a. Send signals to Kristina: "I know you are not working."
   b. Move closer to Kristina to prompt her into action.
   c. Show special interest in Kristina's work.
   d. Employ humor: "I know you want to finish this work sometime during my lifetime!"
   e. Offer assistance to Kristina.
   f. Appraise reality: "Kristina, each incomplete assignment only causes you to fall farther behind, and it hurts your grade!"
   g. Remove Kristina from the situation: "You can return to the group when you show you can complete your work."

Case 2: Sara Cannot Stop Talking

Sara is a pleasant girl who participates in class activities and does most of the assigned work, though she often fails to complete it. She cannot seem to refrain from talking to classmates during lessons. Her teacher, Mr. Gonzales, has to speak to her repeatedly during lessons, which sometimes makes him become exasperated and lose his temper.

What suggestions would Redl and Wattenberg give Mr. Gonzales for dealing with Sara?

Case 3: Joshua Clowns and Intimidates

Joshua, larger and louder than his classmates, always wants to be the center of attention, which he accomplishes through a combination of clowning and intimidation. He makes wise remarks, talks back (smilingly) to the teacher, utters a variety of sound-effect noises such as gunshots and automobile crashes, and makes limitless sarcastic comments and other put-downs of classmates. Other students will not stand up to him, apparently fearing his size and verbal and (perhaps) physical aggression. Joshua's antics have brought his teacher, Miss Pearl, almost to her wit's end.

Using Redl and Wattenberg's suggestions, how would you deal with Joshua?

Case 4: Tom Is Hostile and Defiant

Tom has appeared to be in his usual sour mood all morning. On his way to sharpen his pencil, he bumps into Frank, who complains. Tom tells him loudly to shut up. Miss Baines, the teacher, says, "Tom, go back to your seat." Tom turns to face her and loudly says, "I'll go when I'm damned good and ready!"

How would Redl and Wattenberg have Miss Baines deal with Tom?

Questions
1. Were Kristina, Sara, Joshua, and Tom playing any of the roles identified by Redl and Wattenberg?
2. What psychological roles might the four students expect their teachers to fill?
3. What roles are the following students playing?
   a. Cheryl strolls into Spanish class five minutes late. *«¿Qué pasa?»* she says nonchalantly to the teacher. The class laughs.
   b. The auto shop teacher notices a group of boys squirting oil at one another. The boys point to Shaun, who is watching from the sidelines. "He started it," they all agree. Although their contention is not true, Shaun grins and does not deny it.
4. How do you think Redl and Wattenberg would suggest dealing with Cheryl's and Shaun's situations?

QUESTIONS AND ACTIVITIES

1. Based on Redl and Wattenberg's suggestions, how do you think Mr. Bryant should handle the following situation?

Three girls come into the classroom. Alejandra seems very distracted. Susan appears to be crying. Patricia has an angrily hateful look on her face. The class becomes uneasy, and Mr. Bryant is hesitant to proceed with the lesson. There have been similar previous incidents involving the three girls, though none so severe.

Mr. Bryant has a hunch that Patricia has been attempting to drive a wedge between the other two girls, who have been close friends. He examines the facts: Alejandra and Susan are upset; Patricia glares at Susan; these behaviors have occurred before. From their exchanges Mr. Bryant suspects that Patricia has this time been trying to entice Alejandra into doing something only with her, leaving Susan out.

What should Mr. Bryant do?

2. Examine Scenario 1 in Appendix I. What advice from Redl and Wattenberg would best help Mrs. Miller provide a better learning environment for her students?

REFERENCES AND RECOMMENDED READINGS

Redl, F. (1972). *When we deal with children*. New York: Free Press.

Redl, F., & Wattenberg, W. (1959). *Mental hygiene in teaching* (rev. ed.). New York: Harcourt, Brace & World. (Original work published 1951)

Redl, F., & Wineman, D. (1952). *Controls from within*. Glencoe, IL: Free Press.

Sheviakov, G., & Redl, F. (1956). *Discipline for today's children*. Washington, DC: Association for Supervision and Curriculum Development.

Wattenberg, W. (1955). *The adolescent years*. New York: Harcourt Brace.

———. (1967). *All men are created equal*. Detroit: Wayne State University Press.

CHAPTER 2

The Neo-Skinnerian Model

Discipline through Shaping
Desired Behavior

B. F. Skinner

This model of discipline is drawn from the work of a number of different writers who helped translate for classroom practice B. F. Skinner's discoveries about shaping human behavior. Skinner himself did not set forth a model of discipline, but because his ideas form the substance of what is popularly known as behavior modification—the essence of the model presented here—the label *Neo-Skinnerian* is used to give due credit to Skinner.

BIOGRAPHICAL SKETCH OF SKINNER

B. F. Skinner (1904–1990) is considered by many to have been the greatest behavioral psychologist of all time. Born in Susquehanna, Pennsylvania, he earned his doctorate in psychology at Harvard in 1931 and spent most of his academic career researching and teaching at that university.

Skinner's work in the 1930s consisted primarily of laboratory experiments in learning, in which he used rats and pigeons as subjects. Later, he drew world attention to his ideas about rearing and teaching human beings. Among other things, he proposed raising infants in glass enclosures he called *air cribs*, where the child was kept dry, warm, and comfortable, with all needs satisfied. He raised his own daughter in an air crib.

In 1948 he published a novel, *Walden Two*, in which he described the workings of a utopian community that made systematic application of principles of reinforcement to all aspects of everyday life. That novel, still widely read, served as a model for communes established in the late 1960s.

In 1971 Skinner published his controversial book *Beyond Freedom and Dignity*, which again attracted world attention. In that book he challenged traditional concepts of freedom and dignity, explaining why he considered them to be outmoded, useless, and incorrect. He claimed that we are not really acting freely in most of our decisions but that our choices are made instead on the basis of what has happened to us in the past; that is, our present behavior depends on which of our previous behaviors have been reinforced (rewarded). He urged that rather than worry about the incorrect concept of free choice, humans should turn their efforts to providing conditions that reinforce desired behavior, thus improving human behavior in general.

SKINNER'S CONTRIBUTIONS TO DISCIPLINE

As mentioned, Skinner himself never attempted to set forth a model of discipline, nor did he give attention to the topic of discipline except as it might exist in the larger picture of overall behavior. Nevertheless, the principles Skinner brought to light about shaping human behavior through reinforcement have played major roles in several of the models of discipline developed since 1960.

SKINNER'S CENTRAL FOCUS

Before Skinner, the branch of psychology called *behaviorism* had concerned itself with connections between stimuli that an organism receives and responses the organism makes to those stimuli—an approach commonly known as *S-R*, or *stimulus-response, theory*. Various authorities attempted, though with little success, to explain all of human learning in those terms.

Skinner explored the learning process from a different perspective, investigating how learning was affected by stimuli received by an organism *after* it had performed an act rather than before the act. Contrasted to S-R theory, Skinner's approach can be symbolized as *R-S theory*: the organism performs an act (which Skinner called an *operant* rather than a response), and that operant can be affected by a stimulus applied immediately after the operant. Sometimes the stimulus can make the organism more likely than before to repeat the operant behavior. Skinner called such stimuli *reinforcing stimuli*. Skinner's lifework dealt in large part with discovering how animal and human behavior is affected by patterns and frequencies of reinforcing stimuli.

SKINNER'S PRINCIPAL CONCEPTS AND TEACHINGS

Behavior shaping. Behavior is influenced when reinforcing stimuli are received immediately after an organism performs an act. Reinforcing stimuli can therefore be used to form or shape behavior in desired directions.

Operant behavior. This is an act or group of acts performed by an individual. Operant behavior is not a response, reaction, or reflex but is instead a purposeful voluntary action. Operant behaviors can be any of the immense variety of acts that individuals are able to perform voluntarily, such as speaking, entering a room, taking a seat, raising a hand, or completing an assignment.

Reinforcing stimulus. This is a stimulus an individual receives after performing an operant behavior that increases the likelihood that the individual will repeat the operant. Most stimuli, if they are to have a reinforcing effect, must be received within two or three seconds after the operant. Reinforcing stimuli common in classrooms include knowledge of results, peer approval, awards and free time, and smiles, nods, and praise from the teacher. Teachers normally think of reinforcers as synonymous with rewards (though semantically the two are not the same). When teachers see a student exhibit any behavior (operant) that deserves positive attention, they often give the individual a reward (reinforcer). If receiving the reward is pleasing to the student, the behavior is likely to be repeated.

Reinforcement. This is the process of supplying reinforcing stimuli to individuals who have performed desirable behavior.

Positive reinforcement. This is the technical name for the process of supply-ing something that reinforces student behavior. In classrooms, this process involves teachers' providing reinforcing stimuli that the class desires after they have behaved appropriately. Such reinforcers are typically comments ("Good job," "Nice work"), points, or tangible objects such as stickers.

Negative reinforcement. This is the technical name for the process of remov-ing something, the absence of which then reinforces student behavior. This term is widely misunderstood and misused. Most teachers think that negative reinforcement means some sort of punishment that stifles misbehavior. The opposite is true. Negative reinforcement increases the likelihood of a given behavior's being repeated, just as does positive reinforcement. Negative means taking away something that the student doesn't like rather than adding something that the student does like. Negative reinforcement has only limited application in classrooms. Tauber (1982) illustrates one way of using negative reinforcement with the following examples: "If you score 80 percent or high-er on the exam, you will not have to turn in a final paper." (The final paper is taken away as a reward for scoring well on the exam.) "If you get all of your assignments in on time . . . , you will be allowed to drop your lowest grade" (p. 66). These examples show how negative reinforcement is provided through the removal of an *aversive stimulus* (a stimulus that students dis-like).

Schedules of reinforcement. A schedule of reinforcement refers to when and how often reinforcement is provided when someone (e.g., a teacher) attempts to shape an individual's behavior. Different schedules are known to produce different effects. *Constant reinforcement*, provided every time a desired act is seen, is most effective in establishing new learnings. In class-room use, for example, every time all students enter quietly, sit down, and look at the teacher, they may be awarded a team point that goes toward earn-ing a specific benefit at a later time. Individuals work hard and fast to earn rewards they desire. Once new learning is acquired, it can be maintained indefinitely by using *intermittent reinforcement*, in which reward is sup-plied only occasionally. Individuals believe reward will come sooner or later and so continue trying.

Successive approximations. This phrase refers to a behavior-shaping progres-sion in which actions (operants) come closer and closer to a preset goal. Teachers work toward developing desired student behaviors gradually, realiz-ing that often small improvements are all that can be expected. Successive approximations are gradual modifications that lead to overall learning. For example, the class enters the room and sits down. There is still too much chat-ter, but the teacher gives the class a point for improvement because everyone is seated. Later, the students will have to be seated and also be quiet in order to earn a point.

Extinction. Extinction is the disappearance of a particular behavior. Skinner believes that behaviors become extinguished over time if they are never reinforced. Teachers often attempt to extinguish undesired student behaviors by making sure that reinforcement is withheld. This is often done by ignoring an individual's undesirable behavior and insisting that other students ignore it as well.

Behavior modification. Behavior modification is not one of Skinner's terms but has become the standard label for referring to his overall procedure of shaping behavior intentionally. The term is used in educational settings and various kinds of training efforts everywhere.

ANALYSIS OF THE NEO-SKINNERIAN MODEL

As we explore the Neo-Skinnerian model further, let us again note the following: This model of classroom discipline was not developed by Skinner but only reflects his principles of behavior shaping embedded in practical applications for classroom practice. Most of the educational applications of Skinner's discoveries were formalized by other authorities (here referred to as *Neo-Skinnerians*) who recognized the wide applicability of his discoveries to educational matters. But because this approach to controlling human behavior is unique, has such wide applicability, and has proved to be so successful on a large scale, it is put forth here as a foundational model of classroom discipline. You will find its elements included in various contemporary models of discipline.

The Value of Behavior Modification

You now know that *behavior modification* involves the general use of Skinnerian principles to shape behavior in educational settings. Systems of behavior modification will be described later, but they all function in the same essential way: (1) The teacher observes one or more students displaying desired behavior; (2) the teacher supplies some kind of reinforcement to those students; and (3) the reinforced students, along with others, tend to repeat or improve their behavior.

Behavior modification has been found valuable for speeding the learning of academic material as well as improving personal behavior. It brings the advantage of allowing the teacher to work with students in a supportive rather than adversarial manner. When using behavior modification, teachers need not be cold, harsh, and punitive but can accomplish their intentions in a warm, supportive, and positive manner, a demeanor greatly preferred by teachers and students alike.

Why Punishment Is Not Used in Behavior Modification

Since the beginning of human history, parents and teachers have used *punishment* to motivate the young and teach them to behave properly. Punishment can in fact lead to those outcomes, though it often produces side effects of fear, dislike, and desire for revenge. This punitive approach is still seen today, not only in child-rearing practices but in educational efforts as well. But overall does it accomplish what educators and parents intend?

Skinner discovered in his experiments that animals worked harder and learned more quickly when rewarded for doing something right than when punished for doing something wrong. It is understandable that this should be so for rats and pigeons, because there is no way to explain to them what kind of behavior is desired nor what will happen to them if they don't comply. The question for education, therefore, is not whether punishment works but whether it is desirable for use in motivating learning and behavior.

Skinner's later work with human subjects convinced him that humans also respond better to reward than to punishment. While exceptions were noted, rewards generally served better than threat or punishment in clarifying for students what was expected of them, in spurring their interest and effort, and in shaping their behavior.

Research shows that punishment can motivate good behavior and suppress bad behavior, but it has its dark side. Authorities widely agree that its undesirable side effects can override the best educational intentions. If students see punishment as unwarranted, malicious, or excessive, they develop negative feelings that are very difficult to overcome. Those feelings may discourage students from learning or even provoke retaliation toward the teacher and other students. Worse, punishment teaches students that might makes right, a concept that educators have struggled to discredit.

For these reasons, punishment is incorporated into behavior modification only in rare instances where individuals are exceedingly difficult to teach. Teachers of normal students are advised to use a positive approach instead and to resort to punishment only when everything else fails. That does not mean that teachers shouldn't point out to students what they are doing wrong; students need such knowledge if they are to progress rapidly. However, knowledge of error should be provided in helpful rather than punitive ways.

It should be noted that discipline schemes that make use of behavior modification have tended toward a middle ground as concerns punishment. That middle ground involves the concept of *logical consequences* instead of punishment. Students are informed of behavior rules and the consequences, positive and negative, that will be invoked as students comply with or break the rules. For misbehavior, logical consequences typically involve making right what was done wrong, taking time out from class activities, or giving up a preferred activity.

Types of Reinforcers

Reinforcers, called *reinforcing stimuli* by Skinner, can be anything individuals experience or receive following a certain behavior that serves to strengthen that behavior. In life experience, reinforcers range from such mundane things as a breath of fresh air to such rarities as Pulitzer Prizes. While teachers cannot dispense as reinforcers many things that students might wish to have, they still have a powerful arsenal at their disposal, consisting of social, graphic, activity, and tangible reinforcers.

Social Reinforcers.   *Social reinforcers* are words and behaviors that strengthen students' behavior. Examples of social reinforcers are comments, gestures, and facial expressions, and it should be noted that a great many students will work diligently just to obtain a smile, pat, or kind word from the teacher. Social reinforcers can be verbal or nonverbal. Some examples are the following:

Verbal
"Okay." "Wow!" "Excellent." "Nice going." "Exactly." "Right." "Thank you." "I like that." "Would you share that?"

Nonverbal
Smiles, winks, eye contact, nods, thumbs up, touches, pats, handshakes, walking beside, standing near.

Graphic Reinforcers.   *Graphic reinforcers* include marks of various kinds: numerals, check marks, and symbols such as stars and happy faces. Teachers make these marks with pens and rubber stamps. They may enter the marks on charts or use a paper punch to make holes in cards kept by the students. They often use stickers that are commercially available in large quantities and varieties.

Activity Reinforcers.   *Activity reinforcers* include those activities that students prefer in school. Any school activity can be used as a reinforcer if students prefer it to what they would otherwise be doing. Examples of activities that usually reinforce academic learning are the following:

For Younger Students
Being a monitor. Sitting near the teacher. Choosing the song. Caring for the pet. Sharing a pet or toy.

For Middle Students
Playing a game. Free reading. Decorating the classroom. Having extra recess time. Going to an assembly. Watching a class videotape.

For Older Students
Working or talking with a friend. Being excused from a test. Working on a special project. Being excused from homework.

Tangible Reinforcers.   *Tangible reinforcers* are real objects that students can earn as rewards for desired behavior. They are more powerful than social, graphic, or activity reinforcers for many younger students. They are widely used with students who have special behavior problems. Many elementary teachers make regular use of tangible reinforcers such as popcorn, raisins, chalk, crayons, felt pens, pencils, badges, decals, pennants, used books, magazines, stationery, posters, rubber stamps, certificates, notes, letters, and plastic disks.

Systems of Behavior Modification

Behavior modification produces results even when used sporadically, but it works best when applied in a regular, systematic manner. A random approach to reinforcement has been used for decades, primarily based on letter grades and teachers' praise of students for effort and quality work. Familiarity with those efforts caused many teachers to say, when behavior modification was first introduced as a systematic approach, "But I've always done that." In truth, however, few if any teachers before the mid-1960s used reinforcement systematically as a means of shaping behavior. They did use praise, but on a hit-or-miss basis, and they used grades, though low grades were punitive rather than rewarding.

The term *system of behavior modification* means that the approach is used in an organized and consistent manner. Systems of behavior modification, though similar in essence, can be remarkably varied in detail. Each teacher seems to add a personal twist, and that flexibility allows behavior modification to be used in ways consistent with individual personalities and needs. Behavior modification systems can be grouped roughly into the following five categories, each of which will be explained further: (1) "catch 'em being good", (2) rules-ignore-praise (RIP), (3) rules-reward-punishment (RRP), (4) token economies, and (5) behavior contracts.

Catch 'Em Being Good.   *Catch 'em being good* involves rewarding students who are doing what is expected. The teacher says, "Class, take out your math books." Several students get their books at once. Others waste time talking. The teacher picks out students who behaved as directed and says, "Thank you, Heather, for being ready. Thank you, Shaun. I like the way Ramón got his book out and is paying attention." On hearing these comments, many other students then open their books and pay attention. This strategy offers two benefits. First, it reinforces the proper behavior of Heather, Shaun, and Ramón; and second, it shapes behavior of other students as well.

The "catch 'em being good" approach can be used both in conjunction with specific class rules (e.g., "Thank you for raising your hand before speaking, Christina") and with general behavior such as expeditiously following directions, as was the case in the examples given previously. It is especially effective in primary grades, and teachers up through third grade use it extensively, regardless of the overall discipline system they employ. By fourth grade the approach begins to lose effectiveness, and middle school students react to it with a certain disdain. However, even older students tend to respond positively when reinforced privately or as a group rather than singled out publicly.

Rules-Ignore-Praise (RIP).   The *rules-ignore-praise* (RIP) approach is described by its label. The teacher, with student involvement, formulates a set of rules for class behavior. As an example, the rules might be as follows:

1. Be courteous to others.
2. Keep hands, feet, and objects to yourself.

3. Complete all assignments.
4. Work without disturbing others.
5. Follow all directions.

These rules are made clear and understandable to the students. They may be practiced when first introduced and then posted in the room on a chart. Note that only five are listed in this example, a number sufficient for any class.

Once the rules are established and understood, the teacher watches for students who comply with them. The teacher might say, "Row one is doing an excellent job of following directions." Students who comply with the rules regularly receive attention or praise or other rewards. Students who break the rules are ignored; that is, no direct attention at all is given to them or their behavior. Instead, the teacher finds a student who *is* complying with the rules and praises that student. When Mrs. Jennet sees Tim poke his neighbor, she goes to an adjacent student, Samantha, who is following the rules, gives Samantha a sticker, and says, "Thank you, Samantha, for working without bothering others."

This system serves well at the elementary school level, provided that the class is fairly well behaved to begin with. But it is not effective with older students, who speak derisively of peers who receive public praise from the teacher, calling them pets, kiss-ups, and worse. Generally speaking, secondary school students' behavior is not shaped well through praise given to others. When they misbehave, they usually obtain positive reinforcement in the form of teacher attention, peer attention, and laughter.

Rules-Reward-Punishment (RRP). The *rules-reward-punishment* (RRP) approach builds limits and consequences into behavior modification. As with RIP, this approach begins with rules and emphasizes rewards, but it does not ignore improper behavior. The added factor of consequences for misbehavior makes this approach effective with older students and with students who chronically misbehave.

In RRP, the rules phase is the same as described earlier. Rules, few in number, are established, understood, and put on written display. The teacher explains that compliance with the rules is expected: Students who follow the rules will be rewarded in various ways: they will receive praise if appropriate; they will receive laudatory notes to take home to parents; or they will earn points that count toward a larger reward, either for the individual or for the class.

Students are also clearly informed about what will happen if the rules are broken. They realize it is their prerogative to break the rules but that if they do so, they simultaneously choose the consequences (mild punishments) attached to rule breaking, which will be invoked immediately in accordance with procedures that have been described fully and carefully. When Jane refuses to begin her work, Mr. Trammel tells her that, in accordance with class rules and consequences, she must sit at the table in the rear of the room until she completes her assignment. Teachers point out that such punishments are not imposed on the students but rather that the students are choosing, by their behavior, the consequences that have been agreed to previously; students therefore punish themselves for breaking the rules. In other words, they choose to behave in ways that automatically bring consequences they do not like but of which they are fully aware.

This system is effective with students at all grade levels. It clearly sets expectations, rewards, and punishments. Students consider it fair; they know that they have the power to choose good or bad consequences through their behavior and that the responsibility for good behavior rests on their own shoulders. (You will later find that this RRP approach forms the core of Lee Canter's Assertive Discipline, an application model presented in Chapter 6.)

Token Economies.   *Token economies* are elaborate behavior modification systems that involve student accumulation of graphic or tangible reinforcers that can be saved and traded for other items.

Token economies work as follows: Class rules are established. As students comply with the rules—that is, stay in their seats, raise their hands, complete their work, and so on—they are rewarded systematically with tally marks, stamps on a card, or tokens such as plastic chips. The marks or tokens can be accumulated and later exchanged for other activities or tangible rewards such as toys, comic books, or magazines. Some teachers do nothing at all when students break rules (in other words, they ignore the infraction). Other teachers direct the offending student to return a chip or remove a sticker previously earned. While the plan involves exchanging tokens and marks for presumably more desirable rewards, in actual practice teachers find that the tokens often become sufficiently rewarding in themselves; students would rather accumulate them in quantity than turn them in for something else.

Teachers who use token economies must be sure to award the tokens fairly and consistently and to treat rule transgressions with equal consistency. To implement the program, they must have an adequate supply of tokens, provide a manageable way for students to keep the tokens, and be sure that counterfeiting and extortion do not occur. They must set aside a time every couple of weeks for students to cash in their tokens. For larger prizes, students enjoy buying white elephants that other students have brought from home. Teachers can also obtain free materials from shops and stores, and vouchers can be made for special activities and privileges. Each object and voucher is assigned a price in tokens. Some teachers hold auctions in which students bid for available items.

Teachers who use this plan should explain it very carefully to school principal, students, and parents before putting it into practice. This will ensure that everyone understands and approves what is taking place, thus preventing objections that are otherwise likely to occur through misunderstanding. (For an example of a successful token economy, refer to Specialty System 3 in Chapter 13, contributed by middle school teachers Mike Straus and Roy Allen.)

Behavior Contracts.   *Behavior contracts* are sometimes used with older children, especially those who are difficult to manage. Contracts specify work to be done or behavior to be established and deadlines for completion. They state what the payoff will be for successful accomplishment, and they indicate input the teacher will give. The agreements are signed by teacher and student and sometimes by parents and principal as well. Though they are in no way legal instruments, these contracts do have an air of formality about them, and the signatures tend to promote student compliance.

Mr. Lex's contract with Jesse is an example. Jesse has a history of never completing assigned homework. Mr. Lex prepares a contract in which Jesse agrees to do his homework properly. If he does so five days in a row, Mr. Lex will assign him five points. When Jesse has accumulated 15 points, he can exchange them for a pen bearing his favorite sport team's logo.

Contract forms can be prepared so as to appear very official. Quasi-legal terminology adds a pleasing touch for older children, as do filigree and official stamps of gold-colored foil. While contracts may be fun to use, they must be treated as serious commitments, the terms of which must be complied with by all who have signed.

Behavior Modification in Classroom Use

Teachers who decide to implement behavior modification should plan carefully, first to analyze the specific student behaviors they wish to change, second to develop a careful plan for bringing about the desired changes, and third to decide how they will put the plan into effect.

Analyzing Student Behavior.   Analysis involves clarification of the behaviors that are causing concern, specifying what is wrong with them at present and deciding exactly what they should be like in the future. Analysis should also focus on *antecedents*, conditions existent in the classroom that may be contributing to the problem, and *consequences*, the system of rewards and punishments presently being used, or that should be used, to motivate and guide student behavior. Antecedents include such factors as distractions, boredom, poor peer models, lack of clarity concerning rules, lack of follow-through in enforcing rules, awkward transitions between lessons, and so forth. Consequences include reinforcing stimuli, such as have been described in this chapter, as well as logical consequence punishments that serve to suppress misbehavior. This analysis may at first appear complicated, but in fact it can usually be sketched out in no more than a half hour.

Developing the Behavior Modification Plan.   Developing the plan follows from analysis of misbehavior and specification of desired behavior. The plan should outline behaviors that are to receive special attention and should indicate the rules, reinforcers, and consequences that will be used. The plan should be simple enough that it can be easily understood by students and their parents.

The desired behaviors that the plan is designed to bring about are called *target behaviors*. Those target behaviors will be reached over time by shaping student behavior through systematic reinforcement. If one of the target behaviors is "Students will not talk out during class without permission," the teacher might plan to reinforce students who raise their hands and wait to be called on before speaking. In this case, verbal praise might be used as the reinforcer: "Thank you, María, for raising your hand before speaking." If one of the target behaviors is "Students will remain on task for the entire work period," the teacher might decide to use graphic reinforcers, giving each diligent student a number of points for effort and saying "Thank you" or "Good effort" or "I appreciate your help."

Implementing the Plan.   Implementation of the plan, before it can be accomplished adequately, requires correction of antecedent conditions that might be contributing to poor behavior. Rules should be clarified, reviewed, and discussed. Consequences should be described along with procedures for following through. Personal responsibility should be emphasized. Lessons should be tightened to remove dead time, and instructional activities should be made as interesting as possible.

When antecedent conditions are satisfactory, the teacher should discuss with students the behaviors that are interfering with learning and teaching and should present and discuss the behavior modification plan that will be used to improve behavior. Implementation usually requires the alteration of established habits or conditions. Students who misbehave usually do so in part because their misbehavior brings them reinforcement that is not intended by the teacher, such as teacher attention, peer laughter, or peer admiration. These unintended reinforcers must be removed and, better yet, replaced with negative consequences if better behavior is to be achieved. As we have seen, negative consequences range from ignoring the misbehavior to isolating students from the group to invoking more aversive consequences, such as staying after class or giving up participation in desired activities.

Meanwhile, positive consequences should be applied regularly as students show improved behavior. Teachers can usually find a few students behaving as they are supposed to do, and those students should be reinforced. At the elementary level, compliant students can be called by name and reinforced verbally: "Todd, thank you for getting down to work so quickly." "Therese, your paper is very neat." For older students, good behavior should be reinforced without public fanfare. This can be done anonymously by catching students' eyes and nodding or by reinforcing the entire group: "Class, I really appreciate the way many of you helped us get started by having your materials ready."

Efforts have been made in the past to teach students how to reinforce themselves. Lindsley ("Precision Teaching," 1971) advocated a procedure that he called *precision teaching*, in which students graphed their academic performance and in-class behavior. Reinforcement consisted of students' seeing improvement in their graph lines. Mahoney and Thoresen (1972) taught students to set up their own systems of reward and punishment and apply those consequences to their behavior. Kindergarten students who finished their artwork could go on their own to the play area. Fifth graders who did not disrupt during the entire math period could award themselves 10 minutes of free reading time. High school students who completed assignments accurately before they were due could allow themselves to work together with a friend.

Self-reinforcement is of course subject to abuse. Without frequent review of rules and responsibilities, students tend to become extraordinarily lenient in awarding themselves positive consequences while greatly disinclined to note their own transgressive behavior. A compromise can be reached by having the teacher give an *okay signal* when reinforcement is earned and then allow the student to select the preferred reinforcer.

COMMENTS ON THE NEO-SKINNERIAN MODEL

Behavior modification was, in the past, a favored control strategy for many teachers, and its elements of reinforcement and consequences have been incorporated into many models of discipline. But despite its power, behavior modification has also received a great deal of criticism.

A major point of controversy has to do with whether, and to what extent, behavior modification truly helps students or simply gives teachers a way to place tighter control on student thought and action. Another point of controversy concerns rewards. Most authorities have maintained that rewards strengthen desired learning and behavior, but some contend that rewards are counterproductive in that they reduce intrinsic motivation in students (that is, students work only to get the reward) while supplanting genuine desire to learn with extrinsic motivation and tight behavior control (Hill, 1990; Kohn, 1993).

Certainly not all teachers like behavior modification, for reasons listed by critics and because doling out points and other reinforcers can be quite cumbersome. But those teachers who do like it say it makes students better behaved, which in turn makes teaching easier and more enjoyable. Most teachers find behavior modification to be quite effective in helping prevent misbehavior and providing support for student self-control but admit that it is slow and often ineffective as a means of correcting more serious misbehavior.

In any case, most teachers who implement behavior modification on a systematic basis tend to stick with it, obviously appreciating its powerful effects. They come to see it not as a means to manipulate students but as a method to free students to behave in ways that bring success and positive recognition. When teachers make personal attention and reinforcement a natural part of their teaching style, they assign consequences naturally and spontaneously, not artificially as would an overseeing judge. And when reinforcement is provided in ways appropriate to the developmental levels of students, those students do not see the teacher as manipulating their behavior but simply as being kind, considerate, and helpful.

APPLICATION EXERCISES

REVIEW OF SELECTED TERMINOLOGY

The following terms are central to understanding behavior control based on Skinnerian principles. Check yourself to make sure you can explain their meanings.

behavior shaping	punishment
operant behavior	social reinforcers
reinforcing stimulus	graphic reinforcers
reinforcement	activity reinforcers
positive reinforcement	tangible reinforcers
negative reinforcement	catch 'em being good
schedules of reinforcement	rules-ignore-praise (RIP)
successive approximations	rules-reward-punishment (RIP)
extinction	token economy
behavior modification	behavior contracting

CONCEPT CASES

Case 1: Kristina Will Not Work

Kristina, in Mr. Jake's class, is quite docile. She never disrupts class and does little socializing with other students. But despite all his efforts, Mr. Jake cannot get Kristina to participate in class activities. She rarely makes progress on assignments and never completes one. She is simply there, putting forth no effort.

How would Neo-Skinnerians deal with Kristina? Neo-Skinnerians would suggest that Mr. Jake try the following approaches with Kristina:

1. Try to discover a social reinforcer to which Kristina responds, such as physical proximity, a pat, a smile, or a kind word. Catch her being good (doing anything appropriate) and apply the reinforcer at that time. Continue whenever she participates or works.
2. Reiterate the class rules regarding work and completion of assignments. Praise Kristina publicly or privately, or use any other effective reinforcer whenever she follows the rules.
3. If Kristina does not respond to social reinforcers, look for stronger ones. Try using points, tokens, or tangible objects to reinforce and shape Kristina's improvement.
4. Set up a contract with Kristina and her parent, whose help you request. Identify a reward that is especially attractive to Kristina. Outline what she must do in order to earn the reward. Reinforce every improvement she makes.

Case 2: Sara Cannot Stop Talking

Sara is a pleasant girl who participates in class activities and does most, though not all, of the work assigned to her. She could do much better but cannot seem to refrain from talking to classmates. Mr. Gonzales, her teacher, has to speak to her repeatedly during lessons, to the point that he often becomes exasperated and loses his temper.

What techniques of behavior modification might help Mr. Gonzales in deal-ing with Sara?

Case 3: Joshua Clowns and Intimidates

Joshua, larger and louder than his classmates, always wants to be the center of attention, which he accomplishes through a combination of clowning and intimidation. He makes wise remarks, talks back (smilingly) to the teacher, utters a variety of sound-effect nois-es such as automobile crashes and gunshots, and makes limitless sarcastic comments and put-downs of his classmates. Other students will not stand up to him, apparently fearing his size and verbal aggressiveness. His teacher, Miss Pearl, has come to her wit's end.

What approach to behavior modification do you believe would be most appropriate for working with Joshua?

Case 4: Tom Is Hostile and Defiant

Tom has appeared to be in his usual foul mood ever since arriving in class. On his way to sharpen his pencil, he bumps into Frank, who complains. Tom tells him loud-ly to shut up. Miss Baines, the teacher, says, "Tom, go back to your seat." Tom wheels around and says heatedly, "I'll go when I'm damned good and ready!"

How do you believe Neo-Skinnerians would suggest that Miss Baines deal with Tom?

QUESTIONS AND ACTIVITIES

1. Describe how an effective system of behavior modification for use at the primary grade level would differ from an effective system for use at the high school level.
2. Ms. Wong is having problems in her classroom. The students enter boister-ously and take a long time to settle down. They call out answers and make smart remarks during the lesson. Many do not pay attention when Ms. Wong is talking.
   a. Describe how you would set up an RIP behavior modification plan for Ms. Wong's class. (You may prepare the plan as if Ms. Wong's class were a first-, sixth-, or tenth-grade class.)
   b. Describe how you would set up an RRP behavior modification plan for Ms. Wong's class.
   c. Describe how you would set up a token economy behavior modification plan for Ms. Wong's class.
3. Mr. Chester's seventh-grade student, Alex, arrives tardy to class every day and never brings with him the required materials he needs for class activi-ties. Describe how you would advise Mr. Chester to set up a contract with Alex so that the boy would arrive on time with needed materials.

4. Examine Scenario 7 or 8 in Appendix I. Explain how principles of behavior modification might be used to improve the behaviors of specific students in Mrs. Bates's or Mr. Jaramillo's class.

REFERENCES AND RECOMMENDED READINGS

Firth, G. (1985). *Behavior management in the schools: A primer for parents*. New York: Charles C. Thomas.

Hill, D. (1990). Order in the classroom. *Teacher, 1*(7), 70-77.

Kohn, A. (1993). *Punished by rewards: The trouble with gold stars, incentive plans, A's, praise, and other bribes*. Boston: Houghton Mifflin.

Ladoucer, R., & Armstrong, J. (1983). Evaluation of a behavioral program for the improvement of grades among high school students. *Journal of Counseling Psychology, 30*, 100-103.

Macht, J. (1989). *Managing classroom behavior: An ecological approach to academic and social learning*. White Plains, NY: Longman.

Mahoney, M., & Thoresen, C. (1972). Behavioral self-control—Power to the person. *Educational Researcher, 1*, 5-7.

McIntyre, T. (1989). *The behavior management handbook: Setting up effective behavior management systems*. Boston: Allyn & Bacon.

Precision teaching in perspective: An interview with Ogden R. Lindsley. (1971). *Teaching Exceptional Children, 3*, 114-119.

Sharpley, C. (1985). Implicit rewards in the classroom. *Contemporary Educational Psychology, 10*, 349-368.

Skinner, B. F. (1948). *Walden two*. New York: Macmillan.

———. (1953). *Science and human behavior*. New York: Macmillan.

———. (1971). *Beyond freedom and dignity*. New York: Knopf.

Tauber, R. (1982). Negative reinforcement: A positive strategy in classroom management. *Clearing House, 56*, 64-67.

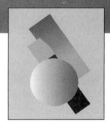

CHAPTER 3

The Kounin Model
Discipline through Classroom Management

Jacob Kounin

BIOGRAPHICAL SKETCH OF KOUNIN

Jacob Kounin was born in Cleveland, Ohio, in 1912. He earned his doctorate at Iowa State University in 1939, and in 1946 he was appointed to a professorship in educational psychology at Wayne State University, where he spent most of his academic career. Kounin made numerous presentations to the American Psychological Association, the American Educational Research Association, and many other professional organizations. He served often as a consultant and visiting professor at other universities.

Kounin is best known for his detailed investigations into the effects of classroom management on student behavior, reported in his book *Discipline and Group Management in Classrooms* (1971, revised 1977). His contributions are frequently cited in scholarly writings that have to do with classroom discipline.

KOUNIN'S CONTRIBUTIONS TO DISCIPLINE

Kounin was the first researcher to present a detailed, scientific analysis of the relationship between certain teaching behaviors and the resultant behavior of students in classrooms. His work led to several conclusions about what teachers should and should not do in order to ensure better student behavior and learning. His work was, and is, very influential, and his teachings have been incorporated into today's most effective models of classroom discipline.

Kounin's research started accidentally one day when he reprimanded a university student for reading a newspaper during the lecture. He noticed that immediately following his reprimand the behavior of other students in the class changed. They sat up straighter and paid closer attention. That started Kounin wondering about the effect teacher *desists* (remarks and reprimands that are intended to stop student misbehavior) might have on other students who were not misbehaving but who only witnessed the desist. He thought that the effect of desists would "ripple out" to other students—he called the phenomenon the *ripple effect*—and might therefore be of considerable value to teachers concerned about classroom discipline.

At first, Kounin conducted his research through interviews, but he found a rather large discrepancy between what was reported and what actually occurred in the classroom. He then changed his research methodology to involve observation in classroom settings. He further refined the procedure by using videotapes of class sessions, which could then be analyzed in detail. Before he completed his research, Kounin had studied thousands of hours of tapes made in 80 different classrooms. He found that the ripple effect of desists, though observable in primary grades, had relatively little influence on the behavior of older students. He redirected his investigations and discovered several other dimensions of teacher behavior that did, in fact, strongly affect student behavior in the classroom.

KOUNIN'S CENTRAL FOCUS

Kounin's central focus evolved over time into a search for teacher behaviors that led to active student involvement in lessons while reducing *deviancy,* or misbehavior. At first, Kounin attempted to determine how teachers responded to misbehavior most effectively, focusing on the characteristics and effects of teacher desists. Before long he concluded that there was little relationship between teacher desists and student behavior.

He then turned attention to teacher behaviors that seemed to affect student attention and participation in lessons, noting that misbehavior rarely occurred when students were engrossed in their lessons. Following up on that lead, he identified a number of classroom management techniques that helped engage students in lessons and thus reduced misbehavior, though he never set forth suggestions concerning how to correct misbehavior once it occurred.

KOUNIN'S PRINCIPAL CONCEPTS AND TEACHINGS

The ripple effect. This is the phenomenon in which teacher words or actions directed at one student tend to spread out and affect the behavior of other students. The ripple effect can be used to advantage in primary grades but has little effect with older students.

Withitness. Kounin used this term to refer to teachers' knowing what was going on in all areas of the classroom at all times, a teacher trait he found especially powerful in reducing the incidence of student misbehavior.

Momentum. Kounin used this term to refer to teachers' starting lessons with dispatch, keeping those lessons moving ahead, bringing them to a satisfactory close, and making transitions from one lesson to another.

Smoothness. This is the term used to indicate steady progression of lessons, with an absence of incidents or changes during a lesson that might abruptly disrupt student work or thought.

Group alerting. This term refers to teachers' efforts to gain student attention and inform students of what they are supposed to do.

Student accountability. This phrase refers to teachers' efforts to keep students on their toes and involved in lessons, usually by calling on students to respond, demonstrate, or explain.

Overlapping. This term refers to the teacher's ability to attend simultaneously to two or more events in the classroom, such as answering questions for students doing independent work while at the same time instructing a small group of students.

Satiation. This is the technical term that Kounin used to refer to students' getting their complete fill of a topic, at least temporarily. Satiation is brought on by boredom, frustration, and repetition.

Valence and challenge arousal. This phrase refers to what teachers do to make instructional activities more enjoyable and challenging, thereby delaying the onset of satiation. Included are teacher enthusiasm, variety in activities, and the use of media, objects, and other props.

Seatwork variety and challenge. Kounin gives this term importance without clearly defining it. One presumes that it is similar to valence and challenge arousal, except that it applies to seatwork activities assigned to students rather than to instructional episodes under the direct control of the teacher.

ANALYSIS OF THE KOUNIN MODEL

The Ripple Effect

It was mentioned that Kounin's research into behavior management grew out of an accidental observation he made while teaching his own university class, in which he noticed that when he reprimanded one of his students, other students were affected by the reprimand and changed their behavior as well.

Intrigued by this observation, Kounin proceeded to investigate the nature of *desists* (remarks and reprimands) and the spread of their effects, which as mentioned previously he called the *ripple effect.* He arranged experiments in four different settings: kindergartens, high school classrooms, university classrooms, and a summer camp group. In those experiments, he tried to determine whether and to what extent the nature of a desist influenced the degree of conforming behavior among students who received the desist and, more important, among those who merely witnessed it.

Kindergarten Level. In the kindergarten studies, Kounin had teachers make desist statements that showed three different qualities: *clarity, firmness,* and *roughness.* Clear desists included the name of the offender, specified the unacceptable behavior, and gave the reason for the desist. Firm desists projected an "I mean it" attitude until the misbehavior stopped. Rough desists included mild punishment and teacher anger. In this set of experiments, Kounin found the following at the kindergarten level:

1. Clarity increased the conforming behavior of all students who witnessed the desist.
2. Firmness increased conformity only in students who were misbehaving at the time.
3. Roughness did not improve behavior at all; it simply upset the members of the class, making them restless and anxious.
4. The ripple effect in general was especially evident on the first day but tended to diminish within a few days.

High School Level.   In the high school study, Kounin explored the following qualities of desists: presence of punishment, amount of threatened harm to the deviant,
clarity, firmness, anger, and presence or absence of humor. In no case did any quality of the desist either decrease or increase the amount of misbehavior among high
school students. Except for their effect on the student being reprimanded, desists
had little effect of any kind on student behavior; however, extremely angry outbursts by the teacher did cause students some emotional discomfort.

While desists had no effect on the behavior of high school students, Kounin did
find that those students' behavior was strongly affected by their liking for the teacher. Students who held the teacher in high regard misbehaved less frequently and less
severely and tended to work more diligently and productively.

University Level.   In the experiment with university students, Kounin presented
the desists somewhat differently than with the other groups. He compared the effects
of a *supporting desist* (offering to help a student whose behavior was inappropriate)
to those of a *threatening desist* (chastising the student). He found that both types of
desists produced a slight ripple effect among adult students, but the effect was too
weak to be of practical value.

Summer Camp.   In the summer camp study, Kounin explored the same qualities
of desists as in the kindergarten experiment. With the camp participants, who
ranged from 7 to 13 years of age, Kounin found no measurable ripple effect following the desists. He acknowledged the possibility, however, that the lack of effect
might have been due to the fact that misconduct at camp was considered more
acceptable than at school and resulted in fewer consequences. The children in the
summer camp setting may simply have not taken the desists seriously.

Conclusions Concerning the Ripple Effect.   Kounin's investigations produced
300 different statistical correlations involving desists and behavior. Only 2 were mar-
ginally significant, while the other 298 were statistically insignificant. That caused
Kounin to write that

> *there is no relationship between the qualities of a teacher's desist tech-
> niques and the degree of her success in handling a deviancy.*

He also wrote that

> *the techniques of dealing with misbehavior, as such, are not significant
> determinants of how well or poorly children behave in classrooms, or
> with how successful a teacher is in preventing one child's misbehavior
> from contaging others.* (p. 70)

Those conclusions caused Kounin to change his research focus away from
desists and toward identification of teacher traits and behaviors that seemed to influ-

ence student involvement in class activities and bring about a corresponding reduction in the amount of misbehavior. Before we proceed to a consideration of what Kounin discovered, let us review the conclusions that can be drawn from his studies of the ripple effect.

1. The ripple effect does influence the behavior of younger children. By correcting one child's misbehavior, a teacher can simultaneously improve the behavior of many others in the group. Therefore, the ripple effect can be included as an important component of elementary teachers' control techniques.

2. At the elementary level, the ripple effect occurs both from positive comments ("Good, I see that many of you are just about to finish your work") and from negative comments ("It looks to me as though some of you are going to have to stay in at recess to complete your work").

3. With older students, the effects of desists do not seem to ripple to other class members, except to make students uncomfortable and anxious.

4. With older students, liking for the teacher has much more influence on behavior than does the ripple effect. Both high school and university students work harder and behave better for teachers they hold in high regard.

We now move ahead to consider factors other than the ripple effect that Kounin found influential in classroom control. Those factors are withitness, momentum and smoothness, group alerting and accountability, overlapping, valence and challenge arousal, and seatwork variety and challenge.

Withitness

In his videotape analyses, Kounin discovered that teachers very good in classroom control seem to have those proverbial eyes in the back of the head that allow them to know what is going on in all areas of the classroom at all times. He calls this awareness phenomenon *withitness* and considers it one of the factors that most clearly differentiate between effective and ineffective teachers.

However, withitness is effective only when students are convinced that the teacher does in fact know what is occurring in every corner of the classroom. Teachers need to communicate their awareness, which they can do with both behaviors and words. If Bob and Bill are not working, the teacher's eye contact will show that awareness. If necessary, the teacher may say, "I see you have not started. This work must be done today."

Kounin identifies several manifestations of withitness that contribute to its effectiveness. One is the ability to select the proper student for correction. Suppose that Bob and Bill are teasing Mary while the teacher is working elsewhere with a small group. Mary protests aloud. The teacher who displays withitness correctly identifies the boys and tells them to get to work. But a teacher who is not fully aware of the situation may only hear Mary and thus incorrectly tell her to stop talking and get to work. If the teacher fails to attend to the instigators of the situation, that teacher communicates to the class a lack of awareness of what is really going on.

A second manifestation of genuine withitness is the ability to attend first to the more serious deviancy when two or more misbehaviors are occurring simultaneously. To illustrate: Jill is playing with something at her desk and is not doing the assigned work. Meanwhile, James and Eric are angrily pushing each other in a corner of the room. The teacher looks up and says, "Jill, put that away and get to work." That teacher failed to identify the more serious misbehavior. If this occurs often, students begin to realize that their teacher is not truly aware of events in the classroom, and as a result they may feel free to misbehave further.

A third manifestation of withitness has to do with timing. Teachers possessing withitness do not allow misbehavior to spread to other students before taking action. Consider this scene: Mark crumples his paper into a ball and throws it at the wastebasket. Ian sees him and decides to try it, too. Before long, several other boys have happily joined the shooting contest. The situation should never have been allowed to progress to that point. The teacher should have noted and corrected the misbehavior when it first occurred.

A similar timing mistake is to allow misbehavior to increase in seriousness before taking action. Consider the following: The second-grade teacher has given two boys permission to go to the drinking fountain. Mark was there first, but Justin rushed around and pushed in ahead of him. Mark pushed Justin in return. The two glared at each other, exchanged words, and postured for a while before beginning to scuffle. Only then did the teacher intervene, but it was too late. This suggested to the class that the teacher was not aware of the situation until it was out of hand. By speaking to the boys earlier, the teacher could have prevented the confrontation and at the same time communicated withitness.

Momentum and Smoothness

Kounin observed that all teachers have to manage a great deal of what he calls *activity movement.* In activity movement, he includes both psychological and physical movement related to the progression of lessons. Kounin draws attention to two other phenomena within activity movement: (1) *momentum,* which refers to teachers' getting activities started promptly, keeping them moving ahead, and bringing them to efficient closure or transition, and (2) *smoothness,* which indicates an absence of abrupt changes that interfere with students' activities or thought processes. Kounin found that momentum and smoothness, which he ultimately investigated as a single combined factor, correlate highly with desired student behavior.

Momentum and smoothness were found to be especially important during lesson presentations and during transitions from one lesson or activity to another, for it is at those times that student misbehavior is most likely to occur. Kounin explains smoothness difficulties in terms of jerkiness and slowdowns.

Jerkiness.   *Jerkiness* describes the failure to move smoothly from one activity to another, as illustrated in the following episodes: Suppose that high school students are working on an art project. Unexpectedly, the teacher says, "Put your supplies away and get ready for a visitor." Half the class does not hear the directions and the other half starts to move around in confusion. Or suppose that an elementary class has just begun a math lesson. The teacher calls on three students to go to the board. On their way up, the teacher suddenly asks, "Just a minute. Class, how many of you brought you money for the field trip?" The teacher counts the raised hands, goes to the desk, and writes down the number.

In the many classrooms he studied, Kounin found that such jerkiness—those abrupt changes that seem to interrupt students' thought processes—promote confusion, unnecessary activity, noise, delay, and various transgressions of class rules. In contrast, smoothness in activity transitions, where students follow routines that do not abruptly interrupt activity or train of thought, keep students at work and cut down on behavior problems.

Slowdowns.   *Slowdowns*, which are also detrimental to momentum and smoothness, are delays that waste time during instruction and between activities. A typical slowdown occurs with what Kounin called *overdwelling*. Overdwelling occurs in many forms, such as spending too much time giving directions and explanations, lecturing students lengthily about inappropriate behavior, and spending too much time on the details of a lesson rather than on its main points. Suppose Mr. Anderson is teaching a composition lesson. He directs students to begin writing, but he stops them frequently with comments such as "Make sure you leave space at the margins," "Remember the sequence we spoke of," "Don't forget to number each paragraph," "Keep your paragraphs fairly short," and "Be sure each paragraph contains a topic sentence." His comments, which are intended to be helpful, break student concentration and slow their progress.

These matters may seem inconsequential in the larger picture of the instructional period or day, but Kounin's investigations led him to conclude that the teacher's ability to manage smooth transitions and maintain momentum is more important to work involvement and classroom control than any other behavior-management technique. In other words, momentum and smoothness do more to maintain good classroom behavior than do any of the discipline techniques Kounin saw teachers use.

Group Alerting and Accountability

Teachers have few opportunities to work exclusively with one student. Mostly they work with groups or with the entire class as a whole. Kounin found that the ability to maintain a concerted group focus—by which he means the ability to keep students alert, attentive, and actively involved in appropriate activities—is essential to a productive, efficient classroom. Group focus is most easily obtained by alerting and accountability.

Alerting.   By *alerting* Kounin means two things: (1) getting students' attention and (2) quickly letting them know what they are supposed to do. Kounin reports that teachers adept in alerting tend to use such attention-getting approaches as such looking around the group in a suspenseful manner and perhaps making statements as the following:

1. "I wonder who can . . ."
2. "Class, look at this odd illustration. What do you think it might mean? If you can guess, raise your hand."
3. "We are now going to have a timed test with thirty problems to solve. Let's see if we can set a new record this morning."
4. "I want you all to listen to Jim as he reads and see if you can guess who took the crystal ball."

Such practices draw the attention of all group members. Kounin contrasts them with what he considers ineffective practices that lead to inattention, such as the following:

1. The teacher focuses on one student at a time and fails to include other students in the discussion.
2. The teacher chooses the person who is to respond before asking the question.
3. The teacher begins a lesson without attempting to get students' minds engaged in the central question, topic, or skill to be learned.

Accountability.   By *accountability*, Kounin means holding each student in the group responsible for active involvement in learning the facts, concepts, or procedures being taught. To encourage accountability, he says, teachers need to know what each student is doing and how each is responding and progressing. Kounin recommends several techniques for holding students accountable, including the following:

1. All students hold up response cards for the teacher to see.
2. The teacher asks all students to observe and check accuracy while one group member performs.
3. The teacher asks all students to write an answer and then, at random, calls on various students to respond aloud.
4. The teacher circulates and observes the responses of nonreciters.

These approaches enable teachers to work with the entire group and still obtain individual evidence of involvement and progress. When students see that the teacher intends to hold them definitely and immediately accountable for the content of the lesson, they pay better attention, involve themselves in the activities, and find fewer reasons to misbehave.

Overlapping

In his studies of classroom practices, Kounin became aware of a group-management technique that skilled teachers used, a technique that he calls *overlapping*. Overlapping refers to attending to two or more issues at the same time. For example, a teacher is meeting with a small group and notices that two students at their seats are playing cards instead of doing their assignment. The teacher could correct the behavior by either:

1. stopping the small-group activity, walking over to the cardplayers and getting them back on task, and then attempting to reestablish the small-group work; or
2. having the small group continue while addressing the cardplayers from a distance, then monitoring the students at their desks while continuing with the small-group activity.

As you can guess, the second approach involves overlapping. Teachers are continually interrupted while working with groups or individuals. For example, if a student approaches with a paper that must be reviewed before the student can continue, teachers adroit in overlapping can check the paper while glancing at the small group and adding encouraging remarks such as "Go on" or "That's correct." Thus, the teacher attends to various issues simultaneously.

Not surprisingly, Kounin found that teachers adept in overlapping are also aware of the broader scope of happenings in the classroom. They are more "with-it," as Kounin would say. Overlapping, in fact, cannot be done effectively if the teacher does not demonstrate withitness. When students working independently know that the teacher is aware of them, they are more likely to remain properly on task.

Valence and Challenge Arousal

Kounin found, as one would expect, that misbehavior is more likely to occur as students become bored and restless (or "satiated," as Kounin would say). To investigate what teachers do that contributes to boredom and restlessness, and conversely what they do to avoid those conditions, Kounin made a concerted effort to explore valence and the satiation effect in class activities.

Valence.   *Valence* refers to whether students are having a positive or negative reaction to a lesson, while *change of valence* refers to whether students, as their involvement with an activity continues, change their attitudes toward the activity. *Satiation* is technically defined as a change of valence of an activity due to repetition. When students become so tired of an activity that they want nothing more to do with it, at least for a while, they are said to be satiated—in other words, they have had all they can stand for the time being.

It is a fact of teaching that prolonged experience with virtually all learning activities leads to satiation. Students become tired and bored with anything if given too much of it. Their growing satiation is evident in behavior as they look elsewhere, make more mistakes, obviously disengage from the lesson, and finally turn for relief to less acceptable behaviors such as sharpening pencils, talking, annoying each other, or getting up and moving about the room.

But many intended learnings can be acquired only through prolonged exposure and repetition. Can the onset of satiation, and the misbehavior it so often permits, be delayed in classroom teaching?

Kounin found that many fine teachers use techniques that spur student interest in learning and rekindle that interest when it lags, thereby postponing satiation and at the same time avoiding considerable misbehavior that would otherwise occur. Kounin identified three categories of teacher techniques that renew interest: (1) routine, (2) positive, and (3) negative.

Routine Techniques.   *Routine techniques* are those that concern familiar classroom and instructional practices, such as having students take turns, providing regular explanations, calling on reciters, and the like—that is, the things that teachers ordinarily do when teaching.

Positive Techniques.   *Positive techniques* are those in which the teacher does something extra, perhaps a bit out of the ordinary, to excite student interest or involvement. Kounin cites building on individual students' previous progress, adding instructional enrichments, and interspersing challenging yet accomplishable subtasks as examples of positive techniques.

Negative Techniques.   *Negative techniques* are those in which teachers repeat explanations, demonstrations, or directions well beyond what is necessary for clarity or use instructional activities that are clearly uninspiring to students.

By analyzing the effects of routine, positive, and negative techniques, Kounin was then able to determine some of the things that more effective teachers do in maintaining student interest. He found that better teachers tend to emphasize challenge, instructional variety, and student awareness of progress.

Challenge Arousal.   Kounin noticed that teachers who offer *challenge arousals* throughout a lesson hold off satiation for a long while. To keep students alert and eager they would say challenging things like "You are going to need your thinking caps for this one; it's tricky" or "I'm going to predict that nobody in the room can figure this one out. Anybody want to try?"

Such challenges nudge students forward, as do simple enthusiastic statements from the teacher such as "This is going to be a magical day for us!" or "This has been my favorite story ever since I was a child" or "You will remember this experience the rest of your life!" or "This is something I bet your parents have never done" or "If you can do this, you can do anything."

Comments of this sort must, of course, reflect the teacher's genuine feelings, and they must have at least some relationship to fact. Teachers quickly lose their credibility if they carry on about how exciting dull activities are going to be.

Variety.   Teachers know that variety is both the spice of life and the spice of lessons, yet many allow themselves to get stuck in routines that do little to stimulate student thinking. Kounin found that more effective teachers offer a *variety* of activities in their instruction. For example, the elementary teachers Kounin observed varied activities so that quiet activities, noisy activities, seated activities, and movement activities were interspersed, thus providing pleasant changes in thought, movement, and use of the senses. Secondary teachers made similar variations within instructional periods, or from day to day, varying reading and analysis with skill practice, discussion, creative production, and purposeful problem solving.

Teachers can also provide variety in the way they present lessons. They can demonstrate, direct an activity, ask questions for discussion, or have students solve problems on their own. When monitoring students at work, teachers may circulate among them or even participate in the activities. Students enjoy such variety in styles and presentation, even when covering material that has otherwise lost its appeal.

Variety can also be provided in other ways—in materials, instructional objects, color, sound, and movement, all of which provide relief from the usual chores of listening, reading, and writing. And, of course, variety can be provided by restructuring study groups. For example, a teacher might begin a lesson with the entire class, break into small groups for interaction, and then reconvene the entire class for group reports, thus alternating leadership between teacher and students.

Progress.   Kounin found students' sense of *progress* to be a factor that helps a great deal in delaying satiation. Students are often very unclear about whether they are making progress. Teachers can reassure students verbally concerning their learning, but it is more helpful if the results can be depicted numerically or graphically.

Seatwork Variety and Challenge

Kounin reported that *seatwork variety and challenge* substantially increase student work involvement while lowering deviancy and that "in fact, seatwork variety correlates higher with work involvement in seatwork than any other single dimension of teacher style" (p. 139). But despite the stated value of variety and challenge in student seatwork assignments, Kounin does not describe or give examples of variety and challenge in the seatwork assignments he analyzed. One might surmise that variety and challenge are of a similar nature to those same elements explained in his discussion of valence and challenge arousal.

KOUNIN'S REFLECTIONS ON HIS INVESTIGATIONS

In commenting on what he had learned from his studies, Kounin explains that he was forced to reconsider the original intentions of his research. He had expected to find a relationship between student behavior and the quality of the desists that teachers use to curb misbehavior. But no such reliable findings for desists emerged, either for their immediate effect on students or for the overall amount of deviancy in the classroom. As Kounin states, that unexpected fact required

> unlearning on my part, in the sense of having to replace the original question by other questions. Questions about disciplinary techniques were eliminated and replaced by questions about classroom management in general [and] preventing misbehavior was given higher investigative priority than handling misbehavior. (p. 143)

Thereafter, Kounin looked for two kinds of student behavior—work involvement and deviancy—and tried to identify teacher behaviors associated with them. He claims success in identifying the elements just presented: withitness, momentum, smoothness, group alerting and accountability, overlapping, valence and challenge arousal, and seatwork variety and challenge. Kounin presents statistical correlations to support the relationships he identified and asserts:

> These techniques of classroom management apply to emotionally disturbed children in regular classrooms as well as to nondisturbed children. They apply to boys as well as to girls. [They] apply to the group and not merely to individual children. They are techniques of creating an effective classroom ecology and learning milieu. One might note that none of them necessitate punitiveness or restrictiveness. (p. 144)

He goes on to say that

> the business of running a classroom is a complicated technology having to do with developing a nonsatiating learning program; programming for progress, challenge, and variety in learning activities; initiating and maintaining movement in classroom tasks with smoothness and momentum; coping with more than one event simultaneously; observing and emitting feedback for many different events; directing actions at appropriate targets; maintaining a focus upon a group; and doubtless other techniques not measured in these researches. (pp. 144–145)

To Kounin's way of thinking, effective discipline has little to do with teachers' reprimanding students. Rather, it has to do with putting in place effective management techniques that, as they contribute to work involvement, prevent the occurrence of misbehavior.

COMMENTS ON THE KOUNIN MODEL

The management techniques described by Kounin are without question effective in creating and maintaining a classroom atmosphere conducive to learning. By keeping students busily and willingly engaged in learning activities, teachers certainly cut down on the number of behavior problems with which they would otherwise have to contend.

Further, the valuable techniques that Kounin identified can clearly be learned and performed by teachers. After all, Kounin identified them by analyzing what effective teachers did in actual practice. It is interesting to note that Kounin did not believe that teachers' personality traits had much to do with classroom control. In reference to teacher traits such as friendliness, helpfulness, rapport, warmth, patience, and the like, he declared that (contrary to popular opinion) such traits are of little value in managing a classroom. Management, he insisted, is a complicated technology consisting of specific techniques applied at the appropriate times and in the appropriate manner so as to provide learning experiences that are nonsatiating.

If we made a list of what Kounin would have teachers do, it would look something like the following:

- Know what is happening in every area of the classroom at all times and communicate that fact to students.
- Be able to deal with more than one issue at a time.
- When misbehavior occurs, deal with the correct person before the misbehavior escalates. Stop the misbehavior before it becomes more serious.
- Maintain group focus through alerting students and holding them accountable.
- Provide nonsatiating learning programs by emphasizing challenge, variety, and progress.

Kounin's ideas have been widely acknowledged and well received. His clarification of the role of management in maintaining good behavior has made an important contribution to school discipline, just as have Redl and Wattenberg's explanations of group behavior and Skinner's explanations of how to shape student behavior. Most systems of discipline in use today incorporate management techniques similar to those Kounin found so valuable.

While there is no doubt about the value of Kounin's suggestions in maintaining a good learning environment that is relatively free from deviancy, his proposals fail to provide teachers a complete program of discipline that can both prevent student misbehavior and correct it expeditiously when necessary. Teachers accept Kounin's advice concerning the prevention of misbehavior but find that he provides them little help when classroom misbehavior must be stopped, dealt with, and redirected.

APPLICATION EXERCISES

REVIEW OF SELECTED TERMINOLOGY

The following terms are central to the Kounin model of discipline. Check yourself to make sure you can explain their meaning:

desists	jerkiness
ripple effect	slowdowns
supporting desist	overdwelling
threatening desist	alerting
withitness	accountability
activity movement	overlapping
momentum	satiation
smoothness	seatwork variety and challenge

CONCEPT CASES

Case 1: Kristina Will Not Work

Kristina, in Mr. Jake's class, is quite docile. She never disrupts class and does little socializing with other students. But despite Mr. Jake's best efforts, Kristina rarely completes an assignment. She doesn't seem to care. She is simply there, putting forth virtually no effort.

How would Kounin deal with Kristina?   Kounin would suggest the following sequence of interventions, hoping to find one that is effective with Kristina.

1. Provide interesting learning activities with variety and challenge. Observe and talk with Kristina about what she most likes to do in school and incorporate some of her favorite activities into the lessons.
2. If this is a primary grade, use the ripple effect: "I see many people have already completed half their work." Look at Kristina and say, "Thank you, Jason, for working so hard. Thank you, Shireen." Comment, "I am afraid a few people will have to stay late to complete their work." If Kristina still doesn't work, ask her what could be done to encourage her to do her work.
3. Call on Kristina in discussions preceding independent work as a means of involving her. If she is reluctant to speak, ask questions that she can at first answer by saying yes or no or by holding her thumb up or down. As she responds, involve her more.

4. When Kristina does some work, acknowledge her progress: "Good for you! Now you are on to it! I can see you are trying hard." Challenge her to do more: "I want to see if you can answer two more problems before the end of the period. What do you think? Can you do that?"
5. Hold Kristina accountable in group activities. Be persistent. Do not ignore her simply because she refuses to work.

Case 2: Sara Cannot Stop Talking

Sara is a pleasant girl who participates in class activities and does most, though not all, of her assigned work. She cannot seem to refrain from talking to classmates, however. Her teacher, Mr. Gonzales, has to speak to her repeatedly during lessons, to the point that he often becomes exasperated and loses his temper.

What suggestions would Kounin give Mr. Gonzales to help stop Sara's misbehavior?

Case 3: Joshua Clowns and Intimidates

Joshua, larger and louder than his classmates, always wants to be the center of attention, which he accomplishes through a combination of clowning and intimidation. He makes wise remarks, talks back (smilingly) to the teacher, utters a variety of sound-effect noises such as automobile crashes and gunshots, and makes limitless sarcastic comments and put-downs of his classmates.

Other students will not stand up to him, apparently fearing his verbal and physical aggression. His teacher, Miss Pearl, has come to her wit's end.

What do you find in Kounin's work that might help Miss Pearl deal with Joshua?

Case 4: Tom Is Hostile and Defiant

Tom has appeared to be in his usual foul mood ever since arriving in class. On his way to sharpen his pencil, he bumps into Frank, who complains. Tom tells him loudly to shut up. Miss Baines, the teacher, says, "Tom, go back to your seat." Tom wheels around and says heatedly, "I'll go when I'm damned good and ready!"

What advice can you glean from Kounin's work that might help Miss Baines deal with Tom?

QUESTIONS AND ACTIVITIES

1. How do you think withitness and the ripple effect would work with Kristina, Sara, Joshua, and Tom?
2. How might Sara's behavior affect others in the class? How could its contagious effects be reduced?

3. According to Kounin's findings, first determine which students in the class would be most affected by the following teacher actions and comments, then describe how those students would be affected.
   a. Mr. Kent (first grade) says, "Kevin, I see you bothering Brian while you are supposed to be working. I need you to get busy working right now."
   b. Mrs. Ames (sixth grade) sees Johnny not working, locates Tina who *is* working, and says, "Some of us are not working. Thank you, Tina, for working as directed."
4. Evaluate the following to determine where, and to what extent, satiation might become a problem. Explain your conclusions.
   a. Mrs. Ames does not allow her class to move ahead into a new unit of work until all students have completed the old unit with grades of C or better. Those who pass early are given review and worksheets for further practice until the others catch up.
   b. Mr. Grant has developed a systematic procedure in which all of his lessons are delivered in the same way—lecture followed by reading followed by worksheets. Mr. Grant contends that this routine helps students feel comfortable in that they know what to do and how to use the materials.
5. One of the things Ms. Alletto's students like best about her is that she never pressures them to move quickly from one activity to the next. She seems to understand their need to talk with each other about nonschool matters. She always waits until all the class gets ready before beginning a new lesson or activity. What would Kounin say about Ms. Alletto's style?
6. Examine scenario 4 or 5 in Appendix I. Which of Kounin's suggestions would be helpful to Mrs. Desmond or Mrs. Reed in establishing a more productive and pleasant learning environment?

REFERENCE

Kounin, J. (1977). *Discipline and group management in classrooms.* (rev. ed.). New York: Holt, Rinehart & Winston. (Original work published 1971)

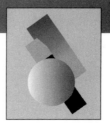

CHAPTER 4

The Ginott Model
Discipline through Congruent Communication

Haim Ginott

BIOGRAPHICAL SKETCH OF GINOTT

Haim Ginott was born in 1922 in Tel Aviv, Israel. A classroom teacher early in his career, he later earned his doctorate at Columbia University and went on to hold professorships in psychology at Adelphi University and at New York University Graduate School. Ginott also served as a UNESCO consultant in Israel, was resident psychologist on television's *Today* show, and wrote a weekly syndicated column titled *Between Us* that dealt with interpersonal communication. He became familiar to teachers through his best-selling books that described how parents and teachers could communicate most effectively with children and teenagers. Ginott's career was cut short by his death in 1973.

GINOTT'S CONTRIBUTIONS TO DISCIPLINE

Ginott was the first strong champion of the role of communication in building sound classroom discipline. When teachers speak with students, Ginott maintained, they should always endeavor to use *congruent communication,* a style of speaking that does not attack students but remains harmonious with students' feelings.

Ginott carried his messages to parents and educators by means of three extremely popular books. In the first two, *Between Parent and Child* (1965) and *Between Parent and Teenager* (1969), Ginott focused on communication break-downs that drive wedges between parents and their offspring and described means of avoiding those breakdowns. He believed that adults, whether parents, teachers, or others, vitally impact children's self-esteem through the messages they send. That impact can be either negative and destructive or positive and constructive.

Ginott showed how communication can provide a desirable positive impact, and he developed specific skills to help parents resolve conflicts they might encounter with their children. The fundamental principle Ginott championed was that when adults speak to children they must always address the situation, not the character of the child. It was Ginott who popularized the notion of parents' showing their children that they still love them even when strongly disapproving of their behavior.

In 1971, Ginott published *Teacher and Child*, a book that explained his ideas on communicating with the young in school settings. In that book he wrote that as a young teacher he came to the frightening conclusion that

> I am the decisive element in the classroom. It is my personal approach that creates the climate. It is my daily mood that makes the weather. As a teacher I possess tremendous power to make a child's life miserable or joyous. I can be a tool of torture or an instrument of inspiration. I can humiliate or humor, hurt or heal. In all situations it is my response that decides whether a crisis will be escalated or de-escalated, and a child humanized or de-humanized. (p. 13)

Ginott was certain that teachers hold the power to make or break a child's self-concept, as do the child's parents, and that teacher power is wielded largely through communication. In *Teacher and Child*, Ginott explained how proper communication in the classroom helps establish and maintain a secure, humanitarian, productive environment for learning.

GINOTT'S CENTRAL FOCUS

Ginott's central focus was on the use of what he called *congruent communication*—communication that addresses the student's situation rather than the student's character and personality. Ginott referred to congruent messages as *sane messages,* and he showed how such messages can be used to guide students away from self-defeating behavior and toward behavior that is appropriate and lasting. For educators who might hope for instantaneous results from his suggestions, he explained that guidance through communication had to be used repeatedly over time for its power to take effect. Ginott did not therefore propose a discipline system that could reach full effectiveness in a single day. True discipline (by which Ginott meant self-discipline) never occurs in that manner, he explained. True discipline occurs over time, in a series of small steps that produce genuine changes within the hearts of students.

GINOTT'S PRINCIPAL CONCEPTS AND TEACHINGS

Present tense. Learning is always in the present tense, meaning teachers do not pre-judge students or hold grudges, and it is always personal to the student.

Congruent communication. This is communication that is harmonious with students' feelings about situations and themselves. The cardinal principle of congruent communication is that it addresses situations rather than students' character and personality.

Teachers at their best. When at their best, teachers make use of congruent communication; they address situations rather than students' character. They do not preach or moralize. They impose no guilt and demand no promises. Instead, they confer dignity on their students.

Teachers at their worst. When at their worst, teachers label students, belittle them, and denigrate their character. They usually do these things inadvertently.

Sane messages. Sane messages are communications from adults that allow the young to trust their own perceptions and feelings.

Inviting cooperation. Effective teachers briefly describe the situation and indicate what needs to be done (which invites cooperation); they do not dictate to students or boss them around (which provokes resistance).

The Ten Commands. This is a term Ginott uses to refer to the unnecessarily detailed work directions that many teachers give their students. Superfluous directions slow work and provoke annoyance.

Acceptance and acknowledgment. These are traits that Ginott would like to see in all teachers—the acceptance and acknowledgment of genuine student comments or behaviors without denying, disputing, deriding, denigrating, derogating, degrading, or arguing. (This does not mean that the teacher must appear to agree with the comments or behaviors or let them go past without comment.)

The hidden asset. Ginott says that teachers have a hidden asset upon which they should always call, namely, "How can I be helpful to my students right now?" Most classroom difficulties are avoided when teachers keep that asset foremost in mind.

Expressing anger: I-messages versus you-messages. Teachers should feel no reluctance to express genuine anger when provoked by student misbehavior. Their anger, however, should not be leveled at students' character. Instead of saying, "You are incredibly inconsiderate!" teachers should tell how they feel: "I am so angry right now that I feel I had better not say anything."

Laconic language. Laconic means short, concise, and brief, which describes the sort of sentences Ginott advocates for responding to or redirecting misbehaving students. Yet he also suggests using long or difficult words that students are not accustomed to hearing, such as "I am aghast!" or "I am appalled!" or "I am dismayed!"

Evaluative praise. This is praise from the teacher that evaluates the student, for example, "You raised your hand. Good boy!" Evaluative praise is worse than none at all, according to Ginott.

Appreciative praise. This is praise in which the teacher shows appreciation for what the student has done, without evaluating the student's character (e.g., "I can almost smell those pine trees when I look at your drawing"). Teachers should make sure all praise they give students is appreciative rather than evaluative.

Labeling is disabling. This is a saying Ginott uses to emphasize that it is harmful to label students derogatorily; students tend to live up to the labels they are given.

Invasion of privacy. Ginott urges teachers to respect students' privacy. They should not pry when students do not wish to discuss personal matters, but should show they are available should students need to talk.

Correcting by directing. This is a saying that Ginott uses to describe how misbehaving students should be dealt with; instead of being reprimanded, students should be (re)directed into appropriate behavior.

Teachers' why questions. These are questions that do not prompt inquiry but are used to make students feel guilty, for example, "Why are you so disorganized?"

Sarcasm. Sarcasm is almost always dangerous. It should be used, if at all, only with greatest care.

Series of little victories. Classroom discipline is attained gradually, as a series of little victories in which the teacher, through continual displays of self-discipline and helpfulness, promotes humaneness and cooperation within students.

Alternatives to punishment. Ginott insists that punishment only produces hostility, rancor, and vengefulness in students and that it never makes students want to improve; he says therefore that punishment should never be used in attempting to control misbehavior but that alternatives should be found.

Teacher self-discipline. In working with students, teachers should strive for self-discipline in which they do not use behaviors they are trying to eradicate in students, such as raising their voice to end noise, using force to break up fighting, showing rudeness to students who are impolite, and berating students who have used bad language.

ANALYSIS OF THE GINOTT MODEL

Teachers Are the Decisive Element

Ginott depicts teachers as the most powerful, most decisive element in setting and maintaining an effective climate in the classroom. As he puts it, teachers create and maintain the environment. Depending on the nature of this environment, teachers are able to humanize or dehumanize their students. Dehumanized students are kept in constant emotional turmoil and, in that condition, find it difficult to learn. It is the teachers' responsibility to reduce this turmoil. They can do so by consistently using what Ginott calls *congruent communication*, a style of speaking that acknowledges and accepts students' feelings about situations and themselves. In order to illustrate what teachers do that promotes positive or negative climates, Ginott contrasts teachers at their best with teachers at their worst.

Teachers at Their Best

Teachers at their best use congruent communication, in which they

- address situations rather than students' characters,
- invite student cooperation,
- accept and acknowledge student feelings,
- confer dignity upon students,
- express anger appropriately,
- use brevity in correcting misbehavior, and
- use appreciative praise rather than evaluative praise.

Teachers at Their Worst

In contrast with teachers at their best, *teachers at their worst* make little if any use of congruent communication, as shown in their inclination to

- name-call and label students as slow, unmotivated, or troublesome;
- ask rhetorical why questions and give long moralistic lectures;

- invade students' privacy;
- make caustic and sarcastic remarks to students;
- attack students' character;
- demand, rather than invite, cooperation;
- deny students' feelings;
- give long and unnecessary moralistic lectures;
- lose their tempers and self-control;
- use evaluative praise to manipulate students; and
- show themselves to be poor models of humane behavior.

Congruent Communication

We have seen that congruent communication is the foundation underlying the Ginott model of discipline. Congruent communication has been defined as communication that is harmonious with students' feelings about situations and themselves. What it entails in actual practice is shown in the following paragraphs.

Sane Messages.   *Sane messages* is the term that Ginott uses for teacher messages that address situations rather than students' character. Such messages communicate that teachers accept and acknowledge how students feel. Ginott explains his use of the word *sane* by pointing out that sanity depends on people's ability to trust their own perceptions of reality. All too often, adults send insane messages, which tell the young to distrust or deny their feelings or perceptions. Adults use insane messages when they blame, preach, command, accuse, belittle, and threaten. Doing these things tells children to deny their feelings about themselves and to base their sense of self-worth upon judgments others make of them.

Ginott (1973) repeatedly reiterates his fundamental principle of the sane message. When a student gets in trouble, the teacher should always address the situation but never judge the student's character or personality. The following is an example of what Ginott means:

> Two students are talking during a quiet study time, in violation of class rules. The teacher says, "This is quiet time. It needs to be absolutely silent."

By simply describing the concern, teachers allow students to appraise the situation, consider what is right and wrong, and decide how they feel about the situation and themselves. An insane teacher message, by contrast, might be the following:

> "Stop that talking. You two are not only breaking rules, you are being very rude. You evidently have no consideration for others who are trying to work."

Ginott continually maintains that teacher communication has the power to build or destroy student self-concept and personal relationships. Poor teacher communication causes students to doubt their own perceptions of themselves. Good teacher communication simply states the facts and lets students decide whether their behavior is in keeping with what they expect of themselves.

Inviting Student Cooperation.   Ginott urges teachers to learn methods of *inviting cooperation* from students rather than demand it. One of the ways he suggests is to decide with the class before an activity what kinds of personal behavior will be needed during the activity. Another is to stop an activity that has gotten out of control and say, "We can watch the film in silence, or we can do another math worksheet. You decide." If the students continue to disrupt, the teacher must follow through with the alternative, making it clear that such was the students' decision.

Teachers who do not invite cooperation usually resort to demanding it by ordering, bossing, and commanding. Ginott urges teachers to avoid direct commands, which tend to provoke student resistance. Once again, Ginott says to describe the situation and let students decide what their course of action should be. Too often, teachers use long, drawn-out directions or explanations. Ginott called such directions the *Ten Commands*. These include statements such as the following:

Close your library books.

Put them on your desks.

Get out your math books.

Get a pencil.

Put your name at the top of your paper.

Turn to page 60.

Do all the problems.

Circle your final answer.

Keep your work neat so I can read it.

Put your papers in the basket when you are finished.

Rather than have teachers spend so much time on needless directions, Ginott would have them simply say, "It is now math time. The assignment is on page sixty." With that kind of message, teachers show that they respect students' ability to behave autonomously. They invite cooperation, promote self-direction, and foster responsibility, all of which help students learn to function on their own.

By inviting cooperation, teachers begin to break down students' dependency on the teacher. Of course, every individual depends on others in many ways, but if that dependency becomes too strong it creates problems, such as inability to direct oneself. This condition is often seen when students are made too dependent on teachers; without teacher presence or prodding, students behave lethargically and indecisively.

Ginott recommends reducing dependency problems by providing many opportunities for students to behave independently. One of his suggestions is to present several possible routes to solving a problem and let students decide which they want to follow. At the same time, students can decide on rules of behavior needed for completing the work they have selected. Providing choice helps students feel that they have control over what happens to them in the classroom. As a result, they depend less on the teacher and become more likely to live up to standards they have set for themselves.

Acceptance and Acknowledgment.   Students' perceptions of reality are often quite different from those of adults. Primary-grade students, for example, routinely fabricate stories, stretch the truth, and express opinions that have no basis in fact. Teachers should not deny or argue with what children say. Students are put in a very awkward position when their own perceptions are contradicted by adults. Ginott suggests that teachers adopt an approach of *acceptance and acknowledgment* of students' feelings. Teachers can minimize student confusion by withholding opinion and merely acting as sounding boards when students give opinions or voice concerns. The following is an example of what Ginott advocates:

> Juan comes running in from the playground crying, "José threw a ball at me and hit me in the head on purpose! Everyone is laughing at me! Nobody likes me!" The teacher could argue with the child's perception, saying, "That's silly. I'm sure it was an accident. The others were laughing at something else." Or the teacher could respond with sympathy and understanding, offering no judgment on the situation, saying, "I can see how upset you are. You feel that nobody likes you. It hurts our feelings when others laugh at us."

These accepting responses acknowledge and show understanding of Juan's feelings. They don't put him on the defensive by telling him how he should think or feel.

Ginott suggests that teachers add another comment to such situations: "How can I help you?" When asked sincerely, this question provides an opportunity for the student to come up with a solution to the problem and reveals the teacher's confidence in the student's ability to cope. Ginott calls this question teacher's *hidden asset* upon which they should always call.

Children's fears should also be treated carefully by teachers. Adults have a tendency to make light of what they see as unreasonable fears, but when doing so they communicate that the student's feelings are not real. They give the standard reply "There is nothing to be afraid of," which only makes the child feel worse, now stuck with the original fear plus a new fear of showing fear. For example,

> Tommy comes running into the classroom terrified, stammering, "There's a wolf out there! Outside! It tried to get me!" Mr. Krales, the teacher, goes to the window and sees a large husky-type dog trotting away from the playground. Mr. Krales can say, "Tommy, there are no wolves here, never have been. It was just a dog, nothing to be afraid of." Or he could say, "That's very frightening, isn't it, Tommy? I think it might have been a big dog, but dogs can sometimes be as scary as wolves."

Telling children not to be afraid, angry, or sad does not dispel their emotion, but it does cause them to doubt their own inner feelings. It may also cause them to doubt the teacher's ability to understand and teach them that adults may not be trustworthy in times of trouble.

Conferring Dignity upon Students.   Teachers wise in the use of congruent communication look for opportunities for *conferring dignity* on their students. Such opportunities often occur when a student is in distress. At such times, teachers should put aside the student's past history and concern themselves only with the immediate situation. Ginott (1972) provides the following example of a situation in which a teacher successfully confers dignity on a distressed student:

> Twelve-year-old Susan had volunteered to help catalog library books on Saturday. But when the weekend came, she realized with dismay that she was overwhelmed with homework. Knowing that she would receive poor grades for delinquent homework, she went to the library anyway but was so obviously distracted that the librarian asked her what was wrong. Susan began to cry as she told her story of overwork and regret. The librarian might have listened and asked, "I was counting on you. Why did you volunteer if you had so much homework?" That would have made Susan feel even more guilty. Instead, the librarian listened attentively and said, "Feeling so disheartened, you still came to work. That's discipline. That's character. That's integrity." The librarian's words showed respect and conferred dignity upon Susan. (p. 44)

Teachers' Expressing Anger: I-Messages versus You-Messages.   Teaching is a demanding job. Fatigue, frustration, and conflict make it inevitable that teachers become angry from time to time. Many people, adults and students alike, do not believe that teachers should allow themselves to show anger. Ginott disagrees. Such expectations, he argues, are wrong and even damaging to teachers. Teachers are bound to become angry at times, and when they do, they should be afforded the same opportunity as anyone else to express that anger. Congruent communication, however, places restrictions on how teacher anger should be expressed.

Teachers should never deny human feelings, whether those feelings are their students' or their own. Accordingly, teacher behavior should always be genuine concerning how they talk, behave, and respond to students. The restrictions on their expressing anger have to do with avoiding attacks on students' character. Consider the following example:

> Mrs. Abel, the art teacher, has obtained art prints of several of the most famous Grecian sculptures of human figures, which she has displayed in the room. During class she is called from the room. She asks students to work on drawings in progress. When she returns, she finds that someone has used a felt-tip marker to draw genitalia on the figures in the art prints. She is flabbergasted and keenly disappointed. Her anger rises. She can say:

> "Class, how could you let this happen? Are you barbarians? Have you lost all sense of decency? Are you nothing but degenerate morons? How can I ever trust you again!"
>
> Or she might say, "I am appalled! I am so angry I could cry! I am so disappointed about this I can't say anything more."

In the first set of responses, though she may feel completely justified in what she says, Mrs. Abel only makes an unfortunate situation worse. Through her use of *you-messages*, she has attacked students' character and made it difficult ever to resolve the situation gracefully.

Compared with her use of you-messages (e.g., "You are . . ."), Mrs. Abel's use of *I-messages* has a much better chance of causing students to think about the right and wrong of the situation. I-messages express emotion in terms of its effect on the person sending the message (e.g., "I am so disappointed . . ."), as contrasted with the character attacks that are inherent in you-messages (e.g., "You are barbarians"). Put another way, when teachers express anger through I-messages, they tell how the situation makes them feel. When they express anger through you-messages, they attack the students.

Using Laconic Language.   Ginott maintains that teachers need to speak succinctly when working with students. Students tend to close their minds to overtalkative teachers. Whenever a problem occurs, teachers should assume what Ginott calls a *solution-oriented focus*; that is, they should be interested only in solving the problem, not in dwelling on philosophies and responsibilities. The following is an example Ginott uses to illustrate his point:

> During a lesson, several students begin talking when they shouldn't. A typical teacher might say the following and even more:
>
> "Some of you are cooperating and some aren't."
> "Now you all know this is not a playground."
> "Good citizens don't bother others who are trying to learn."
> "I want all of you to stop talking. Be good citizens and don't bother others."

Ginott claims that all a teacher needs to say in such a case is

> "It's hard to learn when there's a lot of noise."

The other statements, he believes, only waste time and keep students from learning.

Pontification is endemic among teachers, but it has little effect on students, only going in one ear and out the other. Ginott advises that teachers, instead of carrying on, should talk as reporters write: give headlines, main points, and specific details as briefly as possible. Brevity and succinctness are what Ginott means by the term *laconic language*. Teacher strength, he wrote, is not conveyed by arguing or making long explanations; it is much more convincingly conveyed by brevity.

Providing Appreciative Praise. Ginott regularly admonishes teachers to be positive with their students, rather than negative. Most attempt to do so, and their stock-in-trade is the use of praise. Praise is ubiquitous, and certain adjectives are so overworked that they have lost their meaning. Every few minutes classroom teachers, when reacting to student responses, are heard to say, "Great!" or "Terrific!" or "Super!" According to Ginott, there are two good reasons teachers should not use praise of this type. First, such praise begins to sound silly and insincere, especially when students know their efforts have fallen well short of great or terrific. Second, such praise is evaluative, and evaluative praise is worse than no praise at all, for evaluative praise produces anxiety ("Can I live up to this?") and creates dependency ("I'm no good unless the teacher praises me"). It is interesting to note that Ginott's evaluation of praise is supported strongly by present-day authorities (see Gordon, 1989; Kohn, 1993).

Does this mean that teachers should never use praise at all? Ginott says that praise does have its place, but it should not be used to evaluate students. Instead, praise should show teacher appreciation for student effort. The distinction between evaluative and appreciative praise is akin to that between you-messages and I-messages. The teacher who says, "Great!" or "Super!" is in effect saying, "You are great! You are super!" Students may like this; it may make them feel good—temporarily. But it does not help them. Instead of being helpful, *evaluative praise* creates dependency upon the teacher. The teacher becomes a source of approval who decides whether or not students have worth.

In contrast, *appreciative praise* does not describe the student but instead directs attention to the student's efforts. The following are examples of appreciative praise that a teacher might make after reading a student's poem: "I thought the alliteration was delightful." "I found the descriptive words especially effective." "It was a pleasure to read this work."

This kind of praise does not describe the character of the student but instead indicates that the teacher appreciates the student's work or effort. Ginott emphasizes and reemphasizes this point: Avoid praise that attaches adjectives to a child's character. Use praise that shows your appreciation of specific student acts. Ginott drives this point home by showing that, if we met Leonard Bernstein or Pablo Picasso, we would never say, "You are a great composer, Mr. B!" or "Hey, super painting, Mr. Picasso!" Such evaluative statements would be arrogantly in bad taste. Instead, we would probably say, "I have really enjoyed the music in *West Side Story*" or "Your paintings have given me an appreciation for modern art."

Noncongruent Communication

To this point we have considered what Ginott means by congruent communication. Now let us take a moment to consider some instances of communication that, while typical in classrooms, is *noncongruent communication*; that is, it is not harmonious with students' feelings about situations and themselves and, further, it tends to attack students' character rather than simply deal with the situation at hand.

Name-Calling and Labeling.   Teachers are sometimes heard to make statements to students such as "You're lazy. Your work is sloppy and you are showing no responsibility. Don't you want to amount to anything?"

Ginott claims that such *labeling is disabling*. It tells students how to think about themselves, and if they hear such messages often enough, they begin to believe and live up to them. Teaching should open up vistas for students, not close them off. Most teachers no doubt believe they are encouraging students to do better when they call them lazy and irresponsible. But they are actually accomplishing the opposite. Labeling another's character limits visions of self, worth, and the future. It never serves to provide enlightenment, stimulate imagination, or encourage growth and achievement.

In situations where teachers must deal with difficult matters of student behavior, achievement, or aspiration, they should not say, "You are behaving like an uneducated street punk" or "Your grades show you simply don't care how you do in school" or "Your grades in chemistry are just not good enough for you to get into veterinary medicine school." These labels, inadvertent or not, tend to limit students.

In such situations, teachers should make statements like the following: "There is no more valuable lesson in life than learning self-control" or "Your grades are low now, but if we work together we can improve them" or "You want to be a veterinarian? Did you know there is a career information section in the media center?" Statements such as these do not tell students what the teacher thinks about them but instead encourage students to set goals for themselves. When teachers show that they believe in their students, the students are more likely to believe in themselves.

Teachers' Why Questions.   Teachers who are effective in discipline take care not to do or say anything that makes a student look foolish or feel guilty, angry, or resentful. Those emotions breed resistance and encourage misbehavior. For that reason, Ginott asks teachers to avoid *why questions,* which are in reality hostile inquiries into students' character traits. Ginott (1972) gives the following examples:

- Why do you have to fight with everybody?
- Why must you interrupt everybody?
- Why are you so slow?
- Why are you so disorganized?

Such questions as these, Ginott argues, don't really call for answers. Instead, they are ways of criticizing students. Students learn early that *why* means disapproval, displeasure, or blame.

Ordinarily, teachers can easily avoid asking such condemning questions, but at times they really do want to know the why behind a student's behavior. Ginott (1972) provides the following example to show what teachers can say in such circumstances without making a situation worse:

> A student informs the teacher: "I'm not prepared to take the test." The teacher wants to know why, but resists the temptation to use the damaging why. In its place, the teacher says, "We have a problem. What do you see as the solution?" (p. 89)

Ginott says that this type of response has precisely the opposite effect of why questions. Rather than doing damage, these nondramatic responses convey respect and leave the student responsible for taking corrective steps.

Invasion of Privacy.   We all hear frequently that, when burdened with a problem, it is better to talk the problem out than to keep it bottled up inside. Teachers want to be helpful to students and so sometimes, when they see a student who is uncharacteristically quiet, take the student aside and probe with questions such as "What's the matter today? What's bothering you."

If the student feels like talking about the matter, fine. But if not, the teacher should do nothing more than say, for that student's ears only, "If I can help, let me know." Anything more, says Ginott, is an *invasion of privacy*. Self-disclosure is a personal and sensitive matter, and none of us should be urged to discuss personal matters when we are uncomfortable in doing so. Being thus prodded causes embarrassment and sometimes even resentment.

Correcting by Directing.   Throughout every day, mistakes or misbehaviors occur in the classroom that must be corrected by the teacher. Brian may be working on the wrong page in his workbook. Tim may throw an eraser. A group of girls may be discussing a favorite soap opera instead of working as directed.

Given such situations, teachers' natural inclinations are to say hurtful things to the offending students: "Oh, good grief, Brian. Well, all that work was certainly for nothing" or "Tim, go pick up that eraser and don't let me see anything like that out of you again" or "Girls, let's not have any more of that. No wonder your work has been so poor."

Such noncongruent comments may stop the misbehavior, at least temporarily, but they sting students and produce resentment. Ginott says that instead of correcting with negative comments, teachers should respond by describing the situation and suggesting an acceptable alternative. Usually, students only need be reminded of what they are supposed to be doing. The teacher would do better to respond as follows: To Brian (quietly): "Oh, I'm sorry, Brian. The assignment is on page thirty-four. You certainly worked hard on this one, though." To Tim: "Erasers are not for throwing. This is quiet reading time." To the girls: "Let's finish this assignment now; there will be time for talking later."

You can see that the first set of responses were inappropriate in that they were punitive and therefore likely to provoke undesired effects. The second set of responses simply indicate what is unacceptable and courteously indicate what the students should be doing instead. This approach is what Ginott calls *correcting by directing*. To correct misbehavior, he says, one needs to tell students respectfully what they should be doing instead of the inappropriate behavior.

Overdwelling.   Previously, brevity was described as contributing to congruent communication. Ginott observes that students react much better to teachers who get to the point succinctly than to those who pontificate endlessly. The opposite of brevity is *overdwelling*, a condition mentioned prominently by Kounin, whose teachings were described in Chapter 3. When overdwelling, teachers spend long and needless time in explaining, warning, or reacting to misbehavior.

Ginott, who picked up on Kounin's overdwelling and frequently mentions other aspects of Kounin's work, urges teachers to avoid overdwelling on any topic. Especially when dealing with minor misbehavior, Ginott says, teachers should learn economical responses for correcting the situation. Many teachers do the opposite, using up their energy by overdwelling on every classroom mishap. Wise teachers conserve themselves and at the same time try to avoid wounding students' feelings. Even if the student has talked without permission, forgotten a book, or lost a homework assignment, there is no need to rail about it. Leave the misdeed in the past and suggest a better behavior, thus inviting the student to assume responsibility for behaving appropriately.

Sarcasm.   *Sarcasm* is a chief contributor to teachers' failure to communicate congruently. Many adults use sarcasm as a form of humor. Many teachers do the same with their students, intending to show themselves clever and witty. But sarcasm never sounds witty to students receiving the comments. Too frequently, the result of sarcasm is hurt feelings and damaged self-esteem.

Ginott therefore has a word of advice for teachers inclined to use sarcasm: don't. Offending students can and will feel only that they are belittled and made fun of. Ginott suggests that teachers not use sarcasm at all. The risk of hurting students' feelings is too great.

GINOTT'S SPECIAL VIEWS ON DISCIPLINE

Ginott describes discipline as a *series of little victories* that over time result in student self-direction, responsibility, and concern for others. By that he means that true classroom discipline (that is, student self-discipline) cannot be brought about overnight. Rather, it is a process that grows gradually as teachers treat students humanely and considerately.

Ginott acknowledges that teachers can influence student behavior with threats and punishment, but he attempts to show that aversive techniques inevitably make students resentful toward the teacher and less willing to cooperate.

The essence of discipline, Ginott holds, lies in finding effective *alternatives to punishment*. It is by using those alternatives that teachers achieve the series of little victories. Ginott maintains that the most important factor in that process is *teacher self-discipline*. Teachers show self-discipline by not losing their tempers and by never behaving rudely. They show self-discipline by modeling courtesy and language they want to see in their students. They are polite, helpful, and respectful. They handle crises calmly and reasonably. In times of conflict, they show civilized behavior. All the while, students, even those who are poorly behaved, continually watch to see how teachers handle difficult situations. Given repeated exposure to civil behavior, students begin to display it themselves.

Ginott claims it is easy to identify teachers who lack self-discipline. Such teachers, he said, can be seen to do the following:

1. They lose their tempers: They shout, slam books, and use verbal abuse.
2. They call students names: "You are like pigs! Clean that up!"
3. They insult students' character: "John, you are nothing but lazy."
4. They behave rudely: "Sit down and shut up!"
5. They overreact: When Mary accidentally drops a sheaf of papers being handed out, they exclaim, "Oh, for heaven's sake! Can't you do anything right?!"
6. They show cruelty: "Watch carefully on your way home from school, Shawn. You need to grow some more brains."
7. They punish all for the sins of one: "Since certain people couldn't listen during the assembly, we won't go to the next one."
8. They threaten: "If I hear one more voice, you will all have an extra hour of homework."
9. They deliver long lectures: "It has come to my attention that several of you believe the trash can is a basketball hoop. We can throw things out on the grounds, but here in the classroom . . ."
10. They back students into a corner: "What are you doing? Why are you doing that? Don't you know any better? Apologize at once!"
11. They make arbitrary rules, without student discussion or input.

In contrast, Ginott says that teachers who have good self-discipline are likely to do the following:

1. They recognize student feelings: "I can see that it makes you angry to have to stay in after school."
2. They describe the situation: "I see coats all over the closet floor. They need to be hung up."
3. They invite cooperation: "Let's all see how much we can help by keeping quiet during the performance."
4. They are brief: "We do not throw things in the classroom."
5. They do not argue with students. They make a just decision and stick to it, but remain flexible enough to change if they are wrong. Arguing is always a losing proposition for teachers.

6. They model appropriate behavior. They show through example how they want students to behave.

7. They discourage physical violence: "In our classroom we talk about our problems. We do not hit or yell at each other."

8. They do not criticize, call names, or insult students: When a student interrupts, the teacher says, "Excuse me. I will be with you as soon as I can."

9. They focus on solutions: "I am seeing some very unsportsmanlike conduct. What do you think we can do about it?"

10. They allow face-saving exits: "You may remain at your desk and read quietly, or you may sit by yourself in the back of the room."

11. They allow students to help set standards: "What do we need to remember when we are using this paint?"

12. They are helpful: When Matthew yells, "Roger and Joe are teasing me!" The teacher replies, "You sound upset. What would you like me to do?"

13. They de-escalate conflict: When Susan, crumpling her paper, says, "I am not going to do this assignment! It's too hard!" the teacher replies, "You feel this assignment is too difficult. Would you like me to go over a few problems with you?"

COMMENTS ON THE GINOTT MODEL

Ginott was the first writer to emphasize the strong linkage between the way teachers talk to students and the way students behave in return. He stressed that teachers must provide an environment conducive to learning, and that nothing is more important to quality learning than the socio-emotional atmosphere that pervades the classroom. Discipline problems diminish, Ginott insisted, when teachers show concern for students' feelings and recognize that their comments have strong impact on feelings and self-image.

Ginott's suggestions concerning how teachers function best in the classroom are similar in some ways to Kounin's concept of withitness. When teachers address the situation rather than the students' character, they communicate that (1) they know what is going on, (2) they know what they want changed, and (3) they are aware of the students' feelings.

But to a far greater extent than Kounin, Ginott reminds teachers that students are very sensitive. Being bossed or labeled gives students justification for distrusting adults and for behaving rebelliously. Teachers therefore should treat students as they themselves want to be treated. They should give students choices, be helpful, and invite rather than demand cooperation. They should ask themselves, "How do I want my students to relate to me and to each other, and how should I treat them in order that they will do so?"

By following Ginott's suggestions, most teachers can certainly improve student behavior in the classroom, and teachers and students alike will find greater enjoyment in the educational experience. However, even after becoming adept in the techniques that Ginott advocates, many teachers still feel relatively powerless when they must deal with student defiance, hostility, or verbal abuse, behaviors that were once fairly rare but are now commonplace. While virtually all teachers agree with what Ginott has to say, most do not find Ginott's techniques adequate for dealing with hard-to-manage individuals or classes.

APPLICATION EXERCISES

REVIEW OF SELECTED TERMINOLOGY

The following terms are central to the Ginott model of discipline. Check yourself to make sure you can explain their meanings.

congruent communication	appreciative praise
teachers at their best	noncongruent communication
teachers at their worst	labeling is disabling
sane messages	why questions
inviting cooperation	invasion of privacy
Ten Commands	correcting by directing
hidden asset	overdwelling
conferring dignity	sarcasm
you-messages	series of little victories
I-messages	alternatives to punishment
laconic language	teacher self-discipline
evaluative praise	

CONCEPT CASES

Case 1: Kristina Will Not Work

Kristina, a student in Mr. Jake's class, is quite docile. She does little socializing with other students and never disrupts class. Mr. Jake simply cannot get her to do her work. She never completes an assignment but just sits there, putting forth no effort at all.

How would Ginott deal with Kristina?   Ginott would use a number of gentle tactics to encourage Kristina to do her work. These would include the following:

Using sane messages: "Students in my class are expected to complete all assignments."

Inviting cooperation: "All students who finish their work can then choose to play a game with a friend."

Accepting and acknowledging Kristina's feelings: "Kristina, I can tell that you find it difficult to begin work on your assignment. How can I help you?"

Correcting by directing: "You need to finish ten problems within the next thirty minutes."

Focusing on solutions: "This cannot continue. What do you think we might be able to do about it?"

Case 2: Sara Cannot Stop Talking

Sara is a pleasant girl who participates in class activities and does most, though not all, of her assigned work. She cannot seem to refrain from talking to classmates, however. Her teacher, Mr. Gonzales, has to speak to her repeatedly during lessons, to the point that he often becomes exasperated and loses his temper.

What suggestions would Ginott give Mr. Gonzales for dealing with Sara?

Case 3: Joshua Clowns and Intimidates

Joshua, larger and louder than his classmates, always wants to be the center of attention, which he accomplishes through a combination of clowning and intimidation. He makes wise remarks, talks back (smilingly) to the teacher, utters a variety of sound-effect noises such as gunshots and automobile crashes, and makes limitless sarcastic comments and put-downs of his classmates. Other students will not stand up to him, apparently fearing his size and verbal aggressiveness. His teacher, Miss Pearl, has come to her wit's end.

What do you think Ginott would advise in this case?

Case 4: Tom Is Hostile and Defiant

Tom has appeared to be in his usual foul mood ever since arriving in class. On his way to sharpen his pencil, he bumps into Frank, who complains. Tom tells him loudly to shut up. Miss Baines, the teacher, says, "Tom, go back to your seat." Tom wheels around, swears loudly, and says heatedly, "I'll go when I'm damned good and ready!"

How would Ginott advise Miss Baines to deal with Tom?

Questions and Activities

1. The following statements illustrate some of Ginott's main points about talking with students. Identify the main point with which each statement is associated.

   a. "You boys head the list of my all-time laziest students."
   b. "Yes, I'm just *sure* you didn't do your assignment because your mother was sick last night."
   c. "I am so disappointed and angry I don't know what to do!"
   d. "Alicia, you are the most intelligent kid I have ever known!"

2. Peggy and June are each accusing the other of taking personal items without permission. What would Ginott have the teacher say to the girls?

3. Miss Tykes is dealing with a group of boys who were shouting obscenities in the hall. "That's the worst thing I have ever witnessed!" he yells. "Where do you think you are? Are you allowed to behave like hoodlums at home? You will all report to my room after school for the next two weeks!" How would Ginott advise that Miss Tykes change her approach?

4. Examine Scenario 6 in Appendix I. What specifically would Ginott have Mr. Carnett say to his misbehaving students?

REFERENCES AND RECOMMENDED READINGS

Ginott, H. (1965). *Between parent and child*. New York: Avon.

———. (1969). *Between parent and teenager*. New York: Macmillan.

———. (1971). *Teacher and child*. New York: Macmillan.

———. (1972). I am angry! I am appalled! I am furious! *Today's Education, 61*, 23–24.

———. (1973). Driving children sane. *Today's Education 62*, 20–25.

Gordon, T. (1989). *Discipline that works: Promoting self-discipline in children*. New York: Random House.

Kohn, A. (1993). *Punished by rewards: The trouble with gold stars, incentive plans, A's, praise, and other bribes*. Boston: Houghton Mifflin.

Kounin, J. (1977). *Discipline and group management in classrooms* (rev. ed). New York: Holt, Rinehart & Winston. (Original work published 1971)

The Application Models

The six models of discipline presented in Part II are sufficiently complete in themselves to serve as programs for managing behavior in classrooms at all levels. The models give attention to rules, consequences, prevention, and steps for dealing with misbehavior, and most place emphasis on student input and cooperation. The order in which they are presented corresponds approximately to the chronological order in which they began to influence classroom practice. The six application models are as follows:

5. The Dreikurs Model: Discipline through Democratic Teaching and Confronting Mistaken Goals
6. The Canter Model: Discipline through Assertively Managing Behavior
7. The Jones Model: Discipline through Body Language, Incentive Systems, and Efficient Help
8. The Glasser Model: Discipline through Meeting Needs without Coercion
9. The Gordon Model: Discipline through Developing Self-Control
10. The Curwin and Mendler Model: Discipline through Dignity and Hope

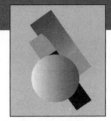

CHAPTER 5

The Dreikurs Model

Discipline through Democratic
Teaching and Confronting
Mistaken Goals

Rudolf Dreikurs

BIOGRAPHICAL SKETCH OF DREIKURS

Rudolf Dreikurs (1897–1972) was born in Vienna, Austria. After receiving his medical degree from the University of Vienna, he entered into a long association with the renowned psychiatrist Alfred Adler, with whom he conducted studies in family and child counseling. Dreikurs immigrated to the United States in 1937 and eventually became director of the Alfred Adler Institute in Chicago. He also served as professor of psychiatry at the Chicago Medical School. Throughout his career, he continued to focus on family-child counseling. He became a recognized authority in the area of classroom behavior through his books *Psychology in the Classroom* (1968), *Discipline without Tears* (1972), coauthored with Pearl Cassel, and *Maintaining Sanity in the Classroom* (1982), coauthored with Bernice Grunwald and Floy Pepper and published posthumously. These books are valuable to teachers for the understandings they provide of student behavior and its guidance.

Dreikurs's work is being carried forward by a former student, Dr. Linda Albert, developer of Cooperative Discipline, a detailed discipline system being used in schools across the country. Cooperative Discipline makes use of Dreikurs' fundamental concepts, with emphasis added on Three C's: Capable, Connect, and Contribute. The program is explained in Albert's book *A Teacher's Guide to Cooperative Discipline* (1989, revised 1996), available along with related materials from American Guidance Service, 4201 Woodland Road, P.O. Box 99, Circle Pines, MN 55014-1796. For workshop presentations and consultation services, Albert can be contacted through the Cooperative Discipline Institute, 27134 Paseo Espada, Suite 302, San Juan Capistrano, CA 92675; telephone 800-WeWin4U.

DREIKURS'S CONTRIBUTIONS TO DISCIPLINE

Dreikurs was among the first to explore the underlying causes of student misbehavior in the classroom. He concluded that virtually all human beings have a primary need to belong, to feel that they have an important place in the group. Dreikurs called that need the *genuine goal* of human social behavior, and he explained that all school students desire more than anything else to feel that they "belong" in the classroom. He maintained that students who have gained that genuine sense of belonging rarely misbehave seriously.

But the sense of belonging does not come easily to all students. When unable to attain it, students turn to a series of *mistaken goals* in an attempt to gain a sense of importance. The pursuit of those mistaken goals often disrupts learning and presents other problems for teacher and students. Dreikurs felt that teachers could ensure acceptable classroom behavior by helping all students reach their genuine goal of belonging. He believed they could best do so by functioning as what he called *democratic teachers* within *democratic classrooms*. But he also recognized that even in the best classrooms, some students will inevitably pursue mistaken goals. To help teachers deal with that eventuality, Dreikurs presented a set of intervention tactics for confronting mistaken goals and reorienting students toward the genuine goal of belonging.

DREIKURS'S CENTRAL FOCUS

Dreikurs's teachings about discipline follow two main thrusts. The first focuses on establishing a democratic classroom and teaching style to help students acquire a sense of belonging. He describes what he means by democracy in the classroom and explains the nature of democratic teaching, which is quite different from autocratic or permissive teaching. Dreikurs's second thrust focuses on identifying and dealing with mistaken goals that students pursue when unable to attain their genuine goal of belonging. Dreikurs explains those mistaken goals, describes the misbehaviors associated with them, and helps teachers learn to recognize and redirect the attendant misbehaviors.

DREIKURS'S PRINCIPAL CONCEPTS AND TEACHINGS

Discipline. This is a process in which students learn to impose reasonable limits on themselves.

Autocratic teacher. This teacher is one who lays down the law in the classroom, feels a strong need to be always in charge, and doles out harsh consequences when rules are broken. Autocratic teachers are relatively ineffective in helping students develop self-discipline.

Permissive teacher. This teacher is one who fails to insist that students comply with reasonable expectations and consequences. Permissive teachers do not help students realize that freedom must be linked to responsibility; they therefore do little to foster student self-discipline.

Democratic teacher. This is a teacher who tries to motivate students from within, helps students develop rules of conduct that will enable the class to prosper, and allows students to exercise freedom coupled with responsibility.

Democratic classroom. This is a classroom in which teacher and students cooperate in making joint decisions about class procedures, rules, and consequences for misbehavior.

Genuine goal of belonging. Almost all students have a prime goal in the classroom, and they expend considerable effort in pursuing it. That prime, or genuine, goal is to feel a sense of belonging in the class.

Mistaken goals. When students are unable to attain the genuine goal of belonging, they turn to any of four mistaken goals in an attempt to feel important. Their efforts in pursuit of the mistaken goals often constitute misbehavior in the classroom.

Misbehavior. Student behavior that chronically disrupts normal teaching and learning is considered misbehavior. It often occurs as students pursue mistaken goals.

Getting attention. This is the first mistaken goal. Students who are not gaining a sense of belonging usually attempt to get attention from peers and teacher.

Seeking power. This is the second mistaken goal. When students are not satisfied in their attempts to get attention, they seek power, usually by refusing to do what the teacher requests.

Seeking revenge. This is the third mistaken goal. When students are thwarted in their attempts to show power over teachers, they try to gain a sense of importance by exacting revenge on the teacher through defacing property, subverting the class, cheating, or spreading lies.

Displaying inadequacy. This is the fourth mistaken goal. When all else has failed, students attempt to shield themselves from further damage by withdrawing and making no attempt to participate in class activities.

Encouragement. This is provided through teacher words or actions that convey respect for students and belief in their abilities. It is differentiated from praise, which Dreikurs considers counterproductive. Praise comes only when a task is done well.

Logical consequences. These are reasonable results that follow behavior. Good behavior brings pleasant consequences, such as opportunities to engage in favorite activities or talk with friends. Misbehavior brings unpleasant consequences linked to rules transgression, such as having to complete work at home that was supposed to be completed in class.

Punishment. This is action taken by the teacher to get back at students and show them who is boss, usually by humiliating or isolating the offending students. Dreikurs advocates logical consequences as the better disciplinary approach.

ANALYSIS OF THE DREIKURS MODEL

The Nature of Discipline

Discipline refers to control of behavior. It is essential to smooth functioning of all aspects of society, including schools. Discipline can be of two kinds, one of them liberating and fulfilling, the other stifling and oppressive. The first, *self-discipline*, grows out of living with reasonable limits on behavior while also recognizing that all behavior produces consequences. Appropriate behavior leads to desirable consequences, while inappropriate behavior leads to undesirable consequences. It is through recognizing the linkage between behavior and consequences that one ultimately acquires self-discipline.

The second kind of discipline, *aversive discipline*, stifles initiative. It imposes unreasonable constraints coupled with harsh consequences when rules are broken. That kind of discipline, sometimes seen in classrooms, does little to teach students self-control. Instead, it is more likely to make students want to subvert the controls and do whatever they feel capable of getting away with.

Aversive discipline remains prevalent because teachers and adults in general retain an either-or concept of discipline: either you make the young behave or they will walk all over you. Many teachers believe that in order to prevent students' walking over them, it is necessary to retain the threat of punishment and be willing to use it when students transgress. But students see this kind of discipline as arbitrary, set up by the teacher to show who is in charge. Teachers who hold this view of discipline find that they cannot always enforce their rules. Over time they tend to become autocratic in demeanor but permissive in enforcement.

Good discipline, Dreikurs maintains, makes no use of punishment. Good discipline requires that students have considerable freedom of choice, though with full understanding of the consequences associated with their choices. The consequences, as will be explained later, are not harshly punitive but are instead logical in that they involve making right what was done wrong. If a student destroys a schoolbook, for example, it is logical that the student pay for a new one. If the student litters the classroom floor with paper, it is logical that he or she clean up the litter.

In this manner, students actually select consequences for themselves by dint of the behavior they choose. They know in advance the consequences associated with misbehavior—in fact, they have helped formulate the consequences. When they behave as the class has agreed, they enjoy pleasant consequences; when they break agreed-upon rules, they must accept the unpleasant consequences they have helped formulate. Students come to see discipline not as dreadful punishment that teachers wait to inflict upon them but as part and parcel of the behavior choices they are free to make, knowing in advance that they must accept the consequences of those choices.

Discipline in the classroom is best accomplished when students and teachers jointly set limits on behavior until students become able to set such limits for themselves. Therefore, it is wise for students to participate in clarifying the kinds of behavior that will best promote the interests of the class. They should also take part in deciding what the consequences should be when behavior agreements are broken. This gives students an understanding of the reasons behind rules and consequences, and it helps them see that social behavior produces consequences that may be desirable or undesirable. As teachers work toward making their classrooms and teaching styles more democratic, Dreikurs reminds them to emphasize the following:

- Students are responsible for their own actions.
- Students must respect themselves and others.
- Students are responsible for helping formulate desirable rules and consequences in their classrooms and for abiding by them.

Discipline and Types of Teachers

We have seen that Dreikurs believes democratic teachers are more likely than others to establish effective classroom discipline. He contrasts democratic teachers with teachers he calls autocratic or permissive, depending on their classroom behavior.

Autocratic Teachers.   *Autocratic teachers* are those who tend to exhibit the following traits (Dreikurs, Grunwald, & Pepper, 1982, p. 76): They boss, use a sharp voice, command, exercise power, exert pressure, demand cooperation, tell you what you should do, impose ideas, dominate, criticize, find fault, punish, and determine all procedures, rules, and consequences.

To illustrate, Mr. Parrons strides into the classroom, eyes the class, and says, "All right, get your books out and open them to page seventy-three. I am going to take you through this chapter, and at the end of the week we will have a test on it. Your grade will depend on how well you do on the test. This is serious business. I will tolerate no talking. If I see you goofing off, I will give you an extra assignment to complete. If your papers are not neat, you will have to do them over."

Mr. Parrons proceeds to lecture over the textual material, explaining what is contained in each paragraph. He asks occasional questions. When he hears an answer he doesn't like, he grills the student for more information and often makes the student appear foolish. Students cast their eyes down, hoping he won't call on them.

Mr. Parrons fits Dreikurs's description of the autocratic teacher, who does little to promote self-discipline in students. In Dreikurs and Cassel's (1972) words, such teachers are

> committed to "making" pupils do as they are told, forcing them to learn, berating them when they don't, punishing any misdemeanor and denying any creative freedom of expression. (p. 15)

Permissive Teachers.   In contrast, *permissive teachers* put few if any limits on student behavior, nor do they invoke logical consequences when misbehavior disrupts the class. In some cases, these teachers are philosophically opposed to imposing controls on students. More often, they have found themselves unable to control students and therefore have stopped trying to do so. We see an illustration of a permissive teacher, Mrs. Samuels, in the following scenario:

> Mrs. Samuels enters the room and smiles tentatively at the students, several of whom do not take their seats as they should. Instead of urging them to get started, she says, "You may visit quietly while you are working. Get together in your groups and select the activities in which you will engage today." Before long, a deafening roar fills the room, but from her desk Mrs. Samuels seems oblivious to it.
>
> Mrs. Samuels does not believe that students ever misbehave intentionally but that when they seem perhaps to do so it is because of their life experiences in a faulted society. She believes that the good in children ultimately will come to

the fore, provided they have a multitude of experiences that are free from adult coercion. For that reason, she allows her students great latitude in deciding what they will study and how. She believes that a noisy and messy classroom is a sign of active student involvement. She encourages students to talk about their efforts, but she does not give tests, which she believes stifle student initiative. It does bother her that students squabble a great deal and destroy materials, but she attributes that to their family backgrounds. She is certainly uncomfortable in her inability to document student progress when conferencing with parents, but she makes up for that concern by telling parents how much she loves their children and how willing she is to do anything possible to help them.

Unfortunately, Mrs. Samuels is even more ineffective than Mr. Parrons in promoting learning and self-discipline. She contributes to problem behavior by allowing students to work in an environment that is inconsistent with everyday reality. Students in her classroom do not learn that living in society requires following rules. They do not learn that failure to follow rules results in undesirable consequences. They do not learn that acceptable behavior requires self-discipline. They do virtually whatever they wish in the classroom, yet at the same time they find classroom life rough and stressful.

Mrs. Samuels needs to learn that discipline and control must be present in the classroom if learning is to occur as intended. Students need and want guidance and leadership. True, they want to be participants and not have regulations forced upon them arbitrarily, but they are incapable of organizing their own education. Without leadership and guidance, they cannot put workable class rules and consequences in place.

Democratic Teachers.   *Democratic teachers* stand in marked contrast to autocratic and permissive teachers. Democratic teachers exhibit the following traits of *democratic teaching*: leadership, friendliness, inviting nature, stimulation, ideas, cooperation, guidance, encouragement, acknowledgment, helpfulness, and shared responsibility. Democratic teachers bring about *democratic classrooms*, which usually reflect the following characteristics (Dreikurs et al., 1982):

- Order necessary for required work is present.
- Rules, responsibilities, and consequences, in which students have collaborated, are in place.
- Mutual trust exists between students and teacher.
- The teacher solicits student help rather than demand it.
- Cooperation is more evident than competition.
- The classroom atmosphere is warm and friendly.
- Group discussions of class concerns are routine.
- The teacher is more concerned with class progress than with personal prestige.
- Students are encouraged and helped to learn from their mistakes.

Democratic teaching and democratic classroom are exemplified in Ms. Taller's class:

> Ms. Tallers enters the room casually, greeting students whose eyes she catches. She gets the class's attention and asks them to settle down. In a warm tone of voice she briefly reviews curricular expectations for a new unit, telling students what she has in mind for them to do but making a point of asking for opinions and suggestions, which she considers carefully. She pauses and sends a meaningful look to a pair of students who are talking in the back of the room; they stop talking and pay attention. She continues discussing the unit with sincerity, encouraging student input and discussion concerning the kind of class behavior that will best allow the work to be done. She is firm in her ideas, which implies self-respect, yet considerate of students, which shows she respects them, too.

Democratic teachers like Ms. Tallers are neither permissive nor autocratic. They provide firm guidance and leadership by giving explanations and involving students in setting rules and consequences. They seek ways of motivating students from within. They maintain order but allow students ample opportunity to interact with others. They continually remind students that freedom is tied to responsibility for adhering to class rules and that transgressions of rules bring undesired consequences. Through this process democratic teachers such as Ms. Tallers help students develop the ability to place limits on their own behavior.

Discipline and Mistaken Goals

Dreikurs makes three very important points in his writings. The first is that students are social beings who want to feel they belong to the groups in which they participate—family, peer, school, class, and other groups. Dreikurs calls this desire a *genuine goal of belonging* that strongly motivates student behavior.

Dreikurs's second point is that students have the *ability to choose* their behavior. Nature does not compel them to behave socially in any particular way.

Dreikurs's third point is that when students fail to achieve their genuine goal of acceptance, they tend to choose other (undesirable) behaviors in the mistaken belief that those behaviors will get them the recognition they seek. Dreikurs calls these erroneous beliefs *mistaken goals*.

It is Dreikurs's contention that all people want to belong, to have a place. They try many kinds of behavior to obtain status and recognition. If they do not receive recognition through socially acceptable means, they turn to mistaken goals, which prompt antisocial behavior. Students' antisocial behavior—called *misbehavior* in the classroom—reflects the mistaken belief that it will bring them the recognition they desire. Dreikurs identifies four mistaken goals to which students turn when unable to satisfy the genuine goal: (1) getting attention, (2) seeking power, (3) seeking revenge, and (4) displaying inadequacy. The names of these goals indicate what the student is attempting to do in order to gain a sense of importance. The goals are usually, though not always, sought in the order listed. If unable to feel accepted, individuals are likely to try to get attention. If they fail in that effort, they turn next to seeking power. If thwarted there, they attempt to get revenge. And if that fails, then they withdraw into themselves and try to show that they are inadequate to accomplish what is expected of them. Let's examine each of these mistaken goals more closely.

Getting Attention. When students are not getting the recognition they desire, they may resort to *getting attention* through misbehavior. They feel important if the teacher pays attention to them and provides them extra services. They may disrupt, ask special favors, raise irrelevant questions, continually call for help with assignments, and refuse to work unless the teacher hovers over them. Good students, as well as poor students, make bids for attention. They function well so long as they have the teacher's approval, but if approval is not forthcoming, they sometimes resort to less acceptable ways of getting attention.

Teachers should understand that giving attention to misbehaving students does not improve their improper behavior; rather, it increases those students' desire for attention and causes them to look for external sources of motivation.

If attention-getting behavior does not provide students the recognition they seek, they turn to the next mistaken goal: seeking power.

Seeking Power. At times students feel that the only way they can get the recognition they desire is through defying the teacher. They may show their attempts at *seeking power* by arguing, contradicting, lying, having temper tantrums, refusing to follow directions, or behaving hostilely. If students can get the teacher to fight with them, they feel they have won whether or not they actually got their way, because they have succeeded in showing they have the power to disrupt the class and put the teacher on the defensive. Even when the teacher wins the contest of wills, the student comes to believe more firmly that power is what matters in life.

If students fail to obtain the recognition they desire through power seeking, they move to the next, more severe, misbehavior: seeking revenge.

Seeking Revenge. Students who move on to *seeking revenge* have failed to gain status through attention or power. The reasoning for their next mistaken goal is "I can only feel significant if I have the ability to hurt others. Hurting others makes up for my being hurt."

Students who seek revenge set themselves up to be punished. They may behave cruelly and, when punished, feel they have renewed cause for vengeful action. The more trouble they cause for themselves, the more justified they feel. They consider it a victory to be disliked.

But underneath their bravado these individuals are deeply discouraged. Their behavior only brings more hurt from others, causing them to feel even more worthless. Finally, they pursue the one mistaken goal left available: displaying inadequacy.

Displaying Inadequacy. Students seeking the goal of *displaying inadequacy* see themselves as abject failures. They see no need to try. They withdraw from situations that might intensify their feeling of worthlessness. They guard what little self-esteem they have left by removing themselves from social tests. Their mistaken belief is "If others see me as inadequate, they will leave me alone."

Students who seek this goal do so by pretending to be stupid. They are unresponsive to teacher urgings and passively refuse to participate in class activities. They sit silently and engage in no interaction. The behavior associated with this mistaken goal is serious and difficult to overcome. Worse, because withdrawn students do not disrupt classes, teachers may not see the depth of the problem and take steps to correct it.

What Can Teachers Do about Mistaken Goals?

Students seek the four mistaken goals in hopes of gaining status. But instead of leading to success, those goals lead to failure. What can the teacher do to redirect students? Dreikurs makes the following suggestions:

Identify the Mistaken Goal.   Dreikurs says that *identifying mistaken goals* is the first thing teachers should do. The easiest way to do so is to note the teacher's own response to the misbehavior. If the teacher feels

- *annoyed*, the student is probably seeking attention;
- *threatened*, the student is probably seeking power;
- *hurt*, the student is probably seeking revenge; or
- *powerless*, the student is displaying inadequacy.

Another way to identify mistaken goals is to observe students' reactions to being corrected.

If Students	*Then Their Goal Is*
stop the misbehavior and then repeat it	attention
refuse to stop or increase the misbehavior	power
become violent or hostile	revenge
refuse to cooperate, participate, or interact	inadequacy

Confront the Mistaken Goal.   After the teacher has identified mistaken goals, the second step is *confronting mistaken goals*. The student should be confronted with an explanation of the goal together with a discussion of the faulty logic involved. By doing this in a friendly, nonthreatening manner, teachers can usually get students to examine and change their behavior. Dreikurs would have teachers ask students the following questions, in order, and observe reactions that might indicate a mistaken goal:

1. "Could it be that you want me to pay attention to you?"
2. "Could it be that you want to prove that nobody can make you do anything?"

3. "Could it be that you want to hurt me (or others)?"

4. "Could it be that you want me to believe you are not capable?"

These questions can open up communication between teacher and student. They can improve misbehavior by removing the fun of provoking the teacher. And they take the initiative away from the student, allowing the teacher to implement actions to change the misbehavior. Dreikurs suggests the following tactics for *reorienting students* toward the genuine goal of belonging.

Redirect Attention-Getting Behavior.   Students who seek attention become very uncomfortable when neglected, so they create disruptions that cannot be ignored by the teacher. Teachers who fall for this ploy tend to nag, coax, and scold, all of which reinforce students' attempts to gain attention and thus only make matters worse. When teachers perceive that students are making undue bids for attention, they should ignore the behavior. When they do so, the students will not get what they need and will be forced to find new ways to gain recognition.

But teachers should strive to give attention to these same students whenever they are not demanding it. This encourages students to develop motivation from within instead of depending on attention from without.

Sometimes it is not feasible for teachers to ignore behavior that is disrupting the class. In such cases, teachers need to give attention in ways that do not reward misbehavior. The teacher may call the student's name and make eye contact without comment. Or the teacher may describe the behavior without any trace of annoyance, saying, for example, "I see that you are not finishing your assignment."

It is sometimes effective to confront the student privately with the goal and ask, "How many times do you think you will need my attention in the next hour?" The student will usually not know what to say. The teacher might then say, "If I give you attention fifteen times, will that be enough?" This will sound like an exaggeration to the student. Then when the student misbehaves, the teacher responds by saying, "Joel, number one," "Joel, number two," and so forth. The teacher does not comment on the behavior or scold, which would give Joel the attention he seeks, but simply lets him know that his misbehavior is being observed.

Avoid Involvement in Power-Seeking Behavior.   When students engage teachers in power struggles, it is natural for teachers to feel threatened and want to fight back. But by participating in power struggles, teachers only cause students to become more rebellious and hostile and to think about getting revenge. Dreikurs urges teachers not to fight with students. The best tactic is to avoid getting involved in power struggles in the first place.

Teachers can do this by withdrawing as an authority figure. The student cannot exert power if there is no one with whom to fight. Teachers may wish to state to the student and the class that they recognize the offending student's need for power. They may decide to stop the entire class and wait for the disruptive behavior to cease, in which case the offending student may receive pressure from peers rather than from the teacher.

Teachers can also redirect students' ambitions for power by inviting them to participate in making decisions or by giving them positions of responsibility. A teacher might take a student aside and say, "The language I am hearing is very offensive to me. The other students look up to you. Do you think you could help out by setting an example?" Or in the same situation the teacher might say, "I have a problem. It concerns the language I am hearing. What do you think I should do?" In this way, teachers admit that the student has power but refuse to be engaged in conflicts.

In some cases, teachers may wish to confront the behavior openly. They might say, "I cannot continue to teach when you are speaking in that manner. Can you suggest ways to express yourself that still allow me to teach?" If students cannot think of suggestions, the teacher can offer some options.

Take Positive Steps against Revenge-Seeking Behavior.   The goal of revenge is closely related to the goal of power. Students seeking revenge may want to hurt others because they have been hurt themselves. What they need most is not retaliation but understanding and acceptance. It is very hurtful for any student to feel unliked by everyone. The teacher may be able to set up situations that allow vengeful students to exhibit talents or strengths, thus helping the students see that they can behave in ways that bring acceptance and status. Teachers can also call on the class to support and encourage offending students. But it must be understood that students who seek revenge at first reject efforts by others to help them. It takes persistence and patience on everyone's part to change such a situation.

Encourage Students Who Display Inadequacy.   Students who have been unable to gain belonging, attention, power, or revenge usually withdraw and want to be left alone. They want the teacher to believe that they are not worth dealing with. These students obviously see themselves as failures and withdraw in order to keep others from reminding them of how inadequate they are. Teachers must never give up on these students. They must always offer encouragement and support for even the smallest efforts. They should also be very sensitive to their own reactions to these students. Any indication of defeat or frustration reinforces a student's sense of worthlessness and desire to appear inadequate.

Four Illustrative Cases of Reorienting Students.   The following cases illustrate teachers' attempts to deal with students who are pursuing mistaken goals.

> ### SALLY'S CASE
>
> Ms. Morton's class is doing independent seatwork. Every few minutes Sally raises her hand to ask for direction: Should she number the sentences? Where should she put her name on the paper? Was this answer right? Ms. Morton has become exasperated with Sally because Sally does this every day and Ms. Morton has to stop and make explanations over and over. Finally, she tells Sally she will not help her any more during work time. She will explain the directions to the class once, and if Sally does not understand them she will have to wait

and do the assignment at recess. Ms. Morton then ignores all of Sally's requests for help. She does, however, encourage Sally when she sees her working without assistance.

Sally's case is an example of attention-getting behavior. The best clue was the teacher's reaction—annoyance—to Sally's behavior. But Ms. Morton did the best thing in this instance. She ignored Sally's bids for attention but reinforced her when she worked independently.

JERRY'S CASE

Jerry and another student are scuffling near dangerous equipment in wood shop class. They know this is against the rules and may result in their being removed temporarily from the class. Mr. Graves approaches and asks them to leave the shop area. Jerry refuses. Mr. Graves is tempted to remove him physically but instead walks to the front of the room, flicks the lights, and tells everyone to stop work. He explains that class cannot continue because Jerry is behaving improperly around dangerous equipment and refuses to follow the class rule and leave the area. The class waits, not without directing looks at Jerry. Jerry soon decides to comply with the rules.

Jerry's was an example of power-seeking behavior. Mr. Graves's first reaction was to feel his authority threatened. He was tempted to get into a power struggle with Jerry. However, he wisely refused to be drawn into a fight. He freely admitted to the class that Jerry had the power to stop the class. Jerry then had no one to struggle against. His power-seeking behavior was thwarted. Later, Mr. Graves asked Jerry to be a member of a group to review the rules for the class. That gave Jerry a position of authority that met his need for power in a constructive manner.

JANETTE'S CASE

Shalee is looking at a book that Miss Allen brought in to read to the class. Janette comes over and grabs it away, saying that she was supposed to get to see it first. Miss Allen takes the book, gives it back to Shalee, and scolds Janette. When Miss Allen is straightening the room after school, she finds the book with pages torn out and the cover ripped. Hurt and angered, she feels certain that Janette destroyed it. Janette has taken revenge for being punished. She has hurt Miss Allen, which was what she hoped to do.

Miss Allen might have handled the situation better by suggesting that Shalee and Janette sit down and read the book together. Janette would have felt accepted and included rather than rejected.

CATRINA'S CASE

Mr. Redding gives the class an assignment to write a composition. Everyone is soon busily writing, except for Catrina. Mr. Redding goes to her and says, "Catrina, you can start by writing your name and the date on your paper."

Catrina does not pick up her pencil but only looks down. Frustrated, Mr. Redding feels like saying, "Fine, if you don't want to work, I won't waste my time on you." Instead he says, "Sometimes writers need time to think before they write. I know you'll start writing when you are ready."

Catrina wanted Mr. Redding to see her as inadequate. If she had wanted attention, she would have responded to him. Instead, she acted as though he were not there. Mr. Redding did not give up on her. He offered encouragement and let her know that he had faith in her ability to do the assignment.

The Critical Difference between Encouragement and Praise

Dreikurs believes that encouragement is a crucial element in the prevention of problem behavior. Through encouragement teachers make learning seem worthwhile and help students develop self-esteem. *Encouragement* consists of words or actions that convey the teacher's respect and belief in students' abilities. It tells students that they are accepted as they are. It recognizes effort, not achievement, and promotes feelings of being a contributing member of the group. It draws on motivation from within and helps students become aware of their strengths, giving them the courage to try while accepting themselves as less than perfect. Teachers should be continually alert for opportunities to recognize effort, regardless of the quality of work that results.

Praise is very different from encouragement. *Praise* is given when a task is done well. It promotes the idea that a product is worthless unless it receives praise. Students who receive steady praise fail to learn to work for self-satisfaction. Praise encourages the attitude "What am I going to get out of it?" Here are some examples showing the differences between praise and encouragement:

> Praise: "You are such a good girl for finishing your assignment."
> Encouragement: "I can tell that you have been working hard."
>
> Praise: "I am proud of you for behaving so well in the assembly."
> Encouragement: "I was so glad that we could all enjoy the assembly."
>
> Praise: "You play the guitar so well!"
> Encouragement: "I can see that you really enjoy playing the guitar."

Dreikurs (Dreikurs & Cassel, 1972) makes the following suggestions for encouraging students:

1. Always be positive; avoid negative comments.
2. Encourage students to strive for improvement, not perfection.
3. Encourage effort. Results don't matter very much so long as students try hard.
4. Emphasize strengths and minimize weaknesses.

5. Teach students to learn from mistakes. Emphasize that mistakes are not failures.
6. Stimulate motivation from within. Do not exert pressure from without.
7. Encourage independence.
8. Let students know that you have faith in their abilities.
9. Offer to help overcome obstacles.
10. Encourage students to help classmates who are having difficulties. This helps them appreciate their own strengths.
11. Send positive notes home, especially concerning effort.
12. Show pride in students' work. Display the work and invite others to see it.
13. Be optimistic and enthusiastic—it is catching.
14. Try to set up situations that guarantee success for all.
15. Use encouraging remarks often, such as:
    You have improved!
    Can I help you?
    What did you learn from that mistake?
    I know you can.
    Keep trying!
    I know you can solve this, but if you really need help . . .
    I understand how you feel, but I am sure you can handle it. (pp. 51–54)

Dreikurs reminds us that there are also pitfalls in using encouragement. He cautions that teachers should not:

Encourage competition or comparison with others.

Point out how much better the student could be.

Use "but" statements, such as "I'm pleased with your progress, but . . ."

Use statements such as "It's about time."

Give up on those who are not responding.

Dreikurs advises teachers always to encourage students consistently and constantly.

Logical Consequences versus Punishment

No matter how much encouragement teachers give, they still encounter behavior problems. Dreikurs advises setting up logical consequences to help deter misbehavior and motivate appropriate behavior. *Logical consequences* are results that consistently follow certain behaviors; they are arranged jointly by teacher and students.

Logical consequences must be differentiated from punishment. *Punishment* is action taken by the teacher to get back at misbehaving students and show them who is boss. It prompts retaliation and makes students feel they have the right to punish in return. Logical consequences, on the other hand, are not weapons used by the teacher. They teach students that all behavior produces a corresponding result. Good behavior brings rewards, while unacceptable behavior brings unpleasant consequences. If a student throws paper on the floor, that student must pick it up. If a student fails to do work as assigned, that student must make up the work on the student's own time.

Logical consequences must be explained, understood, and agreed to by students. If they are sprung on students at the time of conflict, they will be considered punishment. When applying consequences, teachers should not act as self-appointed authorities. They should simply represent the order required by society and enforce the rules agreed to by the students.

To be effective, consequences must be applied consistently. If teachers apply them only when in a bad mood or only to certain students, students will not learn that misbehavior *always* carries unpleasant consequences. They will misbehave and gamble that they can get away with it. Students must be convinced that consequences will be applied each and every time they choose to misbehave. They will have to consider carefully whether misbehaving is worth it. It takes time to break old behavior habits, but teachers should never become discouraged and give up on implementing consequences.

Applying consequences encourages students to make careful choices about how they behave. They learn to rely on their own inner discipline to control their actions. They learn that poor choices invariably result in unpleasant consequences through nobody's fault but their own. Students also learn that the teacher respects their ability to make their own decisions.

Consequences should be related as closely as possible to the misbehavior so that students can see the connection between the two. For example,

1. Students who damage school property have to replace it.
2. Failure to complete an assignment means having to complete it after school.
3. Fighting at recess results in no recess.
4. Disturbing others results in isolation from the group.

Teachers should not show anger or triumph when applying consequences. If an assignment is not completed, they should simply say, "You chose to talk instead of doing math, so you must finish your math after school." This shows that when students choose to misbehave, they also choose the accompanying consequences.

Dreikurs's Dos and Don'ts

Discipline involves ongoing teacher guidance to help students develop inner control. It should not consist of limits imposed from the outside only at times of conflict. Rather, it should be consistent guidance that promotes a feeling of cooperation and team effort. To achieve this feeling, Dreikurs (Dreikurs et al., 1982) suggests that teachers do the following:

1. Give clear-cut directions for the actions expected of students. Wait until you have the attention of all class members before giving directions.
2. Try to establish a relationship with each individual that is built on trust and mutual respect.

3. Use logical consequences instead of traditional punishment. The consequence must bear a direct relationship to the behavior and must be understood by students.
4. See behavior in its proper perspective. In this way, you will avoid making serious issues out of trivial incidents.
5. Let students assume greater responsibility for their own behavior and learning.
6. Treat students as your social equals.
7. Combine kindness and firmness. The student must always sense that you are a friend but that you will not accept certain kinds of behavior.
8. At all times distinguish between the deed and the doer. This permits respect for the student, even when something wrong has been done.
9. Set limits from the beginning, but work toward mutual understanding, a sense of responsibility, and consideration for others.
10. Mean what you say, but keep your requests simple and see that they are carried out.
11. Close an incident quickly and revive good spirits. Let students know that mistakes are corrected, then forgotten.

Dreikurs says teachers should make certain not to do the following:

1. Do not nag and scold, since this fortifies a student's mistaken concept of how to get attention.
2. Do not ask a student to promise anything. Most students will promise to change in order to get out of an uncomfortable situation. It is a sheer waste of time.
3. Do not find fault with students. It may hurt their self-esteem and discourage them.
4. Do not adopt double standards—one for yourself and another for the students.
5. Do not use threat to discipline students. Although some students may become intimidated and conform for the moment, threat has no lasting value; it does not change students' basic attitudes.

COMMENTS ON THE DREIKURS MODEL

The Dreikurs model has great potential for bringing about genuine attitudinal change whereby students ultimately behave better because they see the value of doing so. Dreikurs continually refers to his approach as *democratic discipline*, meaning that teachers and students together decide on rules and consequences and that they take joint responsibility for maintaining a classroom climate conducive to learning.

For teachers to bring about democratic discipline, Dreikurs would have them spend considerable time talking with students about how their actions, efforts, and results affect themselves and others. This puts teachers into a counseling role beyond that called for in other models. Although democratic discipline can produce good results for teachers who have counseling skills, unfortunately most have never had the training that might help them in that regard and so are uncertain how to proceed.

For all its strengths, Dreikurs's system produces its valuable results slowly and must be worked at continually. In addition, it reveals a possible shortcoming that worries teachers of hard-to-manage classes, specifically, what do you do when students defy you? Dreikurs says to acknowledge before the class that you will not engage in power struggles with misbehaving students. But he seems to suggest that the remainder of the class will side with you and thus coerce the misbehaving student into compliance. Experienced teachers know that defiant behavior is often reinforced by other class members and that it is sometimes contagious. They feel that such behavior must be stopped at once.

Dreikurs supplies little to help teachers squelch misbehavior. Thus, teachers see his model as somewhat weak in corrective control though strong in preventive and supportive control.

In summary, Dreikurs's emphasis on mutual respect, encouragement, student effort, and general responsibility sits well with teachers. They consider important his efforts to instill in students an inner sense of responsibility and respect for others. However, most remain somewhat unclear as to how to implement his ideas.

BRIDGING THE GAP BETWEEN DREIKURS AND TEACHERS

The Dreikurs model has not been widely used by teachers, primarily because he did not show how to incorporate the approach into ongoing classroom practice. That shortcoming has been corrected by Dr. Linda Albert, mentioned earlier in the chapter. In 1974, Albert began systematizing Dreikurs's concepts and adding workable strategies and techniques that appeal to teachers. The resultant program, which Albert calls Cooperative Discipline, is explained in books, manuals, and videos that she has developed and tested in cooperation with a wide spectrum of teachers, administrators, and parents.

The principal improvements that Albert has made to Dreikurs's work lie in the following areas:

Democratic Style of Teaching

Albert calls this concept, which is a cornerstone of Dreikurs's model, the "hands-joined" style of teaching. She shows teachers how to encourage student cooperation through code-of-conduct activities, class meetings, and student councils. The style emphasizes giving students choices and regularly soliciting their input during decision making.

Concrete Intervention Strategies

Albert provides over 50 specific strategies for teachers to use when students misbehave. The strategies are categorized in accordance with Dreikurs's mistaken goals and explain the what, when, how, and where of effective teacher responses to misbehavior. This gives teachers the security of always knowing what to say and do when students misbehave.

Encouragement through the Three C Approach

Both Dreikurs and Albert believe that students should be given continual encouragement. Albert stresses giving encouragement through the Three C approach, which helps students feel *C*apable of completing academic work, shows them how to *C*onnect positively with teachers and classmates, and helps them *C*ontribute significantly to the welfare of the class and school. Albert provides specific techniques for the Three C strategy and urges administrators to give it priority for the entire school, involving not only students but teachers and parents as well.

Action Plan for Difficult-to-Control Students

Teachers are always concerned about students who misbehave repeatedly. Albert provides a step-by-step plan that works on behalf of such students by enhancing communication and collaboration between concerned teachers, parents, students, and administrators. The plan unites efforts of parents and professionals in encouraging students to behave more responsibly.

Administrators' Management Action Plan

Albert outlines procedures by which administrators can invite teaching staffs to participate in Cooperative Discipline and evaluate its results. This plan utilizes effective principles from school improvement programs and makes concrete suggestions for supporting teachers over time as they learn to implement the suggested practices.

APPLICATION EXERCISES

REVIEW OF SELECTED TERMINOLOGY

The following terms are central to the Dreikurs model of discipline. Check yourself to make sure you can explain their meanings.

discipline	aversive discipline
self-discipline	autocratic teacher

permissive teacher	seeking revenge
democratic teacher	displaying inadequacy
democratic teaching	identifying mistaken goals
democratic classroom	confronting mistaken goals
genuine goal of belonging	encouragement
mistaken goals	praise
misbehavior	logical consequences
getting attention	punishment
seeking power	democratic discipline

CONCEPT CASES

Case 1: Kristina Will Not Work

Kristina, a student in Mr. Jake's class, is quite docile. She socializes little with other students and never disrupts the class. But despite Mr. Jake's best efforts, Kristina will not do her work. She rarely completes an assignment. She is simply there, putting forth no effort.

How would Dreikurs deal with Kristina? He would suggest that Mr. Jake follow these steps as a means of improving Kristina's behavior:

1. Identify Kristina's mistaken goal: Mr. Jake can do this by checking his own reaction to Kristina's lethargy and by noting the reactions of other students when he attempts to correct her.
2. If Kristina's mistaken goal is getting attention, ignore her.
3. If Kristina's mistaken goal is seeking power, admit that Kristina has power: "I can't make you do your work. What do you think I should do?"
4. If Kristina's goal is seeking revenge, ask other members of the class to be especially encouraging to her.
5. If Kristina's goal is displaying inadequacy, encourage her frequently and give her continual support.
6. Confront Kristina with her mistaken goal and draw her into a discussion about the goal and her behavior.

Case 2: Sara Cannot Stop Talking

Sara is a pleasant girl who participates in class activities and does most, though not all, of her assigned work. She cannot seem to refrain from talking to classmates, however. Her teacher, Mr. Gonzales, has to speak to her repeatedly during lessons, to the point that he often becomes exasperated and loses his temper.

What suggestions would Dreikurs give Mr. Gonzales for dealing with Sara?

Case 3: Joshua Clowns and Intimidates

Joshua, larger and louder than his classmates, always wants to be the center of attention, which he accomplishes through a combination of clowning and intimidation. He makes wise remarks, talks back (smilingly) to the teacher, utters a variety of sound-effect noises such as automobile crashes and gunshots, and makes limitless sarcastic comments and put-downs of his classmates. Other students will not stand up to him, apparently fearing his size and verbal aggression. His teacher, Miss Pearl, has come to her wit's end.

What is Joshua's mistaken goal, and how would Dreikurs have you deal with it?

Case 4: Tom Is Hostile and Defiant

Tom has appeared to be in his usual foul mood ever since arriving in class. On his way to sharpen his pencil, he bumps into Frank, who complains. Tom tells him loudly to shut up. Miss Baines, the teacher, says, "Tom, go back to your seat." Tom wheels around, swears loudly, and says heatedly, "I'll go when I'm damned good and ready!"

What can you find in Dreikurs's work that might help you in this instance?

QUESTIONS AND ACTIVITIES

1. For each of the following cases, first identify the student's mistaken goal and then explain how Dreikurs would have the teacher deal with it.
   a. Joe habitually plays with objects on his desk when he should be listening. This causes his teacher to stop instruction frequently and remind him to listen. He usually complies for only a few minutes.
   b. Lanya seems to have made it her life's goal to taunt and belittle her classmates. If they notify the teacher about her behavior, she harasses them outside the classroom.
   c. Maria sits in the back of the classroom. She stares at her desk. She has never turned in an assignment. She replies only perfunctorily when the teacher speaks to her.
   d. Teresa likes to enter the classroom five minutes late, making enough noise to distract the class. When asked to explain her tardiness, she accuses the teacher of picking on her.

2. Examine Scenario 2 or 1 in Appendix I. Indicate how Dreikurs would advise Mr. Platt or Mrs. Miller to deal with attention-seeking students.

REFERENCES AND RECOMMENDED READINGS

Albert, L. (1996). *A teacher's guide to cooperative discipline* (rev. ed.). Circle Pines, MN: American Guidance Service. (Original work published 1989)

Dreikurs, R. (1968). *Psychology in the classroom* (2nd ed.). New York: Harper & Row.

Dreikurs, R., & Cassel, P. (1972). *Discipline without tears.* New York: Hawthorn.

Dreikurs, R., Grunwald, B., & Pepper, F. (1982). *Maintaining sanity in the classroom.* New York: Harper & Row.

CHAPTER 6

The Canter Model

Discipline through Assertively Managing Behavior

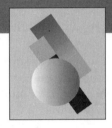

Lee Canter and Marlene Canter

BIOGRAPHICAL SKETCH OF CANTER

Lee Canter is director of Lee Canter & Associates, an organization that provides training in classroom discipline and publishes related materials for educators and parents. His wife, Marlene Canter, collaborates in the work. Canter's system, called Assertive Discipline, is designed to help teachers consistently interact with students in a calm and helpful manner so that order is preserved, personal needs are met, and teaching and learning proceed as intended. Through workshops and graduate courses, Canter has brought Assertive Discipline to over 1 million teachers and administrators, making his program not only the most popular of all such systems but also the most discussed and, possibly, the most controversial.

Canter's company produces quantities of materials on such topics as motivation, homework, dealing with severe behavior problems, and activities for positive reinforcement. The Canter materials are listed in *The Assertive Educator*, a newsletter available from Lee Canter & Associates, P.O. Box 2113, Santa Monica, CA 90406; telephone 310-395-3221.

CANTER'S CONTRIBUTIONS TO DISCIPLINE

Canter has made several major contributions to classroom discipline. He popularized the concept of rights in the classroom—the rights of students to have teachers who help them learn in a calm, safe environment and the rights of teachers to teach without disruption. He reemphasized that students need and want limits that assist proper conduct and that it is the teacher's responsibility to set and enforce those limits. He was the first to insist that teachers have a right to backing from administrators and cooperation from parents in helping students behave acceptably. And he was the first to provide teachers with a workable procedure for correcting misbehavior efficiently through a system of easily administered consequences, both positive and negative.

Canter has progressively modified his approach over the years. He explains that earlier he tried to get across the idea that the teacher must be a strong leader in the classroom. Now he strongly emphasizes that teachers must talk more with troublesome students and actually teach them how to behave. In his materials and programs, Canter explains how these objectives are accomplished.

CANTER'S CENTRAL FOCUS

The central focus of the Canter model is on showing teachers how to take charge responsibly in the classroom and establish a climate in which needs are met, behavior is managed humanely, and learning occurs as intended. This is accomplished through focusing on student needs, establishing good class rules of behavior, teaching students how to behave properly, regularly giving students positive attention, talking helpfully with students who misbehave, and invoking consequences only as a last resort.

CANTER'S PRINCIPAL CONCEPTS AND TEACHINGS

Students' rights. Students need a concerned teacher who is able to set consistent limits on behavior while at the same time providing warmth, personal attention, and support. Students have the right to teachers who work for students' best interests by placing limits on misbehavior while providing support and encouragement.

Teachers' rights. Teachers have the right to teach in a classroom free from disruption and with the support of parents and administrators.

Assertive teacher. This is a teacher who clearly and firmly communicates needs and requirements to students and follows those words with appropriate actions.

Roadblocks to assertive discipline. This phrase refers to the mistaken beliefs that inhibit teachers' establishing good classroom discipline.

Setting limits. This is the process of making plain which behaviors are acceptable and which are unacceptable in the classroom.

Nonassertive responses. These teacher responses to misbehavior fail to back up violations of established standards of behavior with appropriate actions.

Hostile responses. These teacher responses to misbehavior attack and belittle students.

Assertive responses. These teacher responses to misbehavior continually help students comply with established expectations. Words are backed up principally with positive recognition. Consequences are invoked only when all else fails.

Positive recognition. This phrase refers to the sincere, meaningful attention teachers give students who behave according to expectations.

Consequences. These are penalties teachers invoke when students violate class expectations. Consequences must be something students dislike (staying in after class, being isolated from the group) but must never be physically or psychologically harmful.

Teaching responsible behavior. Good behavior management requires that teachers not simply set limits but go well beyond that to actually teach students how to behave responsibly in the classroom.

Positive repetitions. These involve repeating directions as positive statements to students who are complying with class rules, for example, "Fred remembered to raise his hand. Good job."

Moving in. This technique is used when one or two chronically misbehaving students do not respond to normal consequences. It involves moving directly to the student, making eye contact, restating directions to be followed, and indicating what the next consequence will be for further misbehavior.

ANALYSIS OF THE CANTER MODEL

In 1976, Canter first set forth the basic premises and practices of Assertive Discipline. At that time he noted that discipline caused teachers and parents great concern and was much in need of improvement. As societal conditions worsened, teachers became increasingly hesitant and unsure about controlling student behavior. Canter felt that the uncertainty was partly due to teachers' mistaken ideas about discipline.

Mistaken Ideas about Discipline

Teachers had grown confused about what discipline should be, how it should be administered, and the effects it has on students. This confusion resulted in teachers' holding several *mistaken ideas about discipline*, including the following:

1. Good teachers should be able to handle discipline problems on their own without any help.
2. Firm discipline causes students psychological harm.
3. Discipline problems disappear if the curriculum is interesting enough.
4. Misbehavior results from deep-seated causes beyond the influence of the teacher.

Canter says that none of these statements is true and that they should be replaced with correct ideas about discipline.

Students' Rights in the Classroom

Canter (Canter & Canter, 1992, pp. 12–13) says that students have the right to a warm, supportive classroom environment in which to learn, where teachers do all in their power to help students be successful. Specifically, *students' rights* are as follows:

- The right to know the teacher's behavioral expectations clearly, without having to guess
- The right to receive specific instruction concerning how students are expected to behave in all aspects of the program
- The right to receive positive recognition and support (Just as students need to have clear behavior limits, they also need for their teachers to be helpful and to acknowledge proper behavior.)
- The right to have limits set on their behavior (Students do not automatically behave in accord with teachers' expectations. They need to have established limits that indicate what will occur when they fail to comply with expectations.)

Teachers' Rights in the Classroom

Teachers have rights in the classroom as well. Canter mentions the following *teachers' rights*:

- The right to establish optimal learning environments for students that are consistent with the teacher's strengths and limitations
- The right to expect behavior from students that contributes to optimal growth
- The right to backing from administrators and parents

When these basic rights of teachers are recognized, they establish the basis for a climate of positive support and care.

What Assertive Teachers Do

Canter (1978) describes *assertive teachers* as those who care about themselves to the point of not allowing students to take advantage and who care about students to the point of not allowing them to behave in ways that harm themselves. This caring is best conveyed by teachers who are positive, firm, and consistent, not wishy-washy, hostile, abusive, or threatening. Canter (Canter & Canter, 1992) has written:

> We define an assertive teacher as one who clearly and firmly communicates her expectations to her students, and is prepared to reinforce her words with appropriate actions. She responds to students in a manner that maximizes her potential to get her own needs to teach met, but in no way violates the best interest of the students.
>
> Assertive teachers communicate their influence by sending a very clear message to their students: "I am committed to being the leader in this classroom, a leader who will establish an environment where I can teach and my students can learn. To reach this goal, I am committed to teaching and empowering my students to choose the responsible behavior that will allow them to succeed in school, and to succeed later in life.
>
> I care too much about my responsibility as a teacher to allow disruptive behavior to stop me from teaching. I care too much about my students to allow them to behave in a manner that is not in their best interests." (pp. 14–15)

Earlier, Canter (1976) had listed some of the specific things assertive teachers do.

- Identify expectations clearly.
- Be willing to say, "I like that" and "I don't like that."

- Set clear limits concerning classroom behavior.
- Be persistent in stating expectations and feelings.
- Maintain eye contact.
- Use nonverbal gestures in support of verbal statements.
- Use hints and I-messages to request appropriate behavior.
- Interact with students concerning good and bad behavior, why rules are needed, and how behavior can be improved.
- When misbehavior occurs, follow through with established consequences rather than threats.

Steps That Lead to Assertive Discipline

Canter suggests that teachers incorporate the basics of Assertive Discipline into their teaching styles by (1) recognizing and removing roadblocks; (2) practicing assertive response styles; (3) making a discipline plan that contains good rules and clear, effective consequences; (4) teaching the discipline plan to students; and (5) teaching students how to behave responsibly. Let us examine more closely what is involved in these five steps.

Step 1. Recognize and Remove Roadblocks to Assertive Discipline. All teachers have within themselves the potential for expressing their educational needs to students and for obtaining student compliance with those needs. Most teachers have difficulty doing so, however, because of a group of "roadblocks" that hinder their efforts. The first step in Assertive Discipline is to recognize and remove these *roadblocks to discipline*.

The major roadblock to successful classroom management is teachers' *negative expectations* about their ability to deal with disruptive students. They expect some students to behave badly because of health, home, personality, or environment. For example, Victor has a history of bullying other students; Stacy may be a victim of child abuse; no one has ever been able to do a thing with Donald. Therefore those students cannot be expected to behave. Such negative expectations are false and should be replaced with the positive expectation that all students can behave appropriately. The bottom line, Canter (Canter & Canter, 1992) writes, is that "you must believe that if students don't behave, it's because they've chosen not to, or don't know how" (p. 20).

Another prominent roadblock is teachers' presumed *lack of positive influence* on the behavior of their students regardless of the problem. To remove this roadblock, teachers should acknowledge that

- all students need limits, and teachers are responsible for *setting limits*;
- students admire and respect teachers who hold high expectations and high standards but do so humanely; and
- students seldom respect teachers who take a laissez faire approach to teaching.

A third prominent roadblock is teachers' presumed *lack of support*. To the contrary, teachers have the right to request and receive solid backing from principals, parents, and other school personnel. Teachers who have such support will not be intimidated by hostile student behavior.

Step 2. Practice the Use of Assertive Response Styles.   Canter (Canter & Canter, 1992) says that all teachers can learn to function in an assertive manner and that "it is your response style that sets the tone of your classroom . . . and impacts students' self-esteem and their success in school" (p. 25). To help explain what he means by an assertive response style, Canter differentiates between three response styles that teachers are seen to use with misbehaving students.

Nonassertive Response Style.   The *nonassertive response style* is typical of teachers who have given in to students or who feel it is wrong to place strong demands on student behavior. Terry and Rick are laughing and engaging in horseplay that has almost ruined the lesson. Miss Jenkins looks up and says, "For the tenth time, would you two please stop that?" She continues the lesson, but within a few minutes the two boys are disrupting again.

Teachers who use this nonassertive style are approaching discipline passively. Either they do not establish clear standards or they fail to back up their standards with appropriate actions. They hope their good natures will gain student compliance. They often ask students to "please try" to do their work, behave themselves, or do better next time. They are not firm or insistent, and usually they resignedly accept what the students do.

Hostile Response Style.   Mr. Carmody sees Alonso and Shawn talking instead of paying attention. He yells, "All right, you two! That's it for you! Either you pay attention or I guarantee you are going to regret it!"

This *hostile response style* is used when teachers feel they are barely hanging on to class control. They use sarcasm and make threats, believing they must rule with an iron fist or else be overwhelmed with chaos. Most students do what hostile teachers demand of them, but they do so only out of fear. They have little respect for the teacher and dream about getting even.

Assertive Response Style.   Terry and Rick are now in Miss Berard's class. They have continued the horseplay they began in Miss Jenkins's room. Miss Berard looks directly at them, writes their names on her clipboard, and says, "It is against the rules to talk without permission during the lesson. This is a warning." The boys know that, if they continue, Miss Berard will take further steps. The lesson resumes and so does their misbehavior. Miss Berard makes a check mark beside each of their names and tells them they have chosen to remain for two minutes after class. Miss Berard has shown through her *assertive response style* that she follows through on enforcing class rules.

Step 3. Make a Discipline Plan That Contains Good Rules and Clear, Effective Consequences.   All teachers should create a clear, workable discipline plan that includes rules, positive recognition, and consequences.

Rules.   *Rules* must state exactly how students are to behave. The rules should indicate observable behaviors such as "Keep your hands to yourself" rather than vague ideas such as "Show respect to other students." Canter (Canter & Canter, 1992) lists the following as rules needed for good learning in a positive environment:

- Follow directions. (For efficient work.)
- Keep hands, feet, and objects to yourself. (For physical safety.)
- No profanity or teasing. (For psychological safety.) (p. 50)

Canter reminds teachers that their rules must be usable every day, all period long or all day long. They should be limited in number (three to five), apply in every class period, and refer only to behavior, not to academic issues. In accordance with those guidelines, Canter suggests the following for different grade levels:

Grades K–6
- Follow directions.
- Keep hands, feet, and objects to yourself.
- Do not leave the room without permission.
- No swearing or teasing.
- No yelling or screaming.

Grades 7–12
- Follow directions.
- No swearing or teasing.
- Be in your seat when the bell rings. (p. 53)

Positive Recognition.   *Positive recognition* refers to giving sincere attention to students who behave in keeping with class expectations. Canter says recognition should be used frequently because it increases self-esteem, encourages good behavior, and helps build a positive classroom climate. Teachers should make the following special efforts:

- Praise students for behaving appropriately. Canter says giving praise is what most clearly distinguishes the more effective teacher from the less effective one.
- Send positive notes and make positive phone calls to parents. This is the most effective way to secure parental support, and it can be done in five minutes per day.
- Give awards for good behavior. Canter suggests making several such awards each week, using prepared certificates on which student names can be entered.

- Assign special privileges to students who earn them through good behavior. For elementary students, the following are favored privileges:

  —Be first in line.

  —Be allowed to help in the classroom.

  —Read a favorite book.

  —Work on a favorite activity.

  For secondary students, the following are appropriate:

  —Sit by a friend for one period.

  —Have extra computer time.

  —Be excused from a quiz.

- Use classwide positive recognition, in which all students work together to earn a reward for the entire class. The class should be advised of the incentive and what they must do to earn it. Generally, the award should be earnable in a reasonably short time, from one day to one week at the elementary level and from one to two weeks at the secondary level. Progress can be tracked by adding marbles to a jar until it is full, noting progress on a class chart until a finish line is reached, or keeping points on the board until a certain total is reached. The following are examples of classwide awards:

  Elementary Level

  —special video

  —special arts and crafts project

  —extra time on the playground

  Secondary Level

  —video with popcorn

  —free time to talk quietly in class

  —free choice of seating for a day

  —free reading or homework time

- Give tangible awards such as stickers, trinkets, and treats, but do so only if other positive recognition has been ineffective. So that the award will be recognized as a reward for good behavior, give it immediately after observing the desired behavior and pair it with verbal praise: "James, here is a sticker you deserve for working so quietly. I appreciate your help."

Consequences.   *Consequences* are penalties invoked by teachers when students fail to live up to standards of classroom behavior. Consequences are something students do not like, but they are never harmful physically or psychologically. Moreover, students have knowledge of consequences in advance. When consequences must be invoked, students should understand they have chosen them by the way they behaved. Teachers are usually troubled by having to invoke consequences, but Canter (Canter & Canter, 1992) writes:

There is perhaps nothing more harmful we can do to children than allow them to disrupt or misbehave without showing them we care enough to let them know their behavior is not acceptable. (p. 79)

With advance preparation, misbehavior can be dealt with calmly and quickly. Canter advises making what he calls a *discipline hierarchy* that lists consequences and the order in which they will be imposed within the day. (Each day or secondary class period begins afresh.) Each consequence in the hierarchy is a bit more substantial than its predecessor. Canter illustrates the discipline hierarchy as follows:

- *First time a student disrupts.* Consequence: "Bobby, our rule is no shouting out. That's a warning."
- *Second or third time the same student disrupts.* Consequence: "Bobby, our rule is we keep our hands to ourselves. You have chosen 5 minutes' time out at the back table."
- *Fourth time the same student disrupts.* Consequence: "Bobby, you know our rules about hitting others. You have chosen to have your parents called." The teacher informs Bobby's parents. This is best done by phone and is especially effective if Bobby is required to place the call and explain what has happened.
- *Fifth time the same student disrupts.* Consequence: "Bobby, our rule is we keep our hands to ourselves. You have chosen to go to the office to talk with the principal about your behavior."
- *Severe clause.* Sometimes behavior is so severe that the hierarchy is disregarded and the severe clause—being sent to the principal—is invoked on the first offense. Consequence: "Bobby, fighting is not allowed in this class. You have chosen to go to the principal immediately. We will talk about this later." (p. 85)

Teachers are advised to organize hierarchies of discipline in accordance with their needs. For guidance, Canter (Canter & Canter, 1992) provides the following illustrations:

Grades K–3

Rule Is Broken	Consequence
first	warning
second	5 minutes working away from the group
third	10 minutes working away from the group
fourth	call parents
fifth	send to principal
severe clause	send to principal

Grades 4–6

Rule Is Broken	Consequence
first	warning
second	10 minutes working away from group
third	15 minutes working away from group, plus write in the behavior journal
fourth	call parents
fifth	send to principal
severe clause	send to principal

Grades 7–12

Rule Is Broken	Consequence
first	warning
second	stay in class 1 minute after the bell
third	stay in class 2 minutes after the bell, plus write in the behavior journal
fourth	call parents
fifth	send to principal
severe clause	send to principal (p. 88)

The behavior journal referred to in the foregoing suggestions is a log book in which students write accounts of misbehavior, including why the student broke the rule and what alternative action the student might better have taken.

In order to employ the discipline hierarchy, teachers must keep track of offenses students commit. This is easily done by recording on a clipboard students' names and the number of violations. Other options include recording this information in the plan book or, in primary grades, using a system of colored cards that students "turn" or change after each violation.

Step 4. Teach the Discipline Plan to Students. Canter stresses this point: In order to make a discipline plan work effectively, teachers must engage in *teaching the discipline plan* to their students. It's not enough just to read it aloud or display it on a poster. It must be taught directly.

Canter provides a number of sample lessons showing how the plan can be taught at different grade levels (see Canter & Canter, 1992, pp. 98–115). All the suggested plans follow this sequence:

1. Explain why rules are needed.
2. Teach the specific rules.
3. Check for understanding.
4. Explain how you will reward students who follow rules.
5. Explain why you have consequences.

6. Teach the consequences.

7. Check for understanding.

Step 5. Teach Students How to Behave Responsibly.   Canter devotes considerable effort to the subject of *teaching responsible behavior* to students and shows how it can be developed through assertive teaching. He focuses on (1) teaching students how to follow directions, (2) using positive recognition to motivate good behavior, and (3) redirecting nondisruptive off-task behavior.

Teaching Students to Follow Specific Directions.   Canter says that the most important classroom rule is "Follow directions," but students can't be expected to know automatically how to do so in all the many classroom activities. Recognizing that different teachers have their own ways of doing things, Canter (Canter & Canter, 1992) says "Your students need to follow *your* expectations, not another teacher's expectations" (p. 122).

To prevent problems with students' following directions, Canter suggests that teachers identify the academic activities, routine procedures, and special procedures for which directions are needed and then determine the specific directions that students are to follow for each. Canter (Canter & Canter, 1992) gives many examples of where students should be taught to follow directions.

In Academic Activities
- When giving a directed lesson
- When students are doing independent seatwork
- When students are working in small groups
- When the class is having a discussion
- When students are taking a test

In Routine Procedures
- When students enter and exit the classroom
- When students request a drink or ask to use the restroom
- When students sharpen pencils
- When students turn in homework
- When students are in transition from one activity to another

In Special Procedures
- In fire drills
- At school assemblies
- On field trips
- When guests are in the room (pp. 123–124)

Canter (Canter & Canter, 1992) provides sample plans for teaching students to follow directions in situations such as those listed. The following are two examples, one for an academic activity and one for a routine procedure:

Teacher Conducting a Directed Lesson
1. Clear your desks of everything but paper and pencil.
2. Eyes on me. No talking while I'm talking.
3. Raise hand and wait to be called on before speaking.

Routine Procedure for Entering the Room
1. Walk into the room.
2. Go directly to your seat and sit down.
3. No talking after the bell rings. (pp. 126–127)

The best time for teaching directions is immediately prior to the first (or next) time the activity is to take place. For young children, give explanations and have children act them out. Frequent reteaching and reinforcement will be necessary. For older students, explain the reasons behind the directions and the benefits they provide. Canter (Canter & Canter, 1992, pp. 131–138) suggests using the following procedure:

1. Explain the rationale for the direction.
2. Involve the students by asking questions.
3. Explain the specific directions.
4. Check for student understanding (by asking questions or having students role-play).

Once taught, the specific directions should be reinforced regularly through *positive repetition*. This means that rather than identify and correct student who is not following directions, the teacher notes one or more who are following directions and says, "Joshua has remembered to raise his hand. So has Elsa." Directions should be reviewed each time the activity is repeated during the first two weeks. For the next month the directions should be reviewed each Monday as a refresher, and for the remainder of the year they should be reviewed after vacations and before special events such as holidays and field trips.

Using Positive Recognition. Canter (Canter & Canter, 1992) says that the best way to build responsible behavior is to "continually provide frequent positive recognition to those students who are on task" (p. 146). By positive recognition, he means praise and support, both of which should be integrated naturally into lessons being taught.

Canter (Canter & Canter, 1992, pp. 148–150) contends that praise is the most effective technique teachers have for encouraging responsible behavior. He provides guidelines for its use:

- Effective praise is personal. The student's name is mentioned along with the desired behavior: "Jack, thank you for working quietly back there."
- Effective praise is genuine. It must be related to situation and behavior, and the teacher's demeanor should show that it is meant.
- Effective praise is descriptive and specific. It lets students know when and why they are behaving appropriately: "You went right to work on your essay, Susan. Good going."
- Effective praise is age-appropriate. Young children like to be praised publicly. Older students like praise but often prefer to receive it privately.

Canter suggests several techniques helpful in providing positive praise and support, including the following:

- Scanning—looking around the classroom regularly to find students who are working appropriately.
- Circulating around the classroom—moving about the room to give one-on-one attention.
- Writing names on the board—writing on the board the names of students who are behaving responsibly. Set a goal with the class for getting at least 20 names on the board each day.

Redirecting Nondisruptive Off-Task Behavior.   Often students fail to behave responsibly but do not misbehave in a way that disrupts the class. They may look out the window instead of working, read a book instead of doing their assignment, doodle instead of completing their work, do work for another class, or daydream or sleep.

Instead of applying consequences for these benign misbehaviors, teachers should attempt first to redirect students back to the assigned task. Canter (Canter & Canter, 1992, pp. 164–166) describes four techniques teachers should consider.

1. Use "the look": Make eye contact and use an expression that shows awareness and disapproval.
2. Use physical proximity: Move beside the student. Usually there is no need to do more.
3. Mention the offending student's name: Tanya and Michael are not listening. The teacher says, "I want all of you, including Tanya and Michael, to come up with the answer to this problem."
4. Use proximity praise: Jason is not working, but Alicia and Maria, seated nearby, are. The teacher says, "Alicia and Maria are doing an excellent job of completing their work."

Normally, these redirecting techniques are quite effective. If they do not produce the needed results, the teacher should assume that the offending student needs more help for self-control and should turn to the discipline hierarchy and issue a warning.

When Consequences Must Be Invoked

Earlier, consequences were described as unpleasant (but not harmful) penalties students must suffer when they disruptively violate class rules. Students will have been clearly informed of both positive recognition and consequences associated with class rules, and they may even have role-played situations involving both. They realize that consequences naturally follow misbehavior. Canter (Canter & Canter, 1992, pp. 170–186) makes these suggestions for invoking consequences:

1. Provide consequences calmly in a matter-of-fact manner: "Nathan, speaking like that to others is against our rules. You have chosen to stay after class."
2. Be consistent: Provide a consequence every time students choose to disrupt.
3. After a student receives a consequence, find the first opportunity to recognize that student's positive behavior: "Nathan, I appreciate how you are working. You are making a good choice."
4. Provide an escape mechanism for students who are upset and want to talk about what happened: Allow the student to write out feelings or describe the situation in a journal or log.
5. When a younger student continues to disrupt, "move in": Nathan again speaks hurtfully to another student. The teacher moves close to Nathan and quietly and firmly tells him his behavior is inappropriate. She reminds him of the consequences he has already received and of the next consequence in the hierarchy.
6. When an older student continues to disrupt, "move out": Marta once again talks during work time. The teacher asks Marta to step outside the classroom, where she reminds Marta of the inappropriate behavior and its consequences. All the while, the teacher stays calm, shows respect for Marta's feelings, and refrains from arguing.

Dealing with Difficult Students

Canter believes that the techniques described to this point will help almost all students behave in a responsible manner, but he acknowledges that a few students—5 to 10 percent—may require additional steps. Those are the students who disrupt, ignore rules, argue, and do not care about consequences—the students teachers dread to deal with—but they are also the students most in need of attention and adult guidance. Canter describes three approaches to help teachers work with difficult-to-manage students: (1) one-on-one problem-solving conferences, (2) positive support to build relationships, and (3) developing an individualized behavior plan.

The One-On-One Problem-Solving Conference. The *one-on-one problem-solving conference* is a meeting between teacher and student to discuss a specific behavior problem. The goal of the conference is not to punish the student but to gain insight so that more helpful guidance can be provided. Canter (Canter & Canter, 1992, pp. 208–215) makes the following suggestions:

1. Show empathy and concern for the student. Let the student know you care and want to help.
2. Gently question the student to find out why there is a problem: "Did something happen that got you upset? Are other students bothering you? Is the work too difficult? Do you have problems at home?"
3. Determine what you can do to help. Boost your positive attention to the student. Change things in the class that are bothering the student. Contact the parents if there are things they might do to help.
4. Describe how the student can improve behavior.
5. Jointly agree on a course of action. Listen to the student's concerns. Voice yours. Find a common ground.

Use Positive Support to Build Relationships.   You need to show your students that you don't just care about their behavior but that you also care about them as individuals. To accomplish this you must reach out, treating the student as you would want your own child to be treated. Students who believe you really care about them are not so likely to challenge the limits you have set. Canter (Canter & Canter, 1992, pp. 219–225) suggests the following as ways to use *positive support* to build relationships:

1. Take a student interest inventory: Find out about brothers and sisters, friends, preferred activities, hobbies, favorite books and TV shows, future hopes, and what they like their teachers to do.
2. Greet the students personally at the door: Say something special to each of them personally.
3. Spend some individual time with students: Give one-on-one attention during lunch or recess or occasionally before or after school.
4. Make home visits: Home visits can help show that you care about the student and they also teach you much about the student you would otherwise not know.
5. Make a phone call after a difficult day: Make the call to the student, not the parent, and express regret about the difficulty and empathy for the student. And after a positive day at school, a phone call of appreciation can be very helpful.
6. When a student is ill, send a get-well card or use the phone to inquire about the student and convey best wishes.

Develop an Individualized Behavior Plan.   *Individualized behavior plans* can be useful when the general discipline plan is not working with a particular student. This plan should include the behaviors expected of the student, the positive recognition that will come when the student behaves appropriately, and the consequences for failing to comply with the agreements.

Only one or two behaviors should be worked on at a time. The desired behavior should be specified, for example, "No shouting out" or "Always keep your hands to yourself." Also spell out what you will do for positive recognition and follow through consistently. Use praise liberally and look for opportunities to compliment students on their work or behavior.

Consequences will have to differ somewhat from those used with the rest of the class, because the student is obviously not responding to general class agreements. You may wish to skip the warning and go directly to staying after class or even call the parent on the first disruption. This will not surprise parents, because they will have been involved in developing the individualized plan or at least informed about it in detail. In using the individualized plan, it is very important that students know it is for their benefit and that you are willing to do what you can to help them be successful in school.

INITIATING THE CANTER MODEL

Canter's Assertive Discipline can be introduced in the class at any time, though the first few days of a new school year or semester are especially appropriate. Decide on behaviors you want from students, together with positive recognition and consequences. Take your plan to the principal for approval and *administrative support*. At the first meeting with the new class, discuss the kinds of behavior that will make the classroom pleasant, safe, and productive. Solicit student ideas. Jointly formulate three to five rules to govern behavior. Have all students agree to abide by the rules. Discuss with students the recognitions and the hierarchy of consequences associated with the rules. Make sure students realize that the rules apply to every member of the class all the time. Send a copy of the discipline plan home for parents to read. Ask that parents sign and return a slip indicating their approval and *parental support*. With students, role-play rules, recognitions, and consequences, and emphasize repeatedly that the plan helps everyone enjoy a safe, positive environment.

COMMENTS ON THE CANTER MODEL

Canter has developed a system of discipline intended to promote a pleasant, supportive classroom environment that frees teachers to teach and students to learn. His approach is unique in several ways—in ease of implementation, meeting teachers' and students' needs, teaching students how to behave responsibly, and insistence on support from administrators and parents.

A great many teachers are very enthusiastic about Assertive Discipline because it helps them with corrective control and allows them to teach with little interruption. It relieves them of the annoyance, or sometimes agony, of verbal confrontations, preserves instructional time, and is effective in preventive and supportive control. Students are taught how to behave and know in advance the rewards and consequences of both good and poor behavior.

Does Assertive Discipline have shortcomings? In the past it was criticized for being unnecessarily harsh and too focused on suppressing unwanted behavior rather than on helping students learn to control their own behavior. Canter maintains that those criticisms arose only when the program was improperly implemented, and he has taken pains to make sure that teachers understand his central point: students must be taught, in an atmosphere of respect, trust, and support, how to behave responsibly. Assertive Discipline was, and still is, criticized for its extensive use of praise and other rewards, which some authorities believe reduce intrinsic motivation. Debate continues, too, concerning whether research supports the effectiveness of Assertive Discipline. Some writers present evidence that it does (Canter, 1988; McCormack, 1989), while others claim the opposite (Curwin & Mendler, 1989; Render, Padilla, & Krank, 1989; Kohn, 1993). As with anything else, people have different opinions and interpretations. All in all, however, the widespread popularity of Assertive Discipline suggests that it provides educators with effective skills they have been unable to find elsewhere.

APPLICATION EXERCISES

REVIEW OF SELECTED TERMINOLOGY

The following terms are central to the Canter model of discipline. Check yourself to make sure you can explain their meanings.

mistaken ideas about discipline	rules
students' rights	positive recognition
teachers' rights	consequences
assertive teacher	discipline hierarchy
roadblocks to discipline	teaching the discipline plan
negative expectations	teaching responsible behavior
setting limits	positive repetitions
nonassertive response	administrative support
hostile response style	parental support
assertive response	

CONCEPT CASES

Case 1: Kristina Will Not Work

Kristina, a student in Mr. Jake's class, is quite docile. She socializes little with other students and never disrupts lessons. However, despite Mr. Jake's best efforts, Kristina will not do her work. She rarely completes an assignment. She is simply there, putting forth no effort at all.

How would Canter deal with Kristina?   Canter would advise Mr. Jake to do the following:

Quietly and clearly communicate class expectations to Kristina.

Redirect her to on-task behavior.

Have private talks with her to determine why she is not doing her work and what Mr. Jake might do to help.

Provide personal recognition regularly and try to build a bond of care and trust with Kristina.

Contact Kristina's parents about her behavior. See if they can provide insights that will help Mr. Jake work with Kristina.

If necessary, make an individualized behavior plan for helping Kristina do her work.

Case 2: Sara Cannot Stop Talking

Sara is a pleasant girl who participates in class activities and does most, though not all, of her assigned work. She cannot seem to refrain from talking to classmates, however. Her teacher, Mr. Gonzales, has to speak to her repeatedly during lessons, to the point that he often becomes exasperated and loses his temper.

What suggestions would Canter give Mr. Gonzales for dealing with Sara?

Case 3: Joshua Clowns and Intimidates

Joshua, larger and louder than his classmates, always wants to be the center of attention, which he accomplishes through a combination of clowning and intimidation. He makes wise remarks, talks back (smilingly) to the teacher, utters a variety of sound-effect noises such as automobile crashes and gunshots, and makes limitless sarcastic comments and put-downs of his classmates. Other students will not stand up to him, apparently fearing his size and verbal aggression. His teacher, Miss Pearl, has come to her wit's end.

Would Joshua's behavior be likely to improve if Canter's techniques were used in Miss Pearl's classroom? Explain.

Case 4: Tom Is Hostile and Defiant

Tom has appeared to be in his usual foul mood ever since arriving in class. On his way to sharpen his pencil, he bumps into Frank, who complains. Tom tells him loudly to shut up. Miss Baines, the teacher, says, "Tom, go back to your seat." Tom wheels around, swears loudly, and says heatedly, "I'll go when I'm damned good and ready!"

How would Canter have Miss Baines deal with Tom?

QUESTIONS AND ACTIVITIES

1. Each of the following exemplifies an important point in the Canter model of discipline. Identify the point illustrated by each.
   a. Miss Hatcher, on seeing her class list for the coming year, exclaims, "Oh no! Billy Smythe in my class! Nobody can do a thing with him! There goes my sanity!"
   b. "If I catch you talking again during the class, you will have to stay an extra five minutes."
   c. "I wish you would try your best not to curse in this room."
   d. Students who receive a fourth check mark must go to the office and call their parents to explain what has happened.
   e. If the class is especially attentive and hardworking, students earn five minutes they can use for talking quietly at the end of the period.
2. For a grade level and/or subject you select, outline an Assertive Discipline plan that includes
   —four rules,
   —positive recognition and consequences associated with the rules, and
   —the people you will inform about your system, and how you will inform them.
3. Examine Scenario 3 or 4 in Appendix I. How could Assertive Discipline be used to improve behavior in Mrs. Daniels's library or Mrs. Desmond's second grade?

REFERENCES AND RECOMMENDED READINGS

Canter, L. (1976). *Assertive Discipline: A take-charge approach for today's educator*. Seal Beach, CA: Lee Canter & Associates.

———. (1978). Be an assertive teacher. *Instructor, 88(1)*, 60.

———. (1988). Let the educator beware: A response to Curwin and Mendler. *Educational Leadership, 46(2)*, 71-73.

Canter, L., & Canter, M. (1986). *Assertive Discipline Phase 2 in-service media package* [videotapes and manuals]. Santa Monica, CA: Lee Canter & Associates.

———. (1989). *Assertive Discipline for secondary school educators: In-service video package and leader's manual*. Santa Monica, CA: Lee Canter & Associates.

———. (1992). *Assertive Discipline: Positive behavior management for today's classrooms* (2nd ed.). Santa Monica, CA: Lee Canter & Associates.

———. (1993). *Succeeding with difficult students: New strategies for reaching your most challenging students*. Santa Monica, CA: Lee Canter & Associates.

Curwin, R., & Mendler, A. (1988). Packaged discipline programs: Let the buyer beware. *Educational Leadership, 46(2)*, 68-71.

———. (1989). We repeat, let the buyer beware: A response to Canter. *Educational Leadership, 46(6)*, 83.

Hill, D. (1990). Order in the classroom. *Teacher Magazine, 1(7),* 70-77.

Kohn, A. (1993). *Punished by rewards: The trouble with gold stars, incentive plans, A's, praise, and other bribes.* Boston: Houghton Mifflin.

McCormack, S. (1989). Response to Render, Padilla, and Krank: But practitioners say it works! *Educational Leadership, 46(6),* 77-79.

Render, G., Padilla, J., & Krank, H. (1989). What research really shows about Assertive Discipline. *Educational Leadership, 46(6),* 72-75.

CHAPTER 7

The Jones Model

Discipline through Body Language,
Incentive Systems,
and Efficient Help

Fredric H. Jones

BIOGRAPHICAL SKETCH OF JONES

Fredric H. Jones is director of the Classroom Management Training Program, head-quartered in Santa Cruz, California. Jones, a psychologist, has worked for many years to develop training procedures for improving teacher effectiveness in motivating, managing, and instructing school students. His procedures have grown from initial research into classroom practices that he conducted while on the faculties of the UCLA Medical Center and the University of Rochester School of Medicine and Dentistry. An independent consultant since 1978, Jones now devotes full efforts to his training programs, which are widely used for staff development in school districts. Teachers receive his ideas with a good deal of enthusiasm, recognizing in them refinements of practices with which they are already familiar but which they have not seen organized into a systematic approach.

Jones did not publish a book describing his management system until 1987, several years after full development of his "pyramid" training system, which trains teachers to teach fellow teachers. Jones's behavior management book, *Positive Classroom Discipline*, was published in 1987, together with its companion volume, *Positive Classroom Instruction*. Jones also makes available a video course of study called *Positive Classroom Discipline*, the manual for which is authored by Jones's wife, JoLynne Talbott Jones (1993a). These materials and others for Jones's programs are available from Fredric H. Jones & Associates, Inc., 103 Quarry Lane, Santa Cruz, CA 95060; telephone 408-425-8222; fax 408-426-8222.

JONES'S CONTRIBUTIONS TO DISCIPLINE

While other authorities have devoted much attention to the role of verbal communication in promoting classroom discipline, Jones was the first to place major emphasis on the importance of nonverbal communication such as teachers' body language, facial expressions, gestures, eye contact, and physical proximity. He was also the first to emphasize the importance of providing help efficiently when students, during independent activities, stop working because they have encountered problems that require teacher attention. Jones's helpfulness in dealing with such nondramatic yet troublesome classroom matters has attracted a considerable following among teachers.

JONES'S CENTRAL FOCUS

The main focus of Jones's efforts is on helping students support their own self-control (Jones, 1979). Toward that end he emphasizes effective use of body language, describes how to provide incentives that motivate desired behavior, and details procedures for providing efficient help to students during independent work time.

JONES'S PRINCIPAL CONCEPTS AND TEACHINGS

Student misbehavior. This is behavior that disrupts teaching and learning. Approximately 99 percent of such misbehavior in most classrooms consists of talking without permission and generally goofing off, such as daydreaming, making noise, and being out of one's seat.

Massive time wasting. On the average, teachers in typical classrooms lose approximately 50 percent of their teaching time because students are off task or otherwise disrupting learning.

Recouping lost time. Most teaching time that is otherwise lost can be salvaged when teachers make systematic use of effective body language, employ incentive systems, and provide efficient help.

Discipline. This is the process of enforcing standards and building cooperation so that disruptions are minimized and learning is maximized.

Body language. This comprises a group of physical mannerisms that include eye contact, physical proximity, body carriage, facial expressions, and gestures.

Physical proximity. This involves teachers' stationing themselves near students who show an inclination to misbehave.

Body carriage. This term refers to teachers' posture and movement, which can be very effective in communicating authority.

Setting limits. This term refers to the subtle, interpersonal skills that teachers use to convey that they mean business.

Incentives. These are teachers' promises that students will receive, in return for proper behavior, rewards in the form of favorite activities that can be earned by all members of the group for the enjoyment of all members of the group. Group incentives motivate students to remain on task and complete their work.

Genuine incentives. Incentives are genuine when they motivate all students to remain on task and behave properly. Jones emphasizes the difference between genuine incentives and those that teachers hope will be effective. For example, a popcorn party for the class might be a genuine incentive, one for which all members of the class might work. In contrast, a prize for being the first to complete an assignment would probably not be a genuine incentive, since it would motivate only a few of the most capable students.

Grandma's rule. Grandma's rule states: "First eat your vegetables, then you can have your dessert." Jones uses this maxim to remind teachers that students are to receive their rewards for good behavior only after they have behaved properly. They must not be given the reward first based on their promise to behave well.

Group concern. Jones stresses that any incentive must be attractive to the entire group and be available equally to all. Incentives that are available only to certain members of the class will not promote good class behavior.

Dependency syndrome. This refers to students' failure to work on assignments unless the teacher hovers over them and provides constant help. Jones has devised a method of providing help very efficiently to students who call for teacher assistance during independent work. He says efficient help should include (1) mention of anything the student has done correctly, (2) direct suggestion of what needs to be done next, and (3) immediate teacher departure. All this is to be accomplished in 20 seconds or less. Jones says to "be positive, be brief, and be gone."

ANALYSIS OF THE JONES MODEL

Jones's Findings Concerning Misbehavior and Loss of Time

During the 1970s, Jones and his associates conducted thousands of hours of carefully controlled observations in hundreds of elementary and secondary classrooms in various parts of the country. Jones's interest lay in identifying effective methods of classroom management, especially concerning how teachers kept students working on task, how they provided individual help when needed, and how they dealt with *misbehavior.*

Those observations led Jones to several important conclusions. Principal among them was that classroom discipline problems are generally quite different from the way they are depicted in the media and perceived by the public. Even though many of the classrooms studied were located in inner-city schools and alternative schools for students with behavior problems, Jones found no terrorism, no bullying attacks on teachers, and very little hostile defiance—the kinds of behavior that teachers fear and that many people believe predominate in all schools. Instead, Jones found what he called *massive time wasting*, in which students talked when they shouldn't, goofed off, and moved about the room without permission. Jones found that in well-managed classrooms, one of those disruptions occurred about every two minutes. In loud, unruly classes the disruptions averaged about 2.5 per minute. In attempting to deal with those misbehaviors, teachers lost almost 50 percent of the time available for teaching and learning (Jones, 1987a).

Jones also discovered a critical time during lessons in which misbehavior was most likely to occur. He found that most lessons go along fairly well until students are asked to work on their own. That is when, Jones (1987b) says, "the chickens come home to roost" (p. 14). Until that point, students seem to pay attention and give the impression they are learning perfectly. But when directed to continue work on their own, hands go up, talking begins, students rummage around or stare out the window, and some get out of their seats. The teacher doesn't know what to do except nag and admonish. This, Jones says, is "another day in the life of a typical classroom" (1987b, p. 14) where the teacher ends up reteaching the lesson during time that should be devoted to independent work.

Teachers everywhere relate to that scenario as one that repeatedly leaves them feeling frustrated and defeated. When discussing the phenomenon, many express bitterness over never having received training in how to deal effectively with such misbehavior. New teachers say they expected that they would quickly learn to maintain order in their classrooms but were only partially successful and found themselves resorting to punitive measures.

Jones concluded that teachers were correct in their contentions that they had not received training in behavior management and, further, that many, if not most, were unable to develop needed skills while working on the job. Jones decided to observe and document the methods used by the relatively few teachers who were notably successful with discipline. It was out of those observations that the Jones model of discipline took form.

Skill Clusters in the Jones Model

Jones (1993, p. 55) says that the purpose of *discipline* is to engage students in learning in the most positive, unobtrusive fashion possible. His analysis of the numerous classroom observations uncovered three clusters of teacher skills that keep students engaged in learning by forestalling misbehavior or dealing with it efficiently. Those skill clusters have to do with (1) body language, (2) motivation through the use of incentive systems, and (3) providing efficient help to individual students. Let us explore these skill clusters further.

Skill Cluster 1: Body Language. Jones maintains that good discipline depends mostly—90 percent, he says—on effective body language. Therefore, his training program concentrates on helping teachers learn to use physical mannerisms in setting limits on behavior, as specified in the class rules, and enforcing those limits. The *body language* that Jones emphasizes includes (1) eye contact, (2) physical proximity, (3) body carriage, (4) facial expressions, and (5) gestures. At its most effective level, body language communicates that the teacher is calmly in control, knows what is going on, and means business.

Eye Contact. Miss Remy is demonstrating and explaining the process of multiplying fractions. She sees that Jacob has stopped paying attention. She pauses in her explanation. The sudden quiet causes Jacob to look at Miss Remy and find that she is looking directly into his eyes. He straightens up and waits attentively.

Few physical acts are more effective than *eye contact* for conveying the impression of being in control. Skilled teachers allow their eyes to sweep the room continually and engage the eyes of individual students. Locking eyes makes many people uncomfortable, teachers and students alike, and students often avert their eyes when teachers look directly at them. The effect is not lost, however, for the students realize that the teacher, in looking directly at them, takes continual note of their behavior, both good and bad.

Making eye contact does not seem to be a natural behavior for most beginning teachers and must therefore be practiced before it can be used effectively. Inexperienced teachers tend to look over students' heads or between students or dart their eyes rapidly without locking on to individuals. Sometimes while teaching, they stare more or less directly ahead, losing track of students who are at the back and sides of the group, or they find comfort in looking only at the faces of two or three well-behaved, actively responding students, blocking out others who are not so attuned to the lesson.

These tendencies are persistent, and it is common to encounter experienced teachers who do not make good use of eye contact. With practice, however, any teacher can learn to focus the eyes directly on the face of each individual student. This in itself sends a message that the teacher is aware and in control. It further serves to inhibit students who are on the verge of misbehaving and provides an opportunity to send facial expressions of approval or disapproval.

Physical Proximity.   Miss Remy has completed her demonstration of the multiplication of fractions. She has directed students to complete certain exercises on their own. After a time she sees from the back of the room that Jacob has stopped working and has begun talking to Jerry. She moves toward him. Jacob unexpectedly sees Miss Remy's shadow at his side. He immediately gets back to work, without the teacher's having said anything.

In his classroom observations, Jones noted that most misbehavior occurs some distance away from the teacher. Students near the teacher rarely misbehave. This phenomenon has long been recognized by experienced teachers, who have learned to move nearer to students who are prone to misbehave or to seat such students near them.

Jones also noted that teachers who use *physical proximity* do not need to say anything to the offending students to get them to behave. He concluded that verbalization is not needed and that in fact it sometimes weakens the effect, due possibly to defensive reactions engendered in students when they are reprimanded verbally. Teachers who need to deal with minor misbehavior are instructed to move near the offending student, establish brief eye contact, and say nothing. The student will usually return immediately to proper behavior.

To use physical proximity effectively, the teacher must be able to step quickly alongside the appropriate student. This may be difficult in classrooms where students are seated in long rows or in clusters of tables that do not allow the teacher to circulate easily. Jones suggests that teachers seat their students in herringbone patterns or shallow semicircles, no more than three rows deep, with walk space interspersed (Jones, 1987a). The teacher can then operate from within the arc of the semicircle, easily obtain eye contact with students, and move quickly to the side of any student. This arrangement also allows teachers to provide individual help much more quickly, as will be discussed later.

Body Carriage.   Jones also found that posture and *body carriage* are quite effective in communicating authority. Students quickly read body language and are able to tell whether the teacher is well, ill, in charge, tired, disinterested, or intimidated. Good posture and confident carriage suggest strong leadership; a drooping posture and lethargic movements suggest resignation or fearfulness. Effective teachers, even when tired or troubled, tend to hold themselves erect and move assertively. One should note here that on those infrequent occasions when the teacher is feeling ill, it is good to inform the students and ask for their assistance and tolerance. Students usually behave with unexpected consideration at such times, provided the strategy is used sincerely and not too often.

Facial Expressions.   Like body carriage, *facial expressions* communicate much to students. Facial expressions can show enthusiasm, seriousness, enjoyment, and appreciation, all of which tend to encourage good behavior; or they can reveal boredom, annoyance, and resignation, which may encourage misbehavior. Perhaps more than anything else, facial expressions such as winks and smiles demonstrate a sense of humor, the trait that students most enjoy in teachers.

The face can be put to good use in sending other types of nonverbal signals as well. Eye contact has been discussed as a prime example. Very slight shakes of the head can stop much misbehavior before it gets under way. Frowns show unmistakable disapproval. A firm lip line and flashing eyes can indicate powerfully that limits are being strained. These facial expressions are used instead of words whenever possible and are as effective as words in showing approval. For control and disapproval, they have the advantage over verbal rebuffs in that they seldom belittle, antagonize, or provoke counterattacks from students.

Gestures.   Experienced teachers employ a variety of hand signals that they use to encourage and discourage behavior and to maintain student attention. Examples include palm out ("Stop"), palm up flexing fingers ("Continue"), finger to lips ("Quiet"), finger snap ("Attention"), and thumbs up ("Good"). These *gestures* communicate effectively and do not interfere with necessary instructional verbalization.

A Case of Body Language in Use.   The following is an example of body language put to use as suggested by Jones:

1. Sam and Jim are talking and laughing while Mr. Sánchez is explaining the procedure for dividing angles. Mr. Sánchez makes eye contact with them, pauses momentarily, and then continues with his explanation. Sam and Jim probably stop talking when Mr. Sánchez looks at them and pauses. But if they continue . . .
2. Mr. Sánchez again pauses, makes eye contact, and shakes his head slightly but emphatically. He may give a fleeting palm-out signal. Sam and Jim probably stop talking when he sends these signals. But if they continue . . .
3. Mr. Sánchez moves calmly and stands beside Sam and Jim. He asks the class, "Who can go to the board and show us how to divide an angle? Tell us what to do, step-by-step." Sam and Jim will almost certainly stop talking now. But if they continue . . .
4. Mr. Sánchez makes eye contact with them and calmly says, "Jim, Sam, I want you to stop talking right now."

If for any reason the boys defy Mr. Sánchez's direct order, Mr. Sánchez stops the lesson long enough to ask the boys to move to opposite corners of the room or, as a last resort, to call the office to say that the boys are being sent for detention. In any of these cases, a follow-up conference will be necessary with the boys, and if the defiance continues, it will need to be dealt with by the principal, vice-principal, counselor, and/or the boys' parents.

Note that in all cases except the most severe, Mr. Sánchez used only body language. There was no verbal confrontation and only a slight slowdown in the lesson. Instruction continued, students were kept on task, and teaching-learning time was preserved. Jones (1993a) says that effectively *setting limits* involves learning to "do nothing when under pressure." (p. 55). By that he means that teachers are usually most effective in controlling misbehavior when they use their bodies correctly but say nothing and take no other action. He reminds teachers that they cannot discipline with their mouths—that if they could do so, "nagging would have fixed every kid a million years ago" (p. 77). When you open your mouth, he says, you run the risk of slitting your own throat.

Skill Cluster 2: Incentive Systems.   Mr. Sharpe tells his class that if all of them complete their work in 45 minutes or less, they can have the last 10 minutes of class time to talk quietly with a friend. Mr. Dulle tells his class that if they promise to work very hard later on, he will allow them to begin the period by discussing their work with a friend. Which teacher is likely to get the best work from his students?

This question has to do with the use of incentives. An *incentive* is something outside of the individual that prompts the individual to act. It is something that is promised as a consequence for desired behavior but is held in abeyance to occur or be provided later. It might be popcorn, a preferred activity, an unspecified surprise, or the like. It is an effective incentive if students behave as desired in order to obtain it later.

Jones gives a prominent place in his classroom management program to incentives as a means of motivating students. He found that some of the most effective teachers use incentives systematically but that most teachers use them ineffectively or not at all. The ineffective teachers typically made use of giving grades, marks, or stars; having work displayed; being dismissed first; and so forth. Jones points out that the problem with incentives of this type is that they go only to the top achievers; the less able students, once out of contention for the prize, have nothing left for which to work. Moreover, for many students, receiving a badge or being first in line does not compete strongly with the joys of talking or daydreaming.

What, then, are characteristics of effective incentives, and how should they be used? Jones states or implies that teachers should emphasize (1) genuine incentives, (2) Grandma's rule, (3) educational value, (4) group concern, and (5) ease of implementation. Let us examine these suggestions further.

Genuine Incentives.   There is a wide difference between what many teachers hope will be incentives (e.g., "Let's all work in such a way that we will later be proud of what we do") and what students consider genuine incentives (e.g., "If you complete your work on time, you can have five minutes of free time to talk with your friends"). This point may seem obvious, but it is often overlooked. Teachers may say, "The first person to complete a perfect paper will receive two bonus points." This may motivate a few of the most able students, but most know they have little chance to win so they barely try. Or the teacher may say, "If you really try, you can be the best class I have ever had." This usually sounds better to the teacher than to the students. Although the students might like to think of themselves as the best, that thought will not be strong enough to keep them hard at work.

What, then, are some genuine incentives that can be used in the classroom? Generally, students respond well to the anticipation of preferred group activities such as art, viewing a film, or having free time to pursue personal interests or talk with friends. Such group activities are *genuine incentives* in that, first, almost all students desire them sufficiently to make extra effort to obtain them and, second, they are available to all students, not just a few. Many teachers use tangible objects, awards, and certificates as incentives. Jones does not recommend them because they may be costly or difficult to dispense or, worse, because they have little educational value.

Grandma's Rule.   *Grandma's rule* states: "First eat your vegetables, and then you can have your dessert." Applied to the classroom, this rule requires that students first do what they are supposed to do, and then for a while they can do what they want to do. The incentive is the end product of the proposition. In order to obtain it, students must complete designated work while behaving acceptably.

Just as children (and many adults) ask to have their dessert first, promising to eat their vegetables afterward, students ask to have their incentive first, pledging on their honor to work feverishly afterward. As we all know, even the best intentions are hard to fulfill once the reason for doing so is gone. Thus, teachers who wish to use effective incentive systems must, despite student urging, delay the rewards until last and make the reward contingent on the students' doing required work acceptably. In other words, if they don't eat their broccoli, they don't get their pudding.

Educational Value.   To the extent feasible, every class period should be devoted to activities that have educational value. Work that keeps students occupied but teaches them nothing can seldom be justified. This principle applies equally to incentive systems. While few educators would be such Scrooges that they would never allow a moment of innocent frivolity, the opposite extreme of throwing daily or weekly classroom parties as incentives for work and behavior is difficult to condone from an educational standpoint. What then should one do?

There are many activities with *educational value* that students enjoy greatly, both individually and in groups. One of the best for individuals is free time, in which students may read, work on assignments, do art work, plan with other students, or pursue personal interests. Despite the word *free*, students are not left to do just anything, nor do they proceed without rules of guidance. The freedom is that of choosing from a variety of approved activities.

For the total group, activities can be chosen by vote, and all students engage in the same activity during the time allotted. Elementary school students often select physical education, art, music, drama, or construction activities. Frequently, they want the teacher to read to them from a favorite book. Secondary students often choose to watch a film, hold class discussions on special topics, watch performances by class members, or work together on such projects as producing a class magazine. JoLynne Talbott Jones (Jones, 1993a) gives directions for a large number of educationally sound class activities that students of various grade levels enjoy greatly and that therefore serve as excellent preferred activities.

Group Concern. As mentioned earlier, many classroom incentive systems in normal practice contain a fatal flaw, namely, that only a few students—the faster workers or higher achievers—have a genuine opportunity to earn the incentive. Most of the others make only perfunctory effort, having learned that they have little chance of success.

Jones teaches a way around this flaw that involves every class member and yet remains simple to administer. His plan hinges on causing every student to have a stake in earning the incentive for the entire class. This *group concern* motivates all students to keep on task, behave well, and complete assigned work. Here is how it is done.

The teacher agrees to set aside a period of time in which students might be allowed to engage in a preferred activity. In keeping with Grandma's rule, this time period must come after a significant amount of work time has been devoted to the standard curriculum. The time can be at the end of the school day for self-contained classes—perhaps 15 to 20 minutes. For departmentalized classes, the time can be set aside at the end of the week—perhaps 30 minutes on Friday. The students can decide on the activity for their dessert time, and to earn it they have only to work and behave as expected.

The teacher manages the system by using a stopwatch, preferably a large one with hands that the class can see. When any student begins to misbehave, the teacher simply lifts the stopwatch and clicks it on. Every second that ticks off the watch is deducted from the time originally available for the incentive. The teacher must be dispassionately firm in applying this technique. A burst of perfect behavior cannot be allowed to erase previous misbehavior, since that tells students it is all right to misbehave for a while before settling down. The teacher also must not be talked into canceling time lost on the promise of better behavior in the future. The students know the rules of the game from the beginning, and they know that they can choose through their behavior how much incentive time they will earn.

Teachers often think it unfair to penalize the entire class, through loss of time, for the sins of a few or even a single class member. In practice this is rarely a problem, because the class quickly understands that this is a group, not an individual, effort. The group is rewarded together and punished together regardless of who might transgress. A strength of this approach is that it brings peer pressure to bear against misbehavior. Ordinarily a misbehaving student obtains reinforcement from the group in the form of attention, laughter, or admiration. With the stopwatch system the opposite is true. The class is likely to discourage individual misbehavior, because it takes away something the class members want.

Ease of Implementation.   Unlike other incentive systems, that advocated by Jones is notable for two important features that work hand in hand: (1) its effectiveness for all students in that all are brought into the picture, and (2) its ease of implementation. To implement Jones's incentive system, teachers need do only four things.

1. Establish and explain the system.
2. Allow the class to vote from time to time on the teacher-approved activities they wish to enjoy during incentive time.
3. Obtain a stopwatch and use it conscientiously.
4. Be prepared when necessary to conduct the class in low-preference activities for the amount of time that students might have lost from the time allotted to their preferred activity.

When Incentives Do Not Work.   If an incentive system loses effectiveness, it is likely for one of the following reasons:

1. The preferred activities might have grown stale. This is cured by allowing the class to discuss the matter and decide on new preferences.
2. The class may temporarily be overexcited by unsettling occurrences such as unusual weather, a holiday, special events at school, or an accident. In such cases the teacher may suspend the incentive program for a time, giving explanation and allowing discussion.
3. Individual students may occasionally lose self-control or decide to defy the teacher. In this case the offending student should be isolated in the room or removed to the office. The teacher can establish a policy wherein the class will not be penalized for this type of action by individual students.

Skill Cluster 3: Providing Efficient Help.   One of the most interesting, important, and useful findings in Jones's research has to do with the way teachers provide individual help to students who are stuck during seatwork. Suppose that a grammar lesson is in progress. The teacher introduces the topic, explains the concept on the board, asks a couple of questions to determine whether the students are understanding, and then assigns 10 exercises for students to complete at their desks. Very soon a hand is raised to signal that a student is stuck and needs help. If only three or four hands are raised during work time, the teacher has no problem. But if 20 students fill the air with waving arms, most of them sit for several minutes doing nothing while awaiting attention from the teacher. For each student needing help, this waiting time is pure waste and an invitation to misbehave.

Jones asked teachers how much time they thought they spent on the average when providing help to individuals who signaled. The teachers felt that they spent from one to two minutes with each student, but when Jones's researchers timed the episodes, they found that teachers actually spent around four minutes with each student. This consumed much time and made it impossible for the teacher to attend to more than a few students during the work period. Even if the amount of time were only one minute per contact, several minutes would pass while some students sat and did nothing.

Jones noted an additional phenomenon that compounded the problem. He described it as a *dependency syndrome* wherein some students routinely raised their hands for teacher help even when they did not need it. To have the teacher unfailingly come to their side and give personal attention proved rewarding indeed, and that reinforcement further strengthened the dependency.

Based on those observations, Jones concluded that independent seatwork is prone to four inherent problems: (1) insufficient time for teachers to answer all requests for help; (2) wasted student time; (3) the high potential for misbehavior; and (4) the perpetuation of dependency. Consequently, he gives this matter high priority in his training program.

Jones determined that all four problems can be solved through teaching teachers how to give *efficient help*, which is accomplished as follows:

Step 1.   Organize the classroom seating so that students are within easy reach of the teacher. The shallow concentric semicircles previously described are suggested. Without quick, easy passage, the teacher uses too much time and energy dashing from one part of the room to another.

Step 2.   Use graphic reminders, such as models or charts, that provide clear examples and instructions. These reminders might show steps in algorithms, proper form for business letters, or written directions for the lesson. The reminders are posted and can be consulted by students before they call for teacher help.

Step 3.   This step is a hallmark of the Jones model. It involves learning how to cut to a bare minimum the time used for individual help. To see how the process is accomplished, consider that teachers normally give help very inefficiently through a questioning tutorial that proceeds something like this:

> "What's the problem?"
> "All right, what did we say was the first thing to do?" *[Waits; repeats question.]*
> "No, that was the second. You are forgetting the first step. What was it? Think again." *[Waits until student finally makes a guess.]*
> "No, let me help you with another example. Suppose . . ."

Often, in this helping mode, the teacher reteaches the concept or process to each student who requests help. Thus, four minutes can be unexpectedly spent in each interaction. If help is to be provided more quickly, this questioning method must be reconsidered. Jones trains teachers to give help in a very different way, and he insists that it be done in 20 seconds or less for each student, with an optimal goal of about 10 seconds. To reach this level of efficiency, the teacher should do the following when arriving beside the student:

1. Quickly find anything that the student has done correctly and mention it favorably:"Your work is very neat" or "Good job up to here."
2. Give a straightforward hint or suggestion that will get the student going: "Follow step two on the chart" or "Regroup here."
3. Leave immediately. As Jones says, "Be positive, be brief, and be gone."

Help provided in this way solves the major problems that teachers encounter during instructional work time. Every student who needs help can be attended to. Students waste little time waiting for the teacher. Misbehavior is much less likely to occur. The dependency syndrome is broken, especially if the teacher gives attention to students who work without calling for assistance. Rapid circulation by the teacher also permits better monitoring of work being done by students who do not raise their hands. When errors are noted in those students' work, the teacher should help them in the efficient manner Jones suggests for dependent students.

Jones's Reminders for Teachers

The foregoing three skill clusters—body language, incentives, and efficient help—comprise the core of the Jones model of discipline. In a nutshell, the following are reminders for teachers as presented in a report by Rardin (1978):

> Catch misbehavior early and deal with it immediately.
>
> Use body language instead of words. Show you mean business through your posture, eye contact, facial expressions, and gestures.
>
> Use physical proximity in dealing with misbehaving or defiant students.
>
> Use group incentives (following Grandma's rule) to motivate work and good behavior.
>
> Provide individual help efficiently; aim for 10-second interactions.
>
> Do not use threats; establish rules and attend to misbehavior.

INITIATING THE JONES MODEL

Jones (1987a, p. 321) suggests that his model of discipline be initiated as a three-tiered system of closely related management methodologies: (1) limit setting, (2) incentive, and (3) backup systems. All three tiers are planned in advance and introduced simultaneously.

The process begins with a discussion of limit setting, which leads to the formulation of agreements (rules) about what students may and may not do in the classroom. Students are told that when rules are violated, behavior will be corrected with mild social punishment that does nothing more than make the misbehaving student feel uncomfortable, such as eye contact, stares from the teacher, or physical proximity.

To make limit setting work effectively, mild punishment is counterbalanced with incentives and social rewards, such as acknowledgment and approval, in return for students' observing rules and agreements. Desirable incentives are discussed, and procedures for managing incentives are described. Students are reminded that the incentives they select are to have instructional value.

Teachers will also need to discuss with students the *backup systems* they will employ when students misbehave seriously and refuse to comply with positive teacher requests. Such backup sanctions receive relatively little attention in Jones's system, which attempts to move teachers away from reliance on admonition and threat, yet Jones acknowledges that at times the teacher may be unable to get misbehaving students to comply with the rules. At those times, teachers may tell the student, 'If you are not going to do your work, sit there quietly and don't bother others.' And for yet more serious situations of defiance or aggression, teachers must have a plan by which they isolate the student or call for help if needed.

COMMENTS ON THE JONES MODEL

The Jones model provides strong help in preventive and supportive discipline and does so in a balanced way, though teachers may feel that it provides relatively little guidance for dealing with the occasional student who misbehaves seriously. Jones has been successful in identifying and compiling discipline behaviors shown by teachers who are often called "naturals." That is why teachers' heads nod in agreement with his suggestions. Jones has found that the discipline techniques he advocates are all teachable, though many teachers do not learn them well within the pressures of day-to-day teaching. Through specific training episodes, most teachers can acquire the techniques that are usually seen only in their most effective colleagues.

But it is unrealistic to expect that teachers can read Jones's work and then walk into the classroom the next day transformed. The acts he describes must be understood and then practiced repeatedly, which is accomplished best through Jones's training seminars. Fortunately, motivated teachers can assess their classroom behavior in light of Jones's suggestions and isolate certain control tactics on which they would like to improve. They can practice what Jones suggests and then take their new learnings into the classroom to be tested. That is one of the most appealing qualities of Jones's suggestions: they do not have to be put into place as a full-blown total system but can instead be practiced, perfected, and added incrementally.

APPLICATION EXERCISES

REVIEW OF SELECTED TERMINOLOGY

The following terms are central to the Jones model of discipline. Check yourself to make sure you can explain their meanings.

misbehavior	setting limits
massive time wasting	incentives
discipline	genuine incentives
body language	Grandma's rule
eye contact	group concern
physical proximity	dependency syndrome
body carriage	efficient help
facial expressions	backup systems
gestures	

CONCEPT CASES

Case 1: Kristina Will Not Work

Kristina, a student in Mr. Jake's class, is quite docile. She socializes little with other students and never disrupts the class. However, Mr. Jake cannot get Kristina to do any work. She rarely completes an assignment. She is simply there, putting forth almost no effort at all.

How would Jones deal with Kristina? Jones would suggest that Mr. Jake take the following steps to improve Kristina's behavior:

1. Make frequent eye contact with her. Even when she looks down, Mr. Jake should make sure to look directly at her. She will be aware of it, and it may make her uncomfortable enough that she will begin work.
2. Move close to Kristina. Stand beside her while presenting the lesson.
3. Use encouraging facial expressions and gestures every time eye contact can be made.
4. Give Kristina frequent help during seatwork. Check on her progress several times during the lesson. Give specific suggestions and then move quickly on.
5. Set up a personal incentive system with Kristina; for example, a certain amount of work earns an activity she especially enjoys.
6. Set up a system in which Kristina's working can earn rewards for the entire class. This brings her peer attention and support.

Case 2: Sara Cannot Stop Talking

Sara is a pleasant girl who participates in class activities and does most, though not all, of her assigned work. She cannot seem to refrain from talking to classmates, however. Her teacher, Mr. Gonzales, has to speak to her repeatedly during lessons, to the point that he often becomes exasperated and loses his temper.

What suggestions would Jones give Mr. Gonzales for dealing with Sara?

Case 3: Joshua Clowns and Intimidates

Joshua, larger and louder than his classmates, always wants to be the center of attention, which he accomplishes through a combination of clowning and intimidation. He makes wise remarks, talks back (smilingly) to the teacher, utters a variety of sound-effect noises such as automobile crashes and gunshots, and makes limitless sarcastic comments and put-downs of his classmates. Other students will not stand up to him, apparently fearing his size and verbal aggression. His teacher, Miss Pearl, has come to her wit's end.

What specifically do you find in Jones's suggestions that would help Miss Pearl with Joshua?

Case 4. Tom Is Hostile and Defiant

Tom has appeared to be in his usual foul mood ever since arriving in class. On his way to sharpen his pencil, he bumps into Frank, who complains. Tom tells him loudly to shut up. Miss Baines, the teacher, says, "Tom, go back to your seat." Tom wheels around, swears loudly, and says heatedly, "I'll go when I'm damned good and ready!"

How effective do you believe Jones's suggestions would be in dealing with Tom?

QUESTIONS AND ACTIVITIES

1. For each of the following scenarios, first identify the problem that underlies the undesired behavior, then describe how Jones would have the teacher deal with it.
   a. Mr. Anton tries to help all of his students during independent work time but finds himself unable to get around to all who have their hands raised.
   b. Ms. Sevier wants to show trust for her class. She accepts their promise to work hard if they can first listen to a few favorite recorded songs. After listening to the songs, the students talk so much that they fail to get their work done.
   c. Mr. Gregory wears himself out every day dealing ceaselessly with three class clowns who disrupt his lessons. The other students always laugh at the clowns' antics.

2. Examine Scenario 10 or 2 in Appendix I. What changes would Jones suggest that Miss Thorpe or Mr. Platt make in order to provide a more efficient and satisfactory learning environment?

REFERENCES AND RECOMMENDED READINGS

Jones, F. (1979). The gentle art of classroom discipline. *National Elementary Principal, 58,* 26–32.

———. (1987a). *Positive classroom discipline.* New York: McGraw-Hill.

———. (1987b). *Positive classroom instruction.* New York: McGraw-Hill.

———. (1993a). *Instructor's guide: Positive classroom discipline—a video course of study.* Santa Cruz, CA: Fredric H. Jones & Associates.

———. (1993b). *Instructor's guide: Positive classroom instruction—a video course of study.* Santa Cruz, CA: Fredric H. Jones & Associates.

Rardin, R. (1978, September). Classroom management made easy. *Virginia Journal of Education,* 14–17.

CHAPTER 8

The Glasser Model

Discipline through Meeting Needs without Coercion

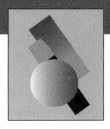

William Glasser

BIOGRAPHICAL SKETCH OF GLASSER

William Glasser, a psychiatrist and educational consultant, has for many years written and spoken extensively on issues related to quality education. Born in Cleveland, Ohio, in 1925, he trained to be a chemical engineer but later turned to psychology and then to psychiatry. He first achieved national acclaim in psychiatry for the theories expressed in his book *Reality Therapy: A New Approach to Psychiatry* (1965), which shifted the focus in treating behavior problems from past events to present reality. Glasser later extended reality therapy to the school arena. His work with juvenile offenders convinced him that teachers could help students make better choices about their school behavior. How that could be done was set forth in his book *Schools without Failure* (1969), acknowledged to be one of the century's most influential books in education.

In 1986, Glasser published *Control Theory in the Classroom*, which gave a new and different emphasis to his contentions concerning discipline, as encapsulated in his pronouncement that if students are to continue working and behaving properly, they must "believe that if they do some work, they will be able to satisfy their needs enough so that it makes sense to keep working" (p. 15). Since the publication of that book, Glasser has emphasized the school's role in meeting basic student needs as the primary means of encouraging work output and desirable behavior. This theme is furthered in his 1992 book *The Quality School: Managing Students without Coercion*.

Because of the different emphases in Glasser's earlier and later works, together with the historical importance of his earlier work, his model of discipline is presented here in two parts: pre-1985 and post-1985. Because the pre-1985 model does not represent Glasser's current thinking, it is presented in highly condensed form. Glasser can be contacted through the Institute for Reality Therapy, 7301 Medical Center Drive, Suite 104, Canoga Park, CA 91307; telephone 818-888-0688; fax 818-888-3023.

GLASSER'S EARLIER WORK

The Central Focus

Prior to 1985, Glasser's primary focus was on helping students make good behavioral choices that would lead to personal success in the classroom and elsewhere.

Principal Concepts and Teachings

Student choice and self-control. Students are rational beings who can control their behavior. They choose to act the way they do.

Good and bad choices. Good choices produce good behavior. Bad choices produce bad behavior.

Teachers and student choices. Teachers must always try to help students make good choices continually throughout each day.

Accepting no excuses. Teachers who truly care about their students accept no excuses for bad behavior.

Consequences of behavior. Teachers must see to it that reasonable consequences should always follow student behavior, good or bad.

Class behavior rules. It is essential that every class have a workable list of rules to govern behavior and that those rules be consistently enforced.

Classroom meetings. Classroom meetings are effective vehicles for addressing matters of class rules, behavior, and consequences. Such meetings of the entire class should be conducted regularly, with teacher and students sitting together in a closed circle, an arrangement that has come to be known as the *Glasser circle*. The purpose of classroom meetings is never to find fault or assign blame but only to seek solutions to problems that concern the class.

ANALYSIS OF THE GLASSER MODEL PRIOR TO 1985

What School Offers

In his earlier views on discipline, Glasser contended that school offers students an excellent opportunity to encounter success and be recognized. Indeed, for many students school affords the only real possibility for meeting those needs. Success in school produces a sense of self-worth and an identity of being successful, both of which mitigate deviant behavior. The road to this identity begins with good relationships with people who care. For students who come from atrocious backgrounds, school may be the only place where they will find adults who are genuinely interested in their well-being.

Yet students often resist entering into quality relationships with their teachers. They may fear teachers, distrust adults in general, or obtain peer rewards by disdaining teachers. Teachers must therefore be very persistent, never waning in their efforts to help students. Glasser maintained that students cannot begin to make better, more responsible choices until they become involved emotionally with people who regularly make such choices in their own lives—people such as teachers.

What Teachers Should Do

Glasser staunchly maintained that teachers hold the key to good discipline. In 1978 he described their responsibilities as follows:

1. Stress student responsibility in making good choices, showing that students must live with the choices they make.
2. Establish class rules that lead to success. Glasser considered class rules essential and wrote disparagingly of teachers who tried to function without them in the mistaken belief that rules stifle initiative, self-direction, and responsibility. Rules should be formulated jointly by teacher and stu-

dents and should always emphasize that students are in school to study and learn.

3. Accept no excuses. A teacher who accepts an excuse says, in effect, that it is all right to break a commitment, that it is all right for students to harm themselves. Teachers who care about their students accept no excuses.

4. Call for value judgments. When students misbehave, they should be required to make value judgments about their actions.

5. Suggest suitable alternatives. If a student is unable to think of alternatives to the inappropriate behavior, the teacher should suggest two or three possibilities and encourage the student to select one of them.

6. Invoke reasonable consequences following student behavior. Glasser stressed that reasonable consequences should follow any behavior the student chooses. Consequences should be desirable when good behavior is chosen and undesirable when poor behavior is chosen. The knowledge that behavior always brings consequences, desirable or undesirable, helps students take charge of their lives and control their own behavior.

7. Be persistent. Caring teachers work toward one major goal: getting students to commit themselves to desirable courses of behavior. They must always help students make choices and have them make value judgments about their bad choices.

8. Continually review the discipline system. Glasser said that any discipline system should be reviewed periodically and revised as necessary.

You can see that in Glasser's earlier work, he depicted the school in a very positive light. While acknowledging problems that students encounter, he maintained that schools afford students the best—often the only—opportunity to associate with quality adults who genuinely care about them. He believed that it is in school that students enjoy the best opportunity many will ever have for finding belonging, success, and positive self-identity. In order to take advantage of this crucial opportunity, students are continually asked to make value judgments about their misbehavior and urged to make good choices and plans that improve the chances for good choices. Meanwhile, they are consistently made to confront the consequences of whatever behavior they choose, good or bad.

GLASSER: POST-1985

Glasser's earlier work had great impact on practices in school discipline, and you probably have recognized several of his earlier teachings incorporated into the Canter and Jones models of discipline (Chapters 6 and 7, respectively). Since 1985, however, Glasser's views on discipline have changed markedly. Previously he depicted the school as a benevolent place that provides unbounded opportunities for students, and he placed responsibility on students for taking advantage of those opportunities. Now, given the fact that student effort has declined and behavior has steadily grown worse,

Glasser has concluded that improvement in education and student behavior can only be accomplished by changing the way classrooms function. Consequently, his present work focuses on approaches to teaching that motivate students to participate willingly in the school program. He says this approach is essential because attempts to force students to learn and behave properly are ultimately bound to fail.

GLASSER'S CENTRAL FOCUS

Glasser says that if schools are to survive, they must be redesigned to emphasize quality in all student work. They must no longer attempt to coerce students, which is increasingly ineffective, but must lead them deeply into learning that addresses what is important in students' lives. The focus of Glasser's work since 1985 has been on describing teaching practices that are most likely to motivate students to engage in worthwhile learning activities. Overall, his emphasis lies in making sure that school activities help satisfy students' basic needs for survival, belonging, power, fun, and freedom. Glasser has moved away from tactics he advocated in his earlier work for confronting student misbehavior, feeling that if students cannot be enticed willingly into learning, it is fruitless to try to make them behave in an orderly manner; they will simply drop out of learning, figuratively if not literally.

GLASSER'S PRINCIPAL CONCEPTS AND TEACHINGS

Motivation and behavior. All of our behavior is our best attempt to control ourselves to meet five basic needs.

The basic needs. The basic needs that students, like everyone else, continually try to satisfy are: survival, belonging, power, fun, and freedom. The school experience is intimately associated with all but survival—and not infrequently survival as well.

Needs and feelings. Students feel pleasure when their basic needs are met and frustration when they are not.

Feelings and motivation. At least half of today's students will not commit themselves to learning if they find their school experience boring, frustrating, or otherwise largely dissatisfying.

Present apathy. Few students in today's schools do their best work. The overwhelming majority is apathetic. Many do no schoolwork at all.

What schools must do. Today's schools must create quality conditions in which fewer students and teachers are frustrated. Students must feel they belong, enjoy a certain amount of power, have some fun in learning, and experience a sense of freedom in the process.

Commitment to quality. What schools require is a new commitment to quality education, which can be accomplished through quality schools where students are encouraged, supported, and helped by the teacher.

Quality curriculum. The school curriculum should be limited to learnings that have usefulness in students' lives and should be delivered by means of activities that attract student interest, involve students actively, provide enjoyment, and lead to meaningful accomplishments.

Quality learning. In the process of quality learning, students acquire in-depth information about topics they recognize as being useful in their lives. They show they have acquired such learning through demonstrating or explaining how, why, and where the learnings are of use.

Quality teaching. In quality teaching, teachers do not scold, punish, or coerce. Instead they befriend students, provide encouragement and stimulation, and show an unending willingness to help.

Boss teachers. These are teachers who dictate procedures, order students to work, and berate them when they do not.

Lead teachers. These are teachers who provide a stimulating learning environment, encourage students, and help them as much as possible.

ANALYSIS OF THE GLASSER MODEL

Glasser remains concerned about student behavior in the classroom, but his focus has moved away from tactics for maintaining discipline in the normal setting and toward quality education, in which students engage themselves willingly and therefore have little reason to misbehave.

Students' Needs

For one who long and staunchly maintained that it was the student's responsibility to make choices that brought success, Glasser's present tack is interesting indeed. What could have prompted such a significant refocusing on the nexus of classroom discipline?

Glasser's present views have grown from his realization that the majority of students are quite satisfied to do low-quality work or even no work at all in school. Glasser (1986) has concluded that "no more than half of our secondary school students are willing to make an effort to learn, and therefore cannot be taught" (p. 3) and, further, "I believe [in light of student apathy] that we have gone as far as we can go with the traditional structure of our secondary schools" (p. 6).

What we must find, he says, is a way to improve instruction. At present, no more than 15 percent of high school students do quality work (Glasser, 1990, p. 5). This situation must be changed "so that a substantial majority do high-quality schoolwork: Nothing less will solve the problems of our schools" (p. 1).

The solution that Glasser proposes involves stimulating students to work while providing encouragement and assistance in such a way as to meet students' needs. This requires only modest changes in curricula, materials, and physical facilities but a significant change in the way teachers work with students.

Glasser (1990) contends that teaching effectively is the hardest job in the world (p. 14) and expresses sympathy for beleaguered secondary teachers who yearn to work with dedicated, high-achieving students but who are continually frustrated by the majority who make little effort to learn. Those teachers report that their main discipline problems are not defiance or disruption but students' overwhelming apathy and resigned unwillingness to participate in classroom activities and assignments. Students, for their part, tell Glasser that the problem with schoolwork is not its difficulty; the problem is that it is too boring (p. 7). For Glasser, this means that schoolwork does not meet students' primary psychological needs.

He has a remedy for this problem, which he puts forth in three fundamental propositions:

1. The school curriculum must be organized to meet students' needs for survival, belonging, power, fun, and freedom.
2. Quality schoolwork and self-evaluation (of quality) by students must replace the fragmented and boring requirements on which students are typically tested and evaluated.
3. Teachers must abandon traditional teaching practices and move toward quality teaching.

Let us examine what Glasser means by these three points.

Students' Needs.   All human beings have genetic needs for (1) survival (food, shelter, freedom from harm); (2) belonging (security, comfort, legitimate membership in the group); (3) power (sense of importance, of stature, of being considered by others); (4) fun (having a good time, emotionally and intellectually); and (5) freedom (exercise of choice, self-direction, and responsibility).

Glasser is adamant in his contention that education which does not give priority to belonging, power, fun, and freedom is bound to fail. Teachers do not have to be psychologists in order to attend to *students' basic needs*. Glasser points out that students sense *belonging* when they are involved in class matters, receive attention from the teacher and others, and are brought into discussions of matters that concern the class. Students sense *power* when the teacher asks them to participate in decisions about topics to be studied and procedures for working in the class. A sense of power comes, too, from being assigned responsibility for class duties, such as helping take attendance, caring for class animals, helping distribute and take care of materials, being in charge of audiovisual equipment, and so forth. Students experience *fun* when they are able to work and talk with others, engage in interesting activities, and share their accomplishments with others. And they sense *freedom* when the teacher allows them to make responsible choices concerning what they will study, how they will do so, and how they will demonstrate their accomplishments. Glasser frequently mentions the value of cooperative learning groups in helping students meet their basic needs.

Curriculum and Quality Work. Glasser (1990, p. 22) says that present-day education is defined in terms of how many fragments of information students can retain long enough to be measured on standardized achievement tests. Students agree, and they resist education of that sort. Glasser finds much fault with the curriculum, the way it is presented, and how student learning is evaluated. School, he says, should be a place where students learn useful information well. To make that possible, a *quality curriculum* is necessary. The old curriculum should be revised so that it consists only of learnings that students find enjoyable and useful; the rest should be discarded as "nonsense" (Glasser, 1992). When teachers introduce new segments of learning, they should hold discussions with students and, if the students are old enough, ask them to identify what they would like to explore in depth. Adequate time should then be spent so that those topics can be learned well. Learning a smaller number of topics very well is always preferable to learning many topics superficially, says Glasser, who calls this type of learning *quality learning*. Evaluation of learning should call upon students to explain why the material they have learned is valuable and how and where it can be used. Students should regularly assess the quality of their own efforts as well.

Quality Teaching. Even teachers who are committed intellectually to quality teaching may find it difficult to identify and make needed changes. It is not easy to change one's teaching style, but Glasser (1993, p. 22 ff) says it can be done by striving for the following, which lead toward *quality teaching* and quality learning as well.

1. Provide a warm, supportive classroom climate. This is done by helping students know and like you. Use natural occasions over time to tell students who you are, what you stand for, what you will ask them to do, what you will not ask them to do, what you will do for them, and what you will not do for them. Show that you are always willing to help them.

2. Ask students to do only work that is useful. *Useful work* consists of skills, as distinct from information, that students see as valuable in their lives. Not infrequently, teachers have to point out the value of new skills, but students must ultimately recognize that value before they will make a sustained effort to learn. Students should be required to memorize no information except that intimately involved in the skill being learned. However, information should be taught and learned provided it meets one or more of the following criteria (p. 48):
   - The information is directly related to an important skill.
   - The information is something that students express a desire to learn.
   - The information is something the teacher believes especially useful.
   - The information is required for college entrance exams.

3. Always ask students to do the best they can. Quality work by students must be nurtured slowly. Glasser (1993, p. 77) suggests that a focus on quality can be initiated as follows:
   - Discuss quality work enough so that students understand what you mean.

- Begin with an assignment that is clearly important enough to do well.
- Ask students to do their best work on the assignment; do not grade it, because grades suggest to students that the work is finished.

Then,

4. Ask students to evaluate their own work and improve it. Quality comes from improvements that result from efforts to improve. Glasser suggests that when students have done a piece of work on a topic they consider important, the teacher should do the following:
   - Ask students to try to improve their work further.
   - Ask students to explain why they feel their work has high quality. As students see the value of improving their work, higher quality will result naturally.
   - Progressively help students begin to use SIR, a process of *s*elf-evaluation, *i*mprovement, and *r*epetition, until quality is achieved.
5. Help students see that quality work makes them feel good. This effect will occur naturally as students learn to do quality work. As Glasser (1993) says,

> There is no better human feeling than that which comes from the satisfaction of doing something useful that you believe is the very best you can do and finding that others agree. (p. 25)

As students begin to sense this feeling, they will want more of it.

6. Help students see that quality work is never destructive to oneself, others, or the environment. Teachers should help students realize that it is not possible to achieve the good feeling of quality work by harming people, property, the environment, or other creatures.

Boss Teachers and Lead Teachers

The preceding framework for quality directs one away from boss teaching and toward lead teaching. Teachers typically function as bosses, Glasser contends, because they do not realize that motivation cannot be furnished to students but must come from within. *Boss teachers*, as Glasser describes them, do the following:

1. Set the task and standards.
2. Talk rather than demonstrate and rarely ask for student input.
3. Grade the work without involving students in evaluation.
4. Use coercion when students resist.

To illustrate how a boss teacher functions, consider the example of Mr. Márquez, who introduces his unit of study on South American geography in the following way:

"Class, today we are going to begin our study of the geography of South America. You are expected to do the following things:

1. Learn the names of the South American countries.
2. Locate those countries on a blank map.
3. Describe the types of terrain typical of each country.
4. Name two products associated with each country.
5. Describe the population of each country in terms of ethnic origin and economic well-being.
6. Name and locate the most important rivers that drain to the north, east, and southeast.

"We will learn this information from our textbooks and encyclopedias. You will have two tests, one at . . ."

Mr. Márquez's boss approach limits both productivity and quality of work. Most students will probably find the work boring and will do only enough, and only well enough, to get by.

Glasser would have teachers forgo Mr. Márquez's style and function not as boss teachers but as lead teachers. *Lead teachers* realize that genuine motivation to learn must arise within students. They also realize that their task in teaching is to use any way they can to help students learn. Glasser says teachers should spend most of their time on two things: organizing interesting activities and providing assistance to students. Such lead teachers would do the following:

1. Discuss the curriculum with the class in such a way that many topics of interest are identified.
2. Encourage students to identify topics they would like to explore in depth.
3. Discuss with students the nature of the schoolwork that might ensue, emphasizing quality and asking for input on criteria of quality.
4. Explore with students resources that might be needed for quality work and the amount of time such work might require.
5. Demonstrate ways in which the work can be done, using models that reflect quality.
6. Emphasize the importance of students' continually inspecting and evaluating their own work in terms of quality.
7. Make evident to students that everything possible will be done to provide them with good tools and a good workplace that is noncoercive and nonadversarial.

To illustrate how lead teaching might proceed, consider the example of Mr. García's introduction to a unit of study on the geography of South America:

"Class, have any of you ever lived in South America? You did, Samuel? Which country? Peru? Fantastic! What an interesting country! I used to live in Brazil. I traveled in the Amazon quite a bit and lived for a while with Indians. Supposedly they were headhunters at one time. But not now. Tomorrow I'll show you a bow and arrow I brought from that tribe. Samuel, did you ever eat monkey when you were in Peru? I think Peru and Brazil are very alike in some ways but very different in others. What was Peru like compared to here? Did you get up into the Andes? They have fabulous ruins all over Peru, I hear, and those fantastic *Chariots of the Gods* lines and drawings on the landscape. Do you have any photographs or slides you could bring for us to see? What a resource you could be for us! You could teach us a lot!

"Class, Samuel lived in Peru and traveled in the Andes. If we could get him to teach us about that country, what do you think you would most like to learn?"

The class discusses this option and identifies topics.

"We have the opportunity in our class to learn a great deal about South America, its mountains and grasslands, its dense rain forests and huge rivers, and its interesting people and strange animals. Did you know there were colonies of English, Welsh, Italians, and Germans living in many parts of South America, especially in Argentina? Did you know there are still thought to be tribes of Indians in the jungles that have no contact with the outside world? Did you know that almost half of all the river water in the world is in the Amazon basin, and that in some places the Amazon River is so wide that from the middle you can't see either shore?

"Speaking of the Amazon, I swam in a lake there that contained piranhas, and look, I still have my legs and arms. Surprised about that? If you wanted to learn more about living in the Amazon jungle, what would you be interested in knowing?"

Discussion ensues.

"How about people of the high Andes? Those Incas, for example, who in some mysterious way cut and placed enormous boulders into gigantic, perfectly fitting fortress walls? Samuel knows about them. The Incas were very civilized and powerful, with an empire that stretched for three thousand miles. Yet they were conquered by a few Spaniards on horseback. How in the world could that have happened? If you could learn more about those amazing people, what would you like to know?"

Discussion continues in this manner. Students identify topics about which they would be willing to make an effort to learn.

"Now let me see what you think of this idea: I have written down the topics you said you were interested in, and I can help you with resources and materials. I have lots of my own, including slides, South American music, and many artifacts I have collected. I know two other people who lived in Argentina and Colombia that we could invite to talk with us. We can concentrate on what you have said you would like to learn about. But if we decide to do so, I want to see if we can make this deal: We explore what interests you; I help you all I can; and you, for your part, agree to do the best work you are capable of. We would need to discuss that to get some ideas of what you might do that would show the quality of your learning. In addition, I hope I can persuade each of you regularly to evaluate yourselves as to how well you believe you are doing. Understand, this would not be me evaluating you, it would be you evaluating yourself—not for a grade but for you to decide what you are doing very well and what you think you might be able to do better.

"What do you think of that idea? Want to give it a try?"

The Relation of Quality Teaching to Discipline

Glasser believes that teachers who learn to function as leaders of quality classrooms avoid the trap of becoming adversaries of their students, a trap that destroys incentive to learn and pleasure in teaching. When teachers stay out of that trap, they not only foster quality learning but at the same time reduce discipline problems to a minimum.

Glasser does admit that no approach to teaching can eliminate all behavior problems. He acknowledges that it is necessary to work with students to establish standards of conduct in the classroom. He makes the following suggestions.

Rules. The teacher should begin with a discussion of the importance of quality work, which is to be given priority in the class, and of how the teacher will do everything possible to help students without forcing them. That discussion should lead naturally into asking students about class *rules* they believe will help them get their work done and truly help them learn. Glasser says that if teachers can get students to see the importance of courtesy, no other rules may be necessary. Mrs. Bentley's second graders decided they needed only two rules in order to do their work well.

1. Be kind to others.
2. Do our best work.

Mr. Jason's physical education class decided on these rules:

1. Be on time.
2. Play safely.
3. Show good sportsmanship.
4. Take care of the equipment.

Teachers should also solicit student advice on what should happen when rules are broken. Glasser says students will suggest punishment, though they know punishment is not effective. If asked further, they will agree that behavior problems are best solved by looking for ways to remedy whatever is causing the rule to be broken. Glasser urges teachers to ask, "What could I do to help?" and to hold *classroom meetings* to explore alternatives to inappropriate behavior. Once the rules and consequences are agreed to, they should be written down. All students sign, attesting that they understand the rules and that, if they break those rules, they will try—with the teacher's help—to correct the underlying problem.

Rules established and dealt with in this way, says Glasser, show that the teacher's main concern lies in quality, not power, and that the teacher recognizes that power struggles are the main enemy of quality education.

When Rules Are Broken.   Every teacher knows that rules will invariably be broken, even in the best classes. Glasser (1990, p. 138) acknowledges that fact and provides specific guidance for teacher intervention—nonpunitive intervention that will stop the misbehavior and refocus the student's mind on class work. Suppose that Jonathan has come into the room obviously upset. As the lesson begins, he turns heatedly and throws something at Michael. Glasser would suggest that the teacher do the following:

TEACHER: It looks like you have a problem, Jonathan. How can I help you solve it? [*Jonathan frowns, still obviously upset.*]

TEACHER: If you will calm down, I will discuss it with you in a little while. I think we can work something out.

Glasser says you should make it clear that you will not help Jonathan until he calms down. You are to speak without emotion, recognizing that your anger will only put Jonathan on the defensive.

If Jonathan doesn't calm down, there is no good way to deal with the problem. Glasser (1990) says to allow him 20 seconds, and if he isn't calm by then, admit that there is no way to solve the problem at that time. Give Jonathan time out from the lesson, but don't threaten or warn.

TEACHER: Jonathan, I want to help you work this out. I am not interested in punishing you. Whatever the problem is, let's solve it. But for now you must go sit at the table. When you are calm, come back to your seat.

Later, at an opportune time, you discuss the situation with Jonathan, approximately as follows (p. 141):

TEACHER: What were you doing when the problem started? Was it against the rules? Can we work things out so it won't happen again? What could you and I do to keep it from happening?

If the problem involves hostilities between Jonathan and Michael, the discussion should involve both boys and proceed along these lines (p. 141):

TEACHER: What were you doing, Jonathan? What were you doing, Michael? How can the three of us work things out so this won't happen anymore?

It is important to note that no blame is assigned to either Jonathan or Michael. No time is spent on trying to find out whose fault it was. You remind the boys that all you are looking for is a solution so that the problem won't occur again.

Glasser contends that if you treat Jonathan and Michael with respect and courtesy, if you show you don't want to punish them or throw your weight around, and if you talk to them as a problem solver, both their classroom behavior and the quality of their work will gradually improve.

INITIATING THE GLASSER MODEL

Suppose you find Glasser's current views on schooling and discipline so persuasive that you want to use them in your classroom. How do you go about putting them into practice? The general framework suggested by Glasser for moving toward quality teaching was presented earlier in the chapter. But for immediate use of his ideas, the implication seems to be that you would begin with class discussions, repeated frequently, in which you help your students understand that you, with their help, wish to do the following:

1. Work to make the curriculum as interesting for students as you possibly can.
2. Involve students in discussions about topics to be pursued, ways of working, procedures for reporting or demonstrating accomplishment, establishment of class rules, and decisions about steps to be taken when misbehavior occurs. You would offer your opinions but give serious attention to student suggestions as well.
3. Make plain to students that you will try to arrange activities they might have suggested and that you will do all in your power to help them learn and succeed.
4. Learn how to be a lead teacher rather than a boss teacher. (The scenario given earlier showing Mr. García's introduction of his unit on South America illustrates lead teaching.)
5. Hold regular class meetings to discuss curriculum, procedures, behavior, and other educational topics. These meetings should always be conducted with an eye to improving learning conditions for students, never as a venue for finding fault, blaming, or criticizing.
6. When students misbehave, discuss their behavior and why it was inappropriate for the class. Ask them what they feel you could do in order to be more helpful to them. If the misbehavior is serious or chronic, talk with the involved student privately at an appropriate time.

     Arranging times and places for these talks can be awkward. Here is how it is done by Maureen Lewnes, who teaches a fourth- and fifth-grade combination class.

> "For conferencing with students I use a 'consultation corner,' which in my room is not a corner at all but rather four feet of wall space to the rear of my desk between a table and file cabinet. A small kindergarten chair is there for students to sit in, which they love to do as I bend down low to converse with them, out of sight of the rest of the class, which creates an impression of closeness between the two of us.
> "I introduce the consultation corner at the beginning of the year, telling my students I may request them to join me there to discuss matters of class work or behavior or to tell them how much I appreciate their help and good work, which I make sure to emphasize.
> "Several benefits have come from use of the corner. When the need arises, I say to the student, 'May I see you in the consultation corner at

study time?' The chat there gives me insights into matters that might be troubling the students, and it encourages shy students to share feelings, interests, and problems.

"Most students react well to the talks, appreciating the privacy, and I find that problems of misbehavior are more easily resolved there. When I ask their opinions, my students say that every room should have a consultation corner because it makes them more comfortable about talking with the teacher."

COMMENTS ON THE GLASSER MODEL

As you have seen, Glasser no longer assigns blame to students when misbehavior occurs. He points out that schools expect students to do boring work while sitting and waiting, which goes strongly against their inherent nature. Glasser wrote that expecting students to do boring work in school "is like *asking someone who is sitting on a hot stove to sit still and stop complaining*" (1986, p. 53, italics added).

Glasser insisted that "teachers should not depend on any discipline program that demands that they do something *to* or *for* students to get them to stop behaving badly in unsatisfying classes. Only a discipline program that is also concerned with classroom satisfaction will work" (p. 56). Glasser expanded on that theme in his 1990 work *The Quality School* by describing how schools can emphasize quality work. This depends on teachers' functioning as lead teachers who provide great support and encouragement but do not coerce, throw their weight around, or punish. In such schools, students find their genetic needs met sufficiently that they will stay in school and do better quality work. Glasser now gives discipline—our concern here—much less attention than before, insisting that if schools and classes are conducted in keeping with his quality concept, discipline problems will be few and relatively easily resolved.

The difficulty for teachers is that schools are not likely to make a sudden transition to the scheme Glasser proposes. Though such a change may well occur over time, for the present it is to be expected that most schools will continue to cover textbook material as broadly as possible, thus enabling students to perform better on the achievement tests currently in use.

Can teachers, then, make any significant use of Glasser's newest model of discipline? The answer is yes. Like Jones's model, Glasser's does not have to be taken as a total system and set into place lock, stock, and barrel. His suggestions for teachers' acting as problem solvers without arguing or punishing should be seriously considered by all teachers. His procedures can be practiced, allowing teachers to evaluate for themselves the effect on classroom climate and morale. Let's remember, too, that Glasser didn't imply that his quality school would wipe out all discipline problems. Students are human beings, and even the best-intentioned students sometimes violate rules, short-change work assignments, and experience conflict with others, including teachers. When such behavior occurs, teachers can practice calmly trying to identify the problem and then, without assigning blame, enlist students' help in correcting its cause.

In the commentary on the Dreikurs model (Chapter 5), it was suggested that Dreikurs's approach, while time-consuming and requiring counseling skills, offered teachers a good procedure for helping students become genuinely self-directing and responsible. Glasser's model seems to possess the same potential.

APPLICATION EXERCISES

REVIEW OF SELECTED TERMINOLOGY

Glasser introduces relatively few unfamiliar terms in his writings on education and discipline. The following, however, are central in understanding Glasser's ideas concerning discipline. Check yourself to be sure you can explain their meanings.

students' five basic needs	quality learning
survival	quality teaching
belonging	useful work
power	boss teacher
fun	lead teacher
freedom	rules
quality curriculum	classroom meetings

CONCEPT CASES

Case 1: Kristina Will Not Work

Kristina, a student in Mr. Jake's class, is quite docile. She socializes little with other students and never disrupts class. However, despite Mr. Jake's best efforts, Kristina never does her work. She rarely completes an assignment. She is simply there, putting forth no effort.

How would Glasser deal with Kristina?   Glasser would first suggest that Mr. Jake think carefully about the classroom and the program to try to determine whether they contain obstacles that prevent Kristina from meeting her needs for belonging, power, fun, and freedom. He would then have Mr. Jake discuss the matter with Kristina, not blaming her but noting the problem of nonproductivity and asking what the problem is and what he might be able to do to help. In that discussion, Mr. Jake might ask Kristina questions such as the following:

You have a problem with this work, don't you? Is there anything I can do to help you with it?

Is there anything I could do to make the class more interesting for you?

Is there anything in this class that you enjoy doing?

Do you think that, for a while, you might like to do only those things?

Is there anything we have discussed that you would like to learn very, very well?

How could I help you do that?

What could I do differently that would help you want to learn?

Mr. Jake would not punish Kristina, nor would he use a disapproving tone of voice. Meanwhile, every day he would make a point of talking with her in a friendly and courteous way about nonschool matters—trips, pets, movies, and so forth—casually, but often, showing he is interested in her and willing to be her friend.

Glasser would remind Mr. Jake that there is no magic formula for success with all students. Mr. Jake can only encourage and support Kristina. Scolding and coercion are likely to make matters worse, but as Mr. Jake befriends Kristina she is likely to begin to do more work and of better quality.

Case 2: Sara Cannot Stop Talking

Sara is a pleasant girl who participates in class activities and does most, though not all, of her assigned work. She cannot seem to refrain from talking to classmates, however. Her teacher, Mr. Gonzales, has to speak to her repeatedly during lessons, to the point that he often becomes exasperated and loses his temper.

What suggestions would Glasser give Mr. Gonzales for dealing with Sara?

Case 3: Joshua Clowns and Intimidates

Joshua, larger and louder than his classmates, always wants to be the center of attention, which he accomplishes through a combination of clowning and intimidation. He makes wise remarks, talks back (smilingly) to the teacher, utters a variety of sound-effect noises such as automobile crashes and gunshots, and makes limitless sarcastic comments and put-downs of his classmates. Other students will not stand up to him, apparently fearing his size and verbal aggression. His teacher, Miss Pearl, has come to her wit's end.

How do you think Glasser would have Miss Pearl deal with Joshua?

Case 4: Tom Is Hostile and Defiant

Tom has appeared to be in his usual foul mood ever since arriving in class. On his way to sharpen his pencil, he bumps into Frank, who complains. Tom tells him loudly to shut up. Miss Baines, the teacher, says, "Tom, go back to your seat." Tom wheels around, swears loudly, and says heatedly, "I'll go when I'm damned good and ready!"

How would Glasser have Miss Baines deal with Tom?

QUESTIONS AND ACTIVITIES

1. Select a preferred grade level and/or subject. As the teacher, outline what you would consider and do, along the lines of Glasser's suggestions, concerning the following:
    a. Organizing the classroom, class, curriculum, and activities so as better to meet your students' needs for belonging, fun, power, and freedom
    b. Your continual efforts to help students improve the quality of their work
2. Do a comparative analysis of Glasser's and Canter's systems of discipline. Explain your conclusions about the models concerning the following:
    a. Effectiveness in suppressing inappropriate behavior
    b. Effectiveness in improving long-term behavior
    c. Ease of implementation
    d. Effect on student self-concept
    e. Effect on bonds of trust between teacher and student
    f. The degree to which each model accurately depicts realities of student attitude and behavior
3. Examine Scenario 9 or 10 in Appendix I. What advice would Glasser give Mr. Wong or Miss Thorpe to help improve learning conditions in the classroom?

REFERENCES AND RECOMMENDED READINGS

Glasser, W. (1965). *Reality therapy: A new approach to psychiatry.* New York: Harper & Row.
———. (1969). *Schools without failure.* New York: Harper & Row.
———. (1977). 10 steps to good discipline. *Today's Education, 66,* 60–63.
———. (1978). Disorders in our schools: Causes and remedies. *Phi Delta Kappan, 59,* 331–333.
———. (1986). *Control theory in the classroom.* New York: Harper & Row.
———. (1990). *The quality school: Managing students without coercion.* New York: Harper & Row. (Reissued with additional material in 1992)
———. (1992). The quality school curriculum. *Phi Delta Kappan 73(9),* 690–694.
———. (1993). *The quality school teacher.* New York: Harper Perennial.

CHAPTER 9

The Gordon Model

Discipline through Developing Self-Control

Thomas Gordon

BIOGRAPHICAL SKETCH OF GORDON

Thomas Gordon, a clinical psychologist, is founder and director of Effectiveness Training International, a network whose instructors offer training worldwide for parents, teachers, physicians, managers, young people, and others. Gordon has authored several books, including *Parent Effectiveness Training: A Tested New Way to Raise Responsible Children* (1970), *Teacher Effectiveness Training* (1974), *P.E.T. in Action* (1976), and *Discipline that Works: Promoting Self-Discipline in Children* (1989). In those books he offers parents and teachers strategies for helping children become more self-reliant, self-controlled, responsible, and cooperative. Catalogs and information about Gordon's programs are available from Effectiveness Training, Inc., 531 Stevens Avenue, Solana Beach, CA 92075; telephone 619-481-8121.

GORDON'S CONTRIBUTIONS TO DISCIPLINE

Gordon has taken a leadership role in the recent trend in school discipline that places primary emphasis on development of student responsibility and self-control. Like Richard Curwin and Allen Mendler (1988), William Glasser (1990), Kay Burke (1992), and Alfie Kohn (1993), Gordon believes that effective discipline cannot be achieved through either coercion or reward and punishment but rather must be developed within the character of each individual.

Gordon first brought his views to public attention in 1962 when he began working with parents in his new program called Parent Effectiveness Training (P.E.T.). Most early parent trainees had been experiencing deteriorating relationships with their offspring, and Gordon's program seemed to help them handle discipline problems better. From the beginning, P.E.T. was a program where parents learned skills not so much for correcting misbehavior as for establishing relationships that prevented its occurrence.

As parents who underwent training saw improvements in home relationships with their children, they brought Gordon's ideas to the attention of schools. Soon, schools began offering effectiveness training to teachers, and a Teacher Effectiveness Training (T.E.T) program evolved that focused on improving interactions between teachers and students.

Gordon's 1989 book, *Discipline That Works*, was built upon ideas formulated for P.E.T. and T.E.T. After examining school discipline policies, Gordon concluded that the punitive actions prevalent in discipline harmed children by leading to self-destructive behavior and antisocial acts. He became convinced that punishment doled out by authoritarian adults could not produce truly effective classroom discipline. But he was quick to state that permissiveness in dealing with children is just as misguided as authoritarianism. In place of power or permissiveness, Gordon offers middle-ground strategies designed to help children make positive decisions, become more self-reliant, and control their own behavior. Gordon (1989) summed up his concerns about current discipline practices and their results as follows:

As a society we must urgently adopt the goal of finding and teaching effective alternatives to authority and power in dealing with other persons—children or adults—alternatives that will produce human beings with sufficient courage, autonomy, and self-discipline to resist being controlled by authority when obedience to that authority would contradict their own sense of what is right and what is wrong. (p. 98)

GORDON'S CENTRAL FOCUS

Gordon maintains that the only truly effective discipline is self-control that occurs internally in each child. The development of such self-control, he says, can be strongly assisted by teachers. To help children control their own behavior and become self-reliant in making positive decisions, teachers must first give up their "controlling" power. As Gordon (1989) says,

You acquire more influence with young people when you give up using your power to control them . . . and the more you use power to try to control people, the less real influence you'll have on their lives. (p. 7)

Precisely how teachers acquire influence with students, and how they can best use that influence, is the central focus of Gordon's work.

GORDON'S PRINCIPAL CONCEPTS AND TEACHINGS

Gordon teaches a number of relatively novel concepts that give meaning and flavor to his work.

Authority. Authority is a condition that can be used to exert influence or control over others. It has at least four definitions: (1) *authority E* is expertise in a given matter; (2) *authority J* is based on job description; (3) *authority C* comes from contracts and agreements; and (4) *authority P* is the power to control others. The first three forms of authority are sources of influence; authority P is a source of control.

Noncontrolling methods of behavior change. These are methods teachers can use to *influence* student behavior positively without resorting to authoritative power or rewards and punishments to *control* them.

Problem. This is a condition, event, or situation that troubles someone.

Problem ownership. The individual troubled by a condition, event, or situation is said to "own" the problem.

Behavior window. This is a visual device that Gordon uses to help clarify whether a problem exists and, if so, who owns it.

Primary feelings. These are fundamental feelings that one experiences following another person's unacceptable behavior.

Secondary feelings. These are manufactured feelings that one senses following the resolution of a difficulty. For example, a teacher is extremely worried (primary feeling) when a child is hurt on the playground. But once the child is found to be all right, the teacher reacts angrily (secondary feeling) because the child violated playground rules.

I-messages. These are statements in which people tell what they personally think or feel about another's behavior and its consequences, for example, "I am having trouble concentrating because there is so much noise in the room."

You-messages. These are blaming statements leveled at others' behavior: "You girls are making too much noise. You know better than that."

Confrontive I-messages. These messages attempt to influence another to cease an unacceptable behavior: "I'm pleased so many of you have something to share about this, but when everyone tries to talk at once, I can't hear what anyone has to say."

Shifting gears. This involves changing from a confrontive to a listening posture. This strategy is helpful when students resist the teacher's I-messages or defend themselves.

Students' coping mechanisms. Students usually deal with coercive power by fighting (combating the person with whom they have the conflict), taking flight (trying to escape the situation), or submitting (giving in to the other person).

Win-lose conflict resolution. This type of conflict resolution ends disputes (temporarily) by producing a "winner" and a "loser," usually with detrimental effects for the loser.

No-lose conflict resolution. This type of conflict resolution ends disputes by enabling both sides to emerge as "winners."

Door openers. These are words and actions that invite others to speak about whatever is on their minds.

Active listening. This involves carefully attending to and demonstrating understanding of what another person says.

Communication roadblocks. These comments by well-meaning teachers shut down student willingness to communicate.

Preventive I-messages.These messages attempt to forestall future actions that may later constitute a problem, for example, "I really hope we can have a quiet room when the principal visits. Can you help us all remember things we can do to help keep the room quiet?"

Preventive you-message. This type of message is to be avoided: "You were very rude the last time our principal visited. You made me feel ashamed. I certainly hope you do better this time."

Participative classroom management. This leadership approach permits students to share in problem solving and decision making concerning the classroom and class rules.

Problem solving. This is a process in which people clarify a problem, put forth possible solutions, select a solution that is acceptable to all, implement the solution, and evaluate the solution in practice.

ANALYSIS OF THE GORDON MODEL

As you have seen, Gordon believes that good classroom discipline ultimately involves students' developing their own inner sense of self-control. The techniques he teaches are designed to help teachers promote self-control in students. He rejects as counterproductive the traditional intervention techniques of power-based authority and win-lose conflict resolution. He also strongly urges teachers not to use rewards or punishments to control student behavior. In order to understand Gordon's overall position more fully, let us examine what he has to say about authority, rewards and punishment, misbehavior, problem ownership, the behavior window, and teacher skills, including confrontive skills, helping skills, and preventive skills.

Authority

Authority is a condition that can be used to exert influence or control over others. Gordon teaches that authority is a complex concept with at least four definitions.

1. *Authority E* (expertise) is inherent in a person's special knowledge, experience, training, skill, wisdom, and education. For example, your expertise as an artist enables you to exert influence over others in matters having to do with art.
2. *Authority J* (job) is based on one's job description. As principal of the school, your position enables you to influence educational decisions made by teachers, parents, and others.
3. *Authority C* (commitments, agreements, or contracts) comes from the daily interactions and subsequent understandings, agreements, and contracts that people make. When students actively participate in setting classroom rules, it strongly influences them to comply.
4. *Authority P* (power) refers to a person's ability to control as opposed to influence others. For example, because of the power you have to give students low grades, you can make them do assignments they would not otherwise do.

Teachers who use authority E, J, or C exert positive influence on students. But when they use authority P to control students rather than influence them, their effectiveness is diminished. The Gordon model of discipline uses *noncontrolling methods* of behavior change that are based on use of the first three types of authority.

Rewards and Punishment

Gordon (1989) summarizes his concerns about discipline based on rewards as follows:

> Using rewards to try to control children's behavior is so common that its effectiveness is rarely questioned. . . . the fact that rewards are used so often and unsuccessfully by so many teachers and parents proves they *don't* work very well. . . . The ineffectiveness of using rewards to control children is due in part to the fact that the method requires such a high level of technical competence on the part of the controller—a level few parents or teachers can ever attain. (pp. 34–35)

> Considering all of the precise conditions that must be met to make this complex method work and the inordinate amount of time it takes, I am convinced that behavior modification with rewards could *never* be a method of any practical use for either parents or teachers. (pp. 37–38).

What does Gordon see as negative effects of behavior modification? He says the following are likely to occur when *rewards* are used to influence behavior:

- Students become concerned only with getting the rewards, not with learning or behaving desirably.
- When rewards are removed, students tend to revert at once to undesirable behavior.
- When students accustomed to receiving rewards are not rewarded, they may equate the lack of reward with punishment.
- Students may receive stronger rewards from classmates for behaving improperly than from the teacher for behaving properly.

And why is *punishment* ineffective in producing self-discipline? According to Gordon, punishment's long-term negative effects include the following:

- Punished students experience feelings of belittlement, rage, and hostility.
- Punished students have a decreased desire to cooperate willingly with the teacher.
- There is an increased likelihood that punished students will lie and cheat in order to avoid punishment.
- Punishment engenders a false notion that might makes right.

What Is Misbehavior, and Who Owns the Problem?

Gordon (1976) sees *misbehavior* as an adult concept in which "a specific action of the child is seen by the adult as producing an undesirable consequence *for the adult*" (p. 107, italics added). It is the teacher, he says, not the student, who experiences the sense of "badness" in student behavior.

If students are to develop self-control, teachers must shift away from their traditional concept of misbehavior. Gordon says that teachers should begin by learning to identify correctly who owns a particular problem, the teacher or the student. The following example illustrates what Gordon means by *problem ownership*: When Kyla becomes morose because she feels other girls have slighted her, she sulks but doesn't bother anyone else. Because no one else is affected, Kyla "owns" the problem; it bothers her but causes no difficulty for teacher or classmates. Her behavior may in fact be entirely acceptable to the teacher, since the class work continues normally. But if Kyla decides to confront the other girls angrily, the resultant squabble causes difficulties for the teacher. Because the teacher is now troubled by the situation (students become inattentive and the lesson is disrupted), the teacher is said to own the problem. When owning a problem of this sort, the teacher feels obliged to deal with it and may take corrective action against Kyla in order to stop the disruption that has ensued.

The Behavior Window

Gordon created a visual device called the *behavior window* to help clarify the concept of problem ownership. Teachers are taught to visualize student behavior through the behavior window, which shows who owns the problem, depending on whether teachers see the behavior as acceptable or unacceptable. The behavior window is shown in Figure 9.1.

FIGURE 9.1

Behavior Window	Acceptability to Teacher
Student's behavior causes a problem for the student only. **Student owns the problem.**	Acceptable behavior
Student's behavior does not cause a problem for either student or teacher. **No problem.**	Acceptable behavior
Student's behavior causes a problem for the teacher. **Teacher owns the problem.**	Unacceptable behavior

SOURCE: Adapted from *PET in Action* (pp. 27, 174, 251) by T. Gordon, 1976, New York: Random House.

The behaviors found in the top section of the behavior window in Figure 9.1 are acceptable to the teacher, though they are troublesome for the student. The student's needs are not being met, or the student is unhappy or frustrated or in trouble, but these behaviors do not much affect the teacher or other students in the class. For example, Mark's failure to appear for his scheduled drama audition (because he is overly self-conscious) affects only Mark, so Mark owns the problem. The drama teacher, Ms. Aldrice, will probably take no action against Mark, but if she is aware of his feelings, she may decide to speak with him using helping skills such as active listening.

Behaviors found in the bottom section of the behavior window are unacceptable to the teacher; that is, they cause a problem for the teacher. Mark observes at the drama auditions and heckles when others read for their parts. His behavior interferes with the tryouts. This bothers Ms. Aldrice, who now owns the problem, and it is up to her to try to change Mark's problem-causing behavior.

In the middle section of the behavior window in Figure 9.1 are student behaviors that are problem-free. Here the teacher and student work together pleasantly. Mark does not want to try out for the play but does want to help with set construction and lighting, which leaves him on good terms with Ms. Aldrice.

The behavior window helps teachers understand problem ownership, but it should be understood that the window is not static. As Gordon (1976) explains, "You inevitably will be inconsistent from day to day, with your different moods, with different children, and in different environments" (p. 18). The window lines that demarcate behavior move in accordance with teacher mood (teacher is rested or upset), student behavior (student is quiet or careful, or aggressive or noisy), and the environment (indoors or outdoors, quiet time or group activity).

By understanding the behavior window and correctly identifying problem ownership, teachers can increase the likelihood of having effective interactions with students. Gordon describes various skills that teachers can use when working with students—skills that apply not only to problem behaviors but to ongoing communication and interactions. Those skills are clustered into three groups.

1. *Confrontive skills,* such as modifying the environment, recognizing and responding to primary feelings, sending I-messages that do not set off the coping mechanisms students use in response to power, shifting gears, and practicing the no-lose method of conflict resolution, are used when the teacher owns the problem.
2. *Helping skills,* such as passive listening, acknowledgment, door openers, active listening, and avoiding communication roadblocks, are used when the student owns the problem.
3. *Preventive skills,* such as rule setting, preventive I-messages, and participative problem solving and decision making, are used when neither the teacher nor the student has a problem with the behavior.

Put another way, confrontive skills help teachers meet their own needs, helping skills assist students in meeting their needs, and preventive skills help ensure mutual satisfaction for both teacher and student. Let us turn now to the relationship between the three sections of the behavior window and their pertinent skill clusters.

Skill Cluster 1: Confrontive Skills.   This skill cluster pertains to the bottom section of the behavior window, as shown in Figure 9.2. Gordon explains that teachers are most likely to take action first at the point where they own the problem. In this instance, teachers can meet their needs by confronting the misbehavior, provided they do so in a positive, nonadversarial manner. Five skills comprise this cluster: (1) modifying the environment, (2) recognizing and responding to primary feelings, (3) sending I-messages that do not trigger the student's coping mechanisms, (4) shifting gears, and (5) using a no-lose method of conflict resolution.

1. Modifying the Environment (Rather than the Student).   By enriching it or, if necessary, by limiting its distractors, teachers may be able to eliminate or minimize problem behavior. To encourage student curiosity and learning, teachers can enrich the room with learning centers and colorful posters, student murals, and displays on the topic being studied. If these effects are too distracting for some students, teachers can provide an area without displays or have study carrels for students who occasionally need a more subdued atmosphere. Teachers can play quiet background music during certain activities and set up areas in the classroom where students study independently or in groups. If the teacher is bothered by the amount of student movement around the room during an art project, sets of supplies can be placed on the students' desks.

2. Identifying and Responding to One's Own Primary Feelings.   In intense situations, people often sense fear, worry, disappointment, or guilt; sometimes these *primary feelings* emerge later as anger. Gordon believes such anger is a manufactured *secondary feeling* that arises as a consequence of the primary feeling. When Maria and Susanna quarrel heatedly in class, Miss Maple feels like shouting at them in

FIGURE 9.2

Behavior Window	Skill Clusters
Student's behavior causes a problem for the student only. **Student owns the problem.**	Helping skills
Student's behavior does not cause a problem for either student or teacher. **No problem.**	Preventive skills
Student's behavior causes a problem for the teacher. **Teacher owns the problem.**	*Confrontive skills*

SOURCE: Adapted from *PET in Action* (pp. 27, 174, 251) by T. Gordon, 1976, New York: Random House.

return. But by pausing, Miss Maple allows herself to realize that she is not so much angry at the girls as disappointed that they show no concern for all the time she has spent talking about this problem in class. So that her disappointment will not be expressed as a secondary feeling of anger, Miss Maple can use an I-message to let the girls know of her disappointment.

3. Sending I-Messages Regularly. When teachers own a problem because student behavior interferes with their needs or rights, instead of scolding students they should express their feelings through I-messages. Complete *I-messages* communicate three things: (1) the behavior that is presenting a problem for the teacher, (2) what the teacher is feeling about the behavior, and (3) why the behavior is causing a problem. Mrs. Watson's I-message is clear: "When class rules are broken as they are now, I feel upset because that keeps us from getting our work done and shows lack of consideration for others."

I-messages contrast with you-messages. I-messages describe situations and teacher feelings and are therefore relatively nonhurtful to students. *You-messages*, on the other hand, carry heavy judgments and put-downs, evident in statements such as "You've been very careless with this work" or "Shame on you for tattling" or "Can't you follow simple directions?"

A special kind of I-message—the *confrontive I-message*—is used to ask students for help and suggestions. The teacher may say, "When I have to wait too long for quiet and readiness, I have to rush through the directions, and then I have to spend more time repeating myself because the directions are not clear. Do you have any suggestions that might help me with this problem?"

4. Shifting Gears. Sometimes the teacher's I-messages provoke defensive responses from students. When teachers see this happen, it is important that they listen sensitively to the resistance and change from a sending/assertive posture to a listening/understanding posture, a change that prompts students to react more positively. Gordon calls this change from assertion to listening *shifting gears*. The change usually improves the likelihood of reaching an acceptable solution, because students feel their needs are being considered and that the teacher understands how they feel. When Mr. Johnson sends a confrontive I-message to Marcos about his irregular attendance, Marcos heatedly responds, "School is not the only thing. I have responsibilities at home. I can't help missing class sometimes." Shifting gears, Mr. Johnson replies, "It sounds like you have some difficult things to deal with outside of school. Is there anything I can do to help?"

Sometimes when I-messages do not work, teachers resort to power to change the student's behavior. This is not likely to be effective because students will in turn resist the controlling power, using *coping mechanisms* that Gordon calls fighting, taking flight, and submitting. For some individuals, the first inclination is one of *fighting* the person with whom they are in conflict. If, however, they see they are unlikely to win the fight, or if they perceive the consequences of fighting as too severe (i.e., harsh punishment or physical or psychological hurt), they will tend to avoid the conflict by *taking flight* from it altogether. If unwilling to fight and unable to escape (as is the case when teachers impose punitive discipline), students generally respond by *submitting*. But they do not do so acceptingly. Indeed, most students would rather lie, cheat, or place blame elsewhere than to accept punishment and loss of dignity. If punished, they are likely to harbor resentment for a long time.

5. Using the No-Lose Method of Conflict Resolution.   When conflict occurs in the classroom, as it inevitably will, Gordon urges teachers to defuse the situation and bring about a solution acceptable to everyone. This can be done, Gordon says, by using a no-lose method to help resolve the conflict.

To see how the no-lose method works, let us first consider the result of *win-lose conflict resolution*. Ego is on the line, and when the conflict is resolved, one person emerges as "winner" and the other as "loser." Suppose Mrs. Penny insists that Marta complete her assigned work before leaving the classroom. Marta complains that she cannot work fast enough to complete it and that it is unfair to make her stay longer than the other students. Mrs. Penny, who thinks Marta procrastinates, says, "You can either complete your work or take a grade of F on the assignment. It is your choice." Marta stays until she finishes but is seething with resentment. In this conflict, Mrs. Penny emerges as winner and Marta as loser, or so it would seem. In reality both may have lost, because their working relationship may have been ruined.

Instead of win-lose conflict resolution, Gordon suggests an approach he calls the *no-lose conflict resolution*. This approach enables both sides to find a mutually acceptable solution to their disagreement. By avoiding use of power, egos are preserved, work continues, and personal relations are undamaged. In this approach, Marta and Mrs. Penny talk about what each feels and about what is causing them to get upset with each other. Then they seek a solution acceptable to both, such as allowing Marta extra time to complete her work in class. This same procedure works well when teachers mediate conflicts between students.

Skill Cluster 2: Helping Skills.   This skill cluster applies to the top section of the behavior window, as shown in Figure 9.3, where the student owns the problem. Gordon's helping skills include (1) listening skills and (2) methods for avoiding communication roadblocks.

1. Using Listening Skills.   Teachers should always listen carefully to students, especially to the problems they voice. But when doing so they should not attempt to solve students' problems for them. Instead of telling students what they ought to do, teachers should make use of four *listening skills*, which Gordon calls passive listening (silence), acknowledgment responses, door openers (invitations), and active listening.

PASSIVE LISTENING   Often nothing but attentive silence is enough to encourage students to talk about what is bothering them. With *passive listening*, the teacher shows attention through posture, proximity, eye contact, and alertness as the student speaks. Mr. Aragon demonstrates this skill when he sits down beside Julian as the boy begins to speak of difficulties at home.

Behavior Window	Skill Clusters
Student's behavior causes a problem for the student only. **Student owns the problem.**	*Helping skills*
Student's behavior does not cause a problem for either student or teacher. **No problem.**	Preventive skills
Student's behavior causes a problem for the teacher.	Confrontive skills

FIGURE 9.3

SOURCE: Adapted from *PET in Action* (pp. 27, 174, 251) by T. Gordon, 1976, New York: Random House.

ACKNOWLEDGMENT RESPONSES   *Acknowledgment responses* can be verbal ("uh-huh", "I see") or nonverbal (nods, smiles and frowns, and other body movements). They demonstrate the teacher's interest and attention. Mrs. Heck smiles and nods as Chris tells his story about his family's recent trip to Washington, D.C.

DOOR OPENERS   *Door openers* are invitations to students to discuss their problems. When the student needs encouragement, the teacher may say, "Would you like to talk about it?" or "It sounds like you have something to say about that." These comments are nonjudgmental and open-ended, and as they are nonthreatening, they invite the student to talk. Sensing that Eduardo is distressed about the math assignment, Mr. Sutton invites him to discuss his concerns: "I think there might be something bothering you about this assignment, Eduardo. Would you like to talk about it?"

ACTIVE LISTENING   *Active listening* involves teachers' mirroring back what students are saying. It confirms that the teacher is attentive and understands the student's message. No judgment or evaluation is made. The teacher simply helps the student verbalize problems and feelings clearly: "You've been late to class this week because you've been working the closing shift at the restaurant, and that makes you so tired you sleep through your alarm."

2. Avoiding Communication Roadblocks.   Gordon points out that when teachers try to communicate with students, they often set up inadvertent roadblocks that shut off student willingness to talk. He goes to some lengths to help teachers learn to recognize and avoid setting up these *roadblocks to communication*, which are 12 in number: giving orders, warning, preaching, advising, lecturing, criticizing, name-calling, analyzing, praising, reassuring, questioning, and withdrawing. The following examples show how a teacher might use each of the 12 roadblocks to respond ineffectively or effectively. At student Del's middle school, all students are required to take physical education. Del, who is very self-conscious about his weight, detests physical education and has been offering various excuses in hopes that he won't be forced to participate.

GIVING ORDERS   When *giving orders*, the teacher tries to help by directing Del on what to do: "You might as well stop complaining about things you can't control. Go ahead and get ready now." A more effective response might be "Do you see any way I might be able to make this easier for you?"

WARNING   When *warning*, the teacher threatens Del: "That's enough. Change into your PE clothes now, or I'll have you running laps." A more effective response might be "I can see this matter is bothering you a great deal. Would you like to discuss it after school?"

PREACHING   When *preaching*, the teacher reminds Del of "shoulds" and "oughts": "You ought to know that exercise is important. You should try to get yourself in shape." A more effective response might be "Some people like to exercise and others don't. How do you think we might help you get the exercise you need?"

ADVISING   When *advising*, the teacher tries to help by offering Del suggestions or giving solutions: "If you feel you can't keep up with the others, try setting your own personal goal and work to meet it." A more effective response might be "Sometimes even good athletes don't like PE classes. Have you heard any of them discuss their feelings?"

LECTURING   When *lecturing*, the teacher presents logical facts to counter Del's resistance: "I can assure you that if you develop a habit for exercise now, you will be pleased and will carry it with you for the rest of your life." A more effective response might be "Sometimes it is certainly tempting to stop exercising and just sit out the class. If you do, what effect do you think it might have on your health?"

CRITICIZING   When *criticizing*, the teacher points out Del's faults and inadequacies: "I can't believe you just said that. That kind of excuse-making is pitiful." A more effective response might be "I think I'm beginning to understand what you are saying. Could you tell me a bit more about that?"

NAME-CALLING   When *name-calling*, the teacher labels or makes fun of Del: "I might expect third graders to argue about dressing out for PE. Aren't you a bit huge for third grade?" A more effective response might be "Frankly, I haven't understood exactly why you are reluctant. Can you help me understand a bit better?"

ANALYZING   When *analyzing*, the teacher diagnoses or interprets Del's behavior: "What you are really saying is that you are afraid others will laugh about your weight." A more effective response might be "Go ahead with that thought. Can you explain it further?"

PRAISING   When *praising*, the teacher uses positive statements and praise to encourage Del: "You have above-average coordination. You'll handle yourself real well out there." A more effective response might be "I understand your concern. What might I do to make physical education more enjoyable for you?"

REASSURING   When *reassuring*, the teacher tries to make Del feel better by offering sympathy and support: "I know how you feel. Remember, there are a lot of boys just like you. You will forget your concerns after a little while." A more effective response might be "Have you known other students with concerns like yours? How did they deal with them?"

QUESTIONING   When *questioning*, the teacher probes and questions Del for more facts: "What exactly are you afraid of? What do you think is going to happen?" A more effective response might be "We often anticipate the worst, don't we? Have you had other experiences like this that troubled you?"

WITHDRAWING   When *withdrawing*, the teacher changes the subject in order to avoid Del's concerns: "Come on, now. Enough of that kind of talk. It's time to get ready and get out there." A more effective response might be "Do you think this matter might be bothering others, too? Do you think I should talk to the class about it, or would you rather keep it between us?"

Skill Cluster 3: Preventive Skills.   This skill cluster is used in connection with the middle, or no problem, section of the behavior window as shown in Figure 9.4. Specific preventive skills addressed by Gordon include (1) preventive I-messages, (2) collaborative rule setting, and (3) participative classroom management, all of which contribute to maintaining harmonious relationships within the classroom.

FIGURE 9.4

Behavior Window	Skill Clusters
Student's behavior causes a problem for the student only. **Student owns the problem.**	Helping skills
Student's behavior does not cause a problem for either student or teacher. **No problem.**	*Preventive skills*
Student's behavior causes a problem for the teacher. **Teacher owns the problem.**	Confrontive skills

SOURCE: Adapted from *PET in Action* (pp. 27, 174, 251) by T. Gordon, 1976, New York: Random House.

1. Using Preventive I-Messages.   *Preventive I-messages* influence students' future actions and thus help avoid problems. The teacher might say, "Next week we're going on our field trip. I need to make sure we all have a good time and don't have any problems. I'd like everyone to be sure to stay together so no one gets lost." By contrast, *preventive you-messages* such as "You behaved very badly on out last field trip, so I hope you can do better this time" are to be avoided.

2. Setting Rules Collaboratively.   Gordon reminds us that rules are necessary in order to make classrooms safe, efficient, and harmonious. He believes those rules should be formulated collaboratively by teacher and students through discussions of what each wants and needs. In a democratic manner, everyone agrees to the rules mutually. *Collaborative rule-setting* is similar to the no-lose method of conflict resolution in that students and teachers both win because everyone's needs receive attention.

3. Using Participative Classroom Management.   Gordon believes that the most effective classrooms are those in which teachers share power and decision making with their students. He suggests *participative classroom management* in which teachers and students make joint decisions about class rules, room arrangement, seating, and preferred activities. That style of management motivates students, gives them greater confidence and self-esteem, and encourages them to take risks and behave more responsibly.

As part of participative management, Gordon (1989) recommends a process of *problem solving* through which teachers show students how to solve problems and make good decisions. The steps in the problem-solving process are as follows:

Step 1. Identify and define the problem or situation. Good solutions depend on accurate identification of the problem at hand. Questions that should be asked at the beginning include "What is really going on here?" "What problems are we having?" "What exactly do we need to solve or do?" and "Is there another deeper problem here?"

Step 2. Generate alternatives. Once the problem is clarified, a number of possible solutions should be generated. To help bring forth ideas, questions and statements such as the following are usually helpful: "What can we do differently to make our work easier or better?" "What rules or procedures do we need to follow?" "Let's see how many ideas we can come up with" and "Are there still more solutions we can think of?"

Step 3. Evaluate the alternative suggestions. When alternatives have been specified, participants are asked to comment on them. The goal is to choose a solution that is agreeable to all. Thus it is appropriate to ask for each proposal, "What do you think of this suggestion?" "What are its advantages and disadvantages?" "What problems does it leave unsolved?" and "If we try this idea, what do you think will happen?"

Step 4. Make the decision. Alternatives are examined. The one that seems to suit most people best is selected for trial.

Step 5. Implement the solution or decision. The trial solution is put into place with the understanding that it may or may not work as anticipated and that it can be changed if necessary.

Step 6. Conduct a follow-up evaluation. The results of the trial solution or decision are analyzed and evaluated. Helpful questions include "Was this a good decision?" "Did it solve the problem?" "Is everyone happy with the decision?" and "How effective was our decision?" If the solution or decision is judged to be satisfactory, it is kept in place. If unsatisfactory, a modified or new solution is proposed and put to the test.

INITIATING THE GORDON MODEL

Suppose it is the beginning of the school year. You like Gordon's ideas and want to use them in your discipline system. What exactly do you do during the first days to put the Gordon model into place? Gordon does not specify how his program should be introduced to the class, but the following steps are implied. (You would of course use language and demonstrations appropriate for your students.)

Step 1. Identify student behaviors. Behaviors that will help, and those that will hinder, learning in your classroom need to be considered. When will you use large group, small group, and individual activities? When is silence desirable? When is quiet talking helpful? When is group discussion and interaction needed? When is movement in the room necessary?

It is also important to think about your own needs concerning student behavior. How much noise can you tolerate? What degree of formal respect do you want students to show to you and to each other? To what extent do you need to structure students' behavior? May they speak out, or should they raise their hands first? How do you expect them to enter and exit the classroom? How much neatness and order do you require?

Step 2. Discuss your concerns with the class. On the first day, describe the curriculum and general expectations concerning work and behavior, but make a point also of asking for student input, to which you give serious consideration as suggested in participative management. In this process, you involve students in clarifying the conditions and working relationships that will make the class profitable and enjoyable. It is important that you use active listening and keep communication open. When students disagree over certain points, you can implement the problem-solving process to help them reach agreement. To culminate this phase, make a written summary of class agreements and post a copy in the classroom.

Step 3. Help students learn to function in keeping with the class agreements. This requires frequent reminders and perhaps practice and role playing. You will need to use preventive, helping, and confrontive skills as suggested by problem ownership. As the weeks pass, you will help students become increasingly self-disciplined as you demonstrate, in daily practice, your own self-discipline, flexibility, and ability to communicate and solve problems.

COMMENTS ON THE GORDON MODEL

By identifying specific alternatives and strategies to promote self-discipline in children, Gordon gives teachers a new strategy for helping students become self-reliant decision makers who exercise control over their own behavior. He moves away from the punitive/permissive extremes of discipline. He shuns behavior management based on reward and punishment and in its place proposes noncontrolling alternatives for influencing, not forcing, student behavior.

But while Gordon's suggestions are well received, they are not immune to challenge. Many teachers, especially those whose classes are hard to manage, do not picture students to be as well intentioned as Gordon seems to imply. Those teachers will be reluctant to abandon discipline techniques that, though controlling of students, nevertheless maintain order and allow instruction to occur.

A second concern has to do with whether teachers can easily acquire the skills that Gordon advocates. Teachers are not trained psychologists, nor are most of them skilled counselors. The Gordon model requires that teachers reconceptualize student behavior as "misbehavior" only when it presents a problem for the teacher. They must be able to examine problems and identify who owns them. They must be good listeners who can help students open up. They must be able to use clear I-messages that reveal their feelings in reaction to behavior. They must be able to shift gears from sending I-messages to listening in order to support successful problem solving. They must be willing to provide a participative classroom and share decision making with students. And they must continually model the decision-making process. Is it realistic to expect that the average, overburdened teacher can or will attempt the significant change of attitude that is needed and, moreover, acquire and implement such an array of new skills? Gordon feels that although the process may be difficult, it is essential. Increasingly, educators find they agree with him.

APPLICATION EXERCISES

REVIEW OF SELECTED TERMINOLOGY

The following terms are central to the in Gordon model of discipline. Check yourself to make sure you can explain their meanings:

authority	authority P
authority E	noncontrolling methods
authority J	rewards
authority C	punishment

misbehavior	coping mechanisms
problem ownership	win-lose conflict resolution
behavior window	no-lose conflict resolution
confrontive skills	passive listening
helping skills	acknowledgment responses
preventive skills	door openers
modifying the environment	active listening
primary feelings	roadblocks to communication
secondary feelings	preventive I-messages
I-messages	preventive you-messages
You-messages	collaborative rule setting
confrontive I-messages	participative classroom management
shifting gears	problem solving

CONCEPT CASES

Case 1: Kristina Will Not Work

Kristina, in Mr. Jake's class, is quite docile. She never disrupts class and does little socializing with other students. But despite Mr. Jake's best efforts, Kristina rarely completes an assignment. She doesn't seem to care. She is simply there, putting forth virtually no effort.

How would Gordon deal with Kristina? Gordon would suggest the following sequence of interventions:

> Recognize that it is the teacher who owns the problem, not Kristina.
>
> Don't try to force Kristina to complete the assignments.
>
> Use I-messages to convey teacher concern to Kristina.
>
> Encourage Kristina to communicate about the assignments. Use active listening skills as she does so. Ask her how you can help.
>
> Invite Kristina into a collaborative problem-solving exploration of why she doesn't work. See if she has suggestions she wishes to make.
>
> Use I-messages to convey to the entire class how important it is that everyone, teacher and students alike, completes the work expected of them in school. But don't single out Kristina.

Case 2: Sara Cannot Stop Talking

Sara is a pleasant girl who participates in class activities and does most, though not all, of her assigned work. She cannot seem to refrain from talking to classmates, however. Her teacher, Mr. Gonzales, has to speak to her repeatedly during lessons, to the point that he often becomes exasperated and loses his temper.

What suggestions would Gordon give Mr. Gonzales to help with Sara's misbehavior?

Case 3: Joshua Clowns and Intimidates

Joshua, larger and louder than his classmates, always wants to be the center of attention, which he accomplishes through a combination of clowning and intimidation. He makes wise remarks, talks back (smilingly) to the teacher, utters a variety of sound-effect noises such as automobile crashes and gunshots, and makes limitless sarcastic comments and put-downs of his classmates. Other students will not stand up to him, apparently fearing his verbal and physical aggression. His teacher, Miss Pearl, has come to her wit's end.

What do you find in Gordon's work that might help Miss Pearl deal with Joshua?

Case 4: Tom Is Hostile and Defiant

Tom has appeared to be in his usual foul mood ever since arriving in class. On his way to sharpen his pencil, he bumps into Frank, who complains. Tom tells him loudly to shut up. Miss Baines, the teacher, says, "Tom, go back to your seat." Tom wheels around and says heatedly, "I'll go when I'm damned good and ready!"

How would Gordon have Miss Baines deal with Tom?

QUESTIONS AND ACTIVITIES

1. Describe how you would use the problem-solving process with your English class if they expressed concern about having too many projects, papers, and other assignments due at about the same time.
2. Refer to Scenario 2 in Appendix I. Which of Gordon's ideas do you think could best be used to improve Mr. Platt's interactions with student Arlene?
3. Refer to Scenario 4 in the Appendix I. Explain how Gordon's ideas might be used to improve conditions in Mrs. Desmond's second-grade class.
4. Which type of authority is most evident in each of the following teacher statements?
   a. "Mr. Youngblood is a member of the Kiowa tribe. He is visiting our class today to share some of the legends of his people."
   b. "Class, I expect you to work quietly and finish before the bell. If not, you'll stay in for recess."
   c. "Officer Santos is with the police department. This morning she will talk to us about what you should do when a stranger tries to talk to you on the street."

5. Decide which of the following statements reflects 1) modifying the environment, 2) participative management, 3) confrontive I-message, or 4) preventive I-message.
   a. "Before we start our art project, let's talk about what we will need to do with the paints and brushes so we have enough time for cleanup before the bell rings."
   b. "Let's sit in our Jungle Hut today, and I'll turn down the lights while I read this story."
   c. "I am feeling tired, so let's all stand up. Is everyone ready? Good. Simon says . . ."
   d. "I feel so disappointed when I see one of my students being disrespectful to another."

REFERENCES AND RECOMMENDED READINGS

Burke, K. (1992). *What to do with the kid who . . . : Developing cooperation, self-discipline, and responsibility in the classroom*. Palatine, IL: IRI/Skylight.

Curwin, R., & Mendler, A. (1988). *Discipline with dignity*. Alexandria, VA: Association for Supervision and Curriculum Development.

Dewey, J. (1938). *Logic: The theory of inquiry*. New York: Holt, Rinehart & Winston.

Glasser, W. (1986). *Control theory in the classroom*. New York: Harper & Row.

———. (1990). *The quality school: Managing students without coercion*. New York: Perennial Library. (Reissued with additional material in 1992)

Gordon, T. (1970). *Parent Effectiveness Training: A tested new way to raise responsible children*. New York: New American Library.

———. (1974). *T.E.T.: Teacher Effectiveness Training*. David McKay.

———. (1976). *PET in action*. New York: Bantam Books.

———. (1989). *Discipline that works: Promoting self-discipline in children*. NY: Random House.

Kohn, A. (1993). *Punished by rewards: The trouble with gold stars, incentive plans, A's, praise, and other bribes*. Boston: Houghton Mifflin.

CHAPTER 10

The Curwin and Mendler Model

Discipline through Dignity and Hope

Richard Curwin

Allen Mendler

BIOGRAPHICAL SKETCHES OF CURWIN
AND MENDLER

Richard Curwin, born in 1944, earned a doctorate in education from the University of Massachusetts in 1972. He began his teaching career in a seventh-grade class of boys whose behavior was seriously out of control. This experience led to a career specialization in school discipline, first as a classroom teacher and later as a university professor and private consultant and writer.

Allen Mendler, born in 1949, earned a PhD in psychology at Union Institute in 1981. His career has been devoted to serving as school psychologist and psychoeducational consultant. He has worked extensively with students and teachers at all levels.

Curwin and Mendler attracted national attention through the book they coauthored in 1983, *Taking Charge in the Classroom* (Mendler & Curwin, 1983). They revised and republished that work in 1988 as *Discipline With Dignity*, a title that more accurately reflects the central concept of their approach. They also coauthored *The Discipline Book: A Complete Guide to School and Classroom Management* (1980) and several journal articles. In 1992 Curwin published *Rediscovering Hope: Our Greatest Teaching Strategy*, a book devoted to helping teachers improve the behavior of difficult-to-control students who are otherwise destined to fail in school.

Curwin and Mendler regularly conduct training seminars across the nation. They can be contacted through Discipline Associates, P.O. Box 20481, Rochester, NY 14602; telephone 800-772-5227.

CURWIN AND MENDLER'S CONTRIBUTIONS
TO DISCIPLINE

Curwin and Mendler's major contributions to school discipline have been strategies for improving classroom behavior through maximizing student dignity and hope. Their ideas have been especially useful to teachers who work with chronically misbehaving students. Those students—about 5 percent of the student population, Curwin and Mendler say—typically disrupt instruction, interfere with learning, and make life miserable for teachers. Described as "without hope," such students are doomed to fail unless treated with special consideration and care. Curwin and Mendler explain what without-hope students need if they are to have a chance for success in school, and they provide strategies to help teachers reclaim those students.

CURWIN AND MENDLER'S CENTRAL FOCUS

The central focus of the Curwin and Mendler model is on improving students' misbehavior while preserving their dignity and providing them with a sense of hope. Included in their model are suggestions for motivating students, ensuring success, and helping students learn to behave responsibly.

CURWIN AND MENDLER'S PRINCIPAL CONCEPTS
AND TEACHINGS

Behaviorally at risk. This phrase describes students whose chronic classroom misbehavior puts them in imminent danger of failing in school.

Hope. Most chronically misbehaving students have lost all hope of encountering anything worthwhile in school. A crucial responsibility of teachers is to help those students believe that school can be of benefit and that they have some control over their lives.

Dignity. Curwin and Mendler use this term to indicate value placed on human life. Students do all they can to prevent damage to their dignity, to their sense of self-value. Much serious misbehavior occurs as students attempt to avoid this damage.

School professionals and clients. Curwin and Mendler strongly make the point that schools exist for students, not for teachers. Teachers are the professionals placed in schools for the benefit of their clients, the students. The teachers' role is basically simple: to do all they can to help students learn and behave responsibly.

Underlying principles of effective discipline. These are five principles which state that (1) discipline is a very important part of teaching, (2) short-term solutions are rarely effective, (3) students must always be treated with dignity, (4) discipline must not interfere with motivation to learn, and (5) responsibility is more important than obedience.

Short-term solutions. Short-term solutions to discipline problems, such as writing offending students' names on the board, often turn into long-term disasters. Damaging student dignity reduces motivation, increases resistance, and promotes desire for revenge.

Responsibility versus obedience. Responsibility, which involves making enlightened decisions, almost always produces better long-term behavior changes than does obedience to teacher demands.

Dimensions of discipline. A thorough approach to classroom discipline has three dimensions: (1) prevention (steps taken to forestall misbehavior), (2) action (steps taken when class rules are broken), and (3) resolution (special arrangements for improving the misbehavior of out-of-control students).

Consequences. Consequences are preplanned actions invoked when class rules are broken. Consequences are planned by the teacher, with student input and agreement.

Insubordination Rule. This is a bottom-line rule included in the social contract. It states that whenever a student refuses to accept the consequence for breaking a rule, that student will not be allowed back into the class until he or she accepts the consequence. This rule requires the support of the school administrator.

The social contract. When class rules and consequences have been formulated, they are written and agreed to by students and teacher. This agreement is called the social contract for classroom behavior.

Creative responses. These are unexpected responses to misbehavior that teachers can at times use effectively. Examples include exchanging roles with the student, taping the class's behavior, and throwing an occasional tantrum.

Preventing escalation. In typical confrontations between teacher and student, both try to "win" the argument. The resulting struggle often escalates to a more serious level. Wise teachers de-escalate these situations by actively listening to the student, using I-messages, and keeping the discussion private.

Motivating the difficult-to-manage student. Students who are very difficult to manage have little motivation to learn in school. Their behavior can be improved through providing them with interesting lessons on topics of personal relevance that permit active involvement and lead to competencies students value.

ANALYSIS OF THE CURWIN AND MENDLER MODEL

Students Who Are Behaviorally at Risk

Behaviorally at risk is a label frequently given to students believed for any of a number of reasons to be in serious danger of failing in school. Like most labels, at risk tends to be misinterpreted and misapplied. Curwin and Mendler point out that the label is useful for communication but can lead to erroneous perception. They therefore make plain that they use the term to refer solely to behavior: "It is what students do under the conditions they are in, not who they are, that puts them at risk" (Curwin, 1992, p. xiii).

The students Curwin and Mendler refer to are those whom teachers consider to be out of control—students often referred to as lazy, turned off, angry, hostile, irresponsible, disruptive, or withdrawn. They are said to have "attitude problems." They make no effort to learn, disregard teacher requests and directions, and provoke trouble in the classroom. Because they behave in these ways, they are unlikely to be successful in school. Curwin and Mendler (1992) describe them as follows:

- They are failing.
- They have received, and do not respond to, most of the punishments and/or consequences offered by the school.
- They have low self-concepts in relation to school.
- They have little or no hope of finding success in school.
- They associate with and are reinforced by similar students.

The number of behaviorally at-risk students is increasing steadily. The reasons for this increase are many: failure of the family unit to provide emotional, social, and intellectual security; increased violence in society; birth of infants addicted to alcohol or cocaine; reemergence of racial tensions; lack of admirable models for children to emulate; replacement of a sense of right and wrong by personal gratification.

These conditions contribute to loss of hope in the young. Many can see no role for themselves in the mainstream. Many do not expect to live very long. Increasingly, adolescents experience depression and contemplate suicide, which accounts for almost one quarter of all adolescent deaths (Curwin, 1992). Students without hope do not care how they behave in the classroom. It does not worry them if they fail, bother the teacher, or disrupt the class.

Helping Students Regain Hope

Teachers can do little about the depressing conditions in society, but they can do a good deal to help students regain a sense of hope. *Hope* is what inspires us. We require it in order to live meaningfully. It provides courage and the incentive to overcome barriers. When hope is lost, there is no reason to try. Students who are behaviorally at risk have, for the most part, lost hope.

Curwin and Mendler contend that such students can be helped to regain hope and, further, that as they do so their behavior will improve. This can be accomplished, they say, by making learning much more attractive.

> If they are to get involved in the learning process, students . . . need something to hope for, something to be gained to make their risk worthwhile. . . . Learning activities can succeed when they promise students competence in doing *what is important to them*. (Curwin, 1992, p. 25, italics added)

Learning must not only be made attractive but must provide student success as well. At-risk students will not persevere unless successful, despite the attractiveness of the topic. To ensure success, teachers can explore ways to redesign the curriculum, encourage different ways of thinking, provide for various learning styles and sensory modalities, allow for creativity and artistic expression, and use grading systems that provide encouraging feedback without damaging the students' willingness to try. In Curwin's (1992) words,

> for students who are alienated, are fearful, or believe that school offers them nothing of importance, we must alter conditions to create hope. (p. 28)

Dignity

While interesting activities and success are crucial to restoring hope among the behaviorally at risk, an equally important consideration has to do with their sense of dignity. *Dignity* refers to respect for life and self, and it has long been at the center of Curwin and Mendler's work. In their book *Discipline with Dignity* (1988a), they point out that students with chronic behavior problems see themselves as losers and have stopped trying to gain acceptance in normal ways, telling themselves it is better not to try than to fail yet again, that it is better to be recognized as a troublemaker than to be seen as stupid.

Dignity cannot be disregarded. Chronically misbehaving students try to protect their dignity at all costs, even with their lives if they are pushed hard enough (Curwin & Mendler, 1988a). Teachers must take pains, therefore, to keep dignity intact and bolster it when possible. Curwin (1992) advises:

> We must . . . welcome high risk students as human beings. They come to school as whole people, not simply as brains waiting to be trained. Our assumptions about their social behavior need to include the understanding that their negative behaviors are based on protection and escape. They do the best they can with the skills they have under the adverse conditions they face. . . . When they are malicious, they believe, rightly or wrongly, that they are justified in defending themselves from attacks on their dignity. (p. 27)

For most teachers, a posture of understanding helpfulness is not easy to maintain, especially when students behave disdainfully and use abominable language. Given a steady dose of defiant hostility, many teachers become cynical and give up on students. Many leave teaching because they don't feel its rewards compensate for the turmoil they must endure.

While very supportive of teachers, Curwin and Mendler make a telling point in their writings: school exists for students, not for teachers. As *professionals*, teachers are there to help their *clients*, the students; they should enter the profession with that understanding. When teachers are able to see their role as supportive of student dignity, rather than confrontive, they can more easily retain their sense of purpose. They must expect to encounter student behavior that reflects society's ills, but they need to accept, as a matter of faith, that they can and will make a difference in their students' lives, even though that difference may not become apparent for a long time.

Why Students Break Rules

All students misbehave at times. They talk without permission, call each other sarcastic names, and laugh when they shouldn't. Some misbehave out of boredom, some because they find certain misbehaviors (such as talking) irresistible. Some break rules simply for expedience's sake. These kinds of misbehavior are relatively benign. They irritate teachers, but they do not place students in danger of failing.

In contrast, students who are behaviorally at risk break rules for more serious reasons, usually related to the sense that their dignity has been damaged. Chronic misbehavior gives students a measure of control over a system that has damaged their sense of dignity (Curwin, 1992, p. 49). They exert their control by refusing to comply with teacher requests, arguing and talking back to the teacher, tapping pencils and dropping books, or withdrawing from class activities. These students have found they can't be very good at learning but that they can be very good at being bad and, by doing so, can meet their needs for attention and power. While such students are relatively few in number, they are not isolated. They find others like themselves with whom to bond, which further encourages misbehavior.

Why At-Risk Students Are Difficult to Discipline

Behaviorally at-risk students are difficult to control for several reasons. They usually, though not always, have a history of academic failure. Unable to maintain dignity through achievement, they protect themselves by withdrawing or acting as if they don't care. They have learned that it feels better to misbehave than to follow rules that lead nowhere. (1992) Curwin illustrates this point.

> Ask yourself, if you got a 56 on an important test, what would make you feel better about failing? Telling your friends, "I studied hard and was just too stupid to pass." Or, "It was a stupid test anyway, and besides I hate that dumb class and that boring teacher." (p. 49)

When students' dignity has been repeatedly damaged in school, it makes them feel good to lash back at others. As they continue to misbehave, they find themselves systematically removed from opportunities to act responsibly. When they misbehave in class, they are made to sit by themselves in isolation. When they fight, they are told to resolve the dispute and make amends. In such cases they are taken out of the very situations in which they might learn to behave responsibly. Curwin (1992) makes the point as follows:

> No one would tell a batter who was struggling at the plate that he could not participate in batting practice until he improved. No one would tell a poor reader that he could not look at any books until his reading improved. In the same way, no student can learn how to play in a playground by being removed from the playground, or how to learn time-management skills by being told when to schedule everything. Learning responsibility requires participation. (p. 50)

Students who are behaviorally at risk know and accept that they are labeled "discipline problems." They know that they can't do academic work as expected and that they are considered bothersome and irritating. Wherever they turn, they receive negative messages about themselves. They have become, in their own eyes, bad persons. How can teachers help students who see themselves as bad persons whose only gratification in school comes from causing trouble?

Discipline Methods That Do Not Work

First, it should be recognized that traditional methods of discipline are ineffective with students who are behaviorally at risk. These students have grown immune to scolding, lecturing, sarcasm, detention, extra writing assignments, isolation, names on the chalkboard, or trips to the principal's office. It does no good to tell them what they did wrong—they already know. Nor does it help to grill them about their ability, to do class work or follow rules. They already doubt their ability, and they know they don't want to follow rules. Sarcastic teacher remarks, because they attack students' dignity, almost always make matters worse. At-risk students need no further humiliation. Punitive acts destroy their motivation to cooperate. They are unwilling to commit to better ways of behaving and therefore cannot achieve the results teachers hope for.

Disciplining the Difficult-to-Control Student

If traditional methods of discipline are ineffective in working with students who are difficult to control, what would be an effective set of methods? What degree of success might the new methods have? And if the entire process is so difficult, is it worth teachers' time to try to help these resistant students?

Curwin and Mendler set forth principles and approaches that, if not effective with all recalcitrant learners, are in their opinion significantly better than the discipline approaches normally used. They acknowledge that dealing with the chronic rule breaker is never easy and admit that the success rate is far from perfect, but they claim it is possible to produce positive changes in 25 to 50 percent of students considered to be out of control (Curwin & Mendler, 1992).

Underlying Principles.   Curwin (1992) would have teachers base their discipline efforts upon the following *principles of effective discipline:*

1. Dealing with student behavior is an important part of teaching (p. 51).

Most teachers do not want to deal with behavior problems, but being a professional means doing whatever one can to help the client. Teachers should therefore look upon misbehavior as an ideal opportunity for teaching responsibility. They should put as much effort into teaching good behavior as they put into teaching content.

2. "Short-term solutions often become long-term disasters" (p. 51).

The discipline techniques that most teachers use are *short-term solutions* that stifle misbehavior in order for the teacher to continue teaching. However, such quick solutions as writing names on boards, scolding, sarcasm, and detention often turn into long-term disasters because they assault students' self-image and thus further reduce desire to learn while provoking additional disobedience.

3. "Always treat students with dignity" (p. 52).

Dignity is a basic need that is essential for healthy life; its importance cannot be overrated. To treat students with dignity is to respect them as individuals, to be concerned about their needs and understanding of their viewpoints. Effective discipline does not attack student dignity but instead offers students hope. Curwin and Mendler advise teachers to ask themselves this question when reacting to student misbehavior: "How would this strategy affect my dignity if a teacher did it to me?"

4. "Good discipline must not interfere with student motivation" (p. 53).

Any discipline technique is self-defeating if it reduces student motivation to learn. Students who are motivated cause few discipline problems. Poorly behaved students are usually unmotivated and badly in need of reason and encouragement to learn. Curwin suggests that teachers, when about to deal with misbehavior, ask themselves this question: "What will this technique do to motivation?"

5. "Responsibility is more important than obedience" (p. 54).

Curwin differentiates between obedience and responsibility as follows: *Obedience* means "do as you are told." *Responsibility* means "make the best decision possible." Obedience is desirable in matters of health and safety, but for most misbehavior it is a short-term solution against which students rebel. Responsibility grows, although slowly, as students have the opportunity to sort out facts and make decisions. Teachers should regularly provide such opportunities.

Outline for a General Discipline Plan. Curwin and Mendler (1988a) maintain that, to be effective, discipline plans should address *three dimensions of disciplines* (1) a prevention dimension, (2) an action dimension, and (3) a resolution dimension. *Prevention* focuses on what can be done to prevent discipline problems. *Action* describes what teachers should do when discipline problems occur. *Resolution* helps chronically misbehaving students learn to make and abide by decisions that serve their needs. All three dimensions are important for discipline in general and especially for students who are behaviorally at risk.

The Prevention Dimension. In prevention, the teacher gives attention to motivation and to establishing a social contract, that is, to formulating class rules and consequences. *Rules* help specify behaviors that are acceptable, or unacceptable, in the classroom. When carefully planned, rules help meet everyone's needs. Curwin and Mendler (1992) say that a good rule should state in behavioral terms what is required, be brief, be clear, and make sense to everyone. The teacher must be willing to enforce rules appropriately when they are broken.

Consequences are steps taken by the teacher when a rule is violated. Curwin and Mendler (1988a) advise that a list of possible consequences be established in advance. From that list the teacher can select an appropriate consequence when a rule is broken. For example, Susan continually fails to turn in homework on schedule. Miss Martin invokes a consequence selected from a list that might include a reminder, a warning, or a conference with Susan and her parents. Unlike other authorities in discipline, Curwin and Mendler do not tie specific consequences to rule violations. They believe it is better to provide teachers with a range of possibilities. The result is what they call *fair is not always equal.* Students have different needs, behave differently, and react differently. They may therefore need to be treated differently.

Curwin and Mendler warn that consequences should not be seen as punishment. Consequences should be logical, which usually involves doing correctly what was done wrong. For example, when James throws wadded paper and fills the corner with clutter, his consequence may be to clean up the mess. It is important that consequences preserve student dignity and allow students the opportunity to make responsible decisions.

One particular rule—the *insubordination rule*—should be made plain to students and enforced when broken. This rule states: "If a student does not accept the consequence after breaking a class rule, then he or she will not be allowed to remain in the class until the consequence is accepted." This is a bottom-line rule that prevents students from defying the teacher with impunity. The insubordination rule must, of course, by agreed to by the principal.

When students and teacher have selected, through group discussions, the rules and consequences that they believe are best for the class, their agreements (which should be written and posted in the room) become the *social contract* for behavior in the classroom. Curwin and Mendler (1992, p. 79) suggest that a "Classroom Social Contract Test" also be used to prevent students' using the excuse that they didn't understand the rules. This test is comprised of items on class rules and consequences, of which the following might be typical:

- When must homework be handed in?
- Name three things you must always bring to class.
- When someone else is speaking and you want to speak, you should first _____.

The Action Dimension.   Taking action refers to what teachers do when rules are broken. Curwin and Mendler advise teachers to select and apply, from alternatives previously identified, the consequence that best fits the situation. They see this not as a mechanical process of fitting consequence to offense but as an opportunity to interact productively with the student. They say that the method of implementation is at least as important as the consequence itself, and they remind teachers to avoid power struggles while remaining positive and mindful of student dignity.

The Resolution Dimension.   The resolution dimension is used to formulate plans of positive action for students who misbehave chronically. As noted, such students have given up hope and have grown immune, through repeated exposure, to tactics normally used. As teachers interact with noncooperative students, they should attempt to find out what is needed to prevent the problem's occurring again, work out a mutually agreeable plan with the student, implement and monitor the plan, and use creative approaches as necessary—approaches that will be explained later in the chapter.

More about Consequences

Curwin and Mendler give considerable attention to the nature of consequences and how they should be invoked. They maintain that students must have a very accurate idea of what is likely to happen if they break rules. Consequences should therefore be stated clearly and specifically and must always protect and maintain the dignity of the child. There is no reason ever to use a consequence that is humiliating or dehumanizing.

If teachers apply consequences as Curwin suggests, they are certain to treat individual students differently. Students and parents may complain about this inequality, but it is fair, Curwin and Mendler say. Curwin (1992) suggests that teachers say the following to parents who might complain about unequal treatment their child has received:

> Thank you for coming in, Mr. and Mrs. Blake. I am glad you are here to talk about your daughter. It is true that I have treated your daughter differently . . . My goal is to teach her how to behave responsibly, and I will do anything to help her learn. If you think my method is not appropriate in this case, I will be glad to listen to any suggestions you have. . . . However, . . . please do not ask me to treat your child just like everybody else. Your child deserves a lot better than that. (pp. 74-75, abridged)

Curwin and Mendler differentiate between four types of consequences: (1) logical, (2) conventional, (3) generic, and (4) instructional.

Logical Consequences.   *Logical consequences* are those in which students must make right what they have done wrong. If they make a mess, they must clean it up. If they willfully damage material, they must replace it. If they speak hurtfully to others, they must practice speaking in ways that are not hurtful.

Conventional Consequences.   *Conventional consequences* are those that are commonly in practice, such as time out, removal from the room, and suspension from school. Curwin and Mendler suggest modifying conventional consequences so as to increase student commitment. For time out, they suggest that instead of banning the student for a specified length of time, teachers should say something like "You have chosen time out. You may return to the group when you are ready to learn." When students must be removed from the room, they should not be embarrassed or humiliated. They may be sent to another teacher's room, where they sit in the back but do not participate. For suspension, sending students home is counterproductive. In-school suspension is preferable, in which students go to a designated room and complete assignments. Students are readmitted to their class only after they have made a plan for working and learning.

Generic Consequences.   *Generic consequences* are reminders, warnings, choosing, and planning that are invoked for almost all misbehavior. Often, simple *reminders* are enough to stop misbehavior: "We need to get this work completed." *Warnings* are very firm reminders: "This is the second time I have asked you to get to work. If I have to ask you again, you will need time out." *Choosing* allows students to select from three or four options a plan for improving their behavior. *Planning*, which Curwin (1992) calls "the most effective consequence that can be used for all rule violations" (p. 78), requires that students plan their own solution to a recurring behavior problem. Planning conveys that the teacher has faith in the student's competence. That faith often engenders a degree of commitment. The plan should name specific steps the student will follow and should be written, dated, and signed.

Instructional Consequences.   *Instructional consequences* teach students how to behave properly. Simply knowing what one ought to do does not ensure correct behavior. Some behaviors, such as raising one's hand or speaking courteously, are learned more easily when taught and practiced.

Invoking Consequences.   Curwin (1992, pp. 79–80) makes a number of suggestions for helping teachers use consequences. They include the following:

- Always implement a consequence when a rule is broken.
- Select the most appropriate consequence from the list of alternatives, taking into account the offense, situation, student involved, and the best means of helping that student.
- State the rule and consequence to the offending student. Nothing more need be said.
- Be private. Only the student(s) involved should hear.
- Do not embarrass the student.
- Do not think of the situation as win-lose. This is not a contest. Do not get involved in a power struggle.
- Control your anger. Be calm and speak quietly, but accept no excuses from the student.
- Sometimes it is best to let the student choose the consequence.
- The professional always looks for ways to help the client.

Creative Responses to Chronic Misbehavior.   Curwin and Mendler (1988a, pp. 151-155) suggest that when normal consequences are no longer effective with behaviorally at-risk students, teachers may wish to try creative responses. *Creative responses*, of which there are seven, include (1) role reversal, (2) humor and nonsense, (3) agreement with put-downs, (4) improbable answers, (5) paradoxical behavior, (6) teacher tantrums, and (7) taping classroom behavior.

Reverse Roles.   With *role reversal*, you give the student the responsibility of teaching the class for a time, a quarter hour for primary students, an hour or two for middle-grade students, and entire periods for secondary students. You take the student's place and behave as the student usually does. Afterward, discuss the situation in a private conference in which the student retains the teacher role and you the student role.

Use Humor and Nonsense.   Make a list of sayings you find humorous and/or nonsensical. When a chronically misbehaving student commits another rule violation, surprise him or her with one of the sayings. Curwin and Mendler give this example:

When Jack comes into the class late for the third day in a row, say, "Jack! Did you know that Peter Piper picked a peck of pickled peppers?" While Curwin and Mendler acknowledge that this tactic will not produce long-term behavior change, *humor and nonsense* may ease tensions and provide an opportunity for better communication.

Agree with Put-downs.   *Agreement with put-downs* works this way: When a student makes a nasty comment about you, you defuse the situation by acknowledging that the comment may have some truth, and then return to the matter of concern. For example, if a student says, "This assignment is stupid and so are you!" you might say, "Well, you may be right. I haven't had my IQ checked lately. But the assignment still needs to be completed."

Answer Improbably.   Sometimes when a student defies you, you can defuse the situation by giving an *improbable answer*. For example, if when you tell the student to go to the in-school suspension room, the student says, "I'm not going. What are you going to do about it?" then in reply you might say, "Well, I think maybe I'll pack my bags and catch the next plane for a long vacation. But before I do, I hope you will help us both by honoring my request that you go to the suspension room."

Use Paradoxical Behavior.   Teachers behave paradoxically by sending messages that ask students to behave in an undesirable manner. Curwin and Mendler (1988), who feel *paradoxical behavior* is an especially effective way of dealing with chronically misbehaving students, provide the following contrast between typical teacher behavior and paradoxical behavior:

> *Typical:* "This is the third day that you have not done your homework. The consequence is that you will have to remain after school."
>
> *Paradoxical:* "This is the third day that you have not done your homework. Your assignment for tonight is to try your best to forget to do tomorrow's homework." [This statement is made sincerely, not sarcastically or jokingly.] (p. 153)

Naturally, one must be cautious about using paradoxical behavior. You would not want to use it for misbehaviors that damage property, hurt students, or interfere drastically with teaching.

Throw an Occasional Tantrum.   Very occasionally, when highly provoked, you may find it helpful to throw a temper tantrum for the class's benefit. With *teacher tantrums* you may shout, slam books, show great exasperation, and carry on about discourtesy or lack of effort. While doing so, you must make sure that you do not attack individual students. You can use I-messages such as: "I am so furious I can barely speak!" "Am I ever going to get this message across?!" and "My Lord, I am dumbfounded!" Curwin and Mendler say that if you throw a tantrum more than three or four times a year, the tactic loses its impact.

Audio- or Videotape the Class.   Behavior usually improves markedly when students know they are being taped. If when *taping classroom behavior* you happen to record bothersome disruptions, meet with the offending student privately to consider the misbehaviors. Discuss with the student how he or she feels about the behavior. See if you can jointly come up with a specific plan for change. Keep track for a week to see whether improvement has occurred, and again discuss the result with the student. For especially troublesome behaviors, particularly those that the student denies committing, Curwin and Mendler (1988a, p. 155) suggest that you say to the student, "Beginning today, I will keep the tape recorder on 'record.' Since I think it important that you and your parents understand the problem we have here, I will make the tape available to your parents when we get together to discuss your progress. Good luck!"

Preventing Escalation.   When teachers respond to student misbehavior, students often dig in their heels and a contest of wills ensues, from which neither teacher nor students will back down. Curwin and Mendler remind teachers that their duty is not to "win" such contests but to do what they can to help the student. The way to help is to keep channels open for rational discussion of problem behavior. That cannot be done if the teacher humiliates, angers, embarrasses, or demeans the student. This point is critical for high-risk students, who are predisposed to responding negatively. Curwin (1992) suggests that teachers do the following toward *preventing escalation* of incipient conflicts:

1. Use active listening. Teachers acknowledge and/or paraphrase what students say without agreeing, disagreeing, or expressing value judgment.
2. Arrange to speak with the student later. Allow a time for cooling off. It is much easier to have positive discussions after anger has dissipated.
3. Keep all communication as private as possible. Students do not want to lose face in front of their peers and so are unlikely to comply with public demands. Nor do teachers like to appear weak in front of the class. When communication is kept private, the chances for productive discussion are much better because egos are not so strongly on the line.
4. If a student refuses to accept a consequence, invoke the insubordination rule.

Motivating the Difficult-to-Manage Student

Rules, consequences, and enforcement are necessary in all classrooms, but the key to better student behavior lies elsewhere—in *motivation to learn*. Most students are somewhat motivated to learn and behave properly in school, whether because they find school interesting, like to please the teacher, or simply want to avoid failure. Such is not the case for students behaviorally at risk, who have exceptionally low levels of motivation.

It would be foolish to suggest that a magical set of techniques exists for helping such students. But teachers do know what motivates students in general. Students who are behaviorally at risk have the same general needs and interests as other students, but they have encountered so much failure that they have turned to resistance and misbehavior to bolster their egos. Curwin (1992, pp. 130–144) makes the following suggestions for increasing motivation among students who are behaviorally at risk:

1. Select for your lessons as many topics as you can that have personal importance and relevance to the students.
2. Set up learning goals that are real—goals that lead to genuine competence that students can display and be proud of.
3. Help students interact with the topics in ways that are congruent with their interests and values.
4. Involve students actively in lessons. Allow them to use their senses, move about, and talk. Make the lessons as much fun as possible. The lessons don't need to be easy if they are important and enjoyable.
5. Give students numerous opportunities to take risks and make decisions without fear of failure.
6. Show your own genuine energy and interest in the topics being studied. Show that you enjoy working with students. Try to connect personally with them as individuals.
7. Each day, do at least one activity that you love. Show pride in your knowledge and ability to convey it to your students. Don't be reluctant to ham it up.
8. Make your class activities events that students look forward to. Make them wonder what might happen next.

INITIATING THE CURWIN AND MENDLER MODEL

Suppose you teach a class that contains several chronically misbehaving students, and you decide that the Curwin and Mendler model might help you deal with them more effectively. How do you put the model in place?

Principles You Must Accept

Before using the approaches Curwin and Mendler propose, you must subscribe to certain principles that undergird their model, as described earlier in this chapter. A primary principle is that student dignity must be preserved. You must understand that students will do all in their power to protect their dignity against threat. They don't want to appear stupid. They don't want to feel incapable. They don't want to be denigrated, especially in front of their peers. When faced with threat, students, especially the chronically misbehaved, use antisocial behavior to deflect it. You must be willing to guard against threatening students' dignity, even when they threaten yours.

A second principle is that dealing with misbehavior is an important part of teaching. You are in the classroom to help your students. Those whose behavior puts them at risk of failure especially need your help, though their behavior may suggest that they want nothing to do with you. The best thing you can do for them is to find ways to encourage prosocial behavior.

A third principle is that lasting results are achieved only over time. There are no quick-fix solutions to chronic misbehavior, but by finding ways to motivate students and help them learn, you will enable many to make genuine improvement.

A fourth principle is that responsibility is more important than obedience. The ability to weigh facts and make good decisions is far more valuable in students' lives than is obedience to demands. You must be willing to put students into situations where they can make decisions about matters that concern them, be willing to allow them to fail, and then help them try again. Progressively, they will learn to behave in ways that are best for themselves and others.

The Social Contract

You will have given much thought to the kind of classroom you want and how you want your students to behave. When you first meet the students, spend as much time as necessary discussing goals for the class, activities that might be helpful, and class behavior that will improve enjoyment and accomplishment. In those discussions, class rules and consequences should be agreed to. It is important that students contribute heavily to those decisions and that you obtain their agreement to abide by them. The rules and consequences should be written out, dated, and signed by teacher and students. The document should be posted in the room and copies sent to parents and administrators.

Motivation and Helpfulness

From the outset you must seek to structure lessons to help students be active and successful. It is far more important that students engage in activities of interest than that they be dragged perfunctorily through the standard curriculum. Your own energy, enjoyment of learning, and pride in teaching will affect students positively, while your willingness to help without confrontation will slowly win them over.

COMMENTS ON THE CURWIN AND MENDLER MODEL

All teachers experience misbehavior in their classrooms. Most have found ways to deal with minor infractions such as talking, speaking out, chewing gum, and failing to complete homework. But all teachers dread dealing with students whose behavior is so chronically poor that they not only disrupt learning but are likely to fail in school. Dealing with such students makes teachers feel trapped and overwhelmed. The Curwin and Mendler model seems to provide realistic help for working with chronically misbehaving students. They say that school is for students. Like that of all good professionals, teachers' primary responsibility is to help their clients, the students, by helping them learn and behave in socially acceptable ways.

Curwin and Mendler point out the ineffectiveness of traditional methods of discipline, the damage that school has done to student dignity, and the self-defeating nature of power struggles between teacher and student. They do not pretend that all out-of-control students can be reformed by the teaching approach they advocate, but they insist that many can and that they are worth saving from failure.

But can teachers make the adjustments Curwin and Mendler advocate? Can they calmly accept being called nasty names, acknowledge that slanderous expletives leveled at them may be partially correct, and all the while keep trying to help students who spurn their every effort? Can they wait weeks or months to see their efforts bear fruit, if indeed they ever do? Human nature does not seem attuned to what Curwin and Mendler ask of teachers.

Yet there is strength in their argument that teachers are professionals and that their job is to help students however they can. If teachers accept that premise, they can also accept that student misbehavior comes from defense of dignity, not from maladaptive pleasure in defying the teacher. And teachers know that Curwin and Mendler's warning about slowly emerging effects is true, even though they always hope for instant success.

The way for teachers ultimately to appraise Curwin and Mendler's approach is to try it in the classroom. They have little to lose and potentially a good deal to gain.

APPLICATION EXERCISES

REVIEW OF SELECTED TERMINOLOGY

The following terms are central to the Curwin and Mendler model of discipline. Check yourself to make sure you can explain their meanings.

behaviorally at risk	three dimensions of discipline
hope	rules
dignity	consequences
professionals	fair is not always equal
clients	insubordination rule
principles of effective discipline	social contract
short term solutions	creative responses
obedience	preventing escalation
responsibility	

CONCEPT CASES

Case 1: Kristina Will Not Work

Kristina, in Mr. Jake's class, is quite docile. She never disrupts class and does little socializing with other students. But despite Mr. Jake's best efforts, Kristina rarely completes an assignment. She doesn't seem to care. She is simply there, putting forth virtually no effort.

How would Curwin and Mendler deal with Kristina?   They would suggest the following sequence of interventions:

> Consider that Kristina's behavior might be due to severe feelings of incapability. She may be protecting herself by not trying.
>
> Relate to Kristina as an individual. Chat with her informally about her life and interests.
>
> Find topics that interest Kristina. Build class lessons around them. Assign Kristina individual work that helps her become more competent in her areas of special interest.
>
> Have a private conversation with Kristina. Ask for her thoughts about how you could make school more interesting for her. Show her you are interested and willing to help.
>
> As Kristina begins to work and participate, continue private chats that help her see herself as successful.

Case 2: Sara Cannot Stop Talking

Sara is a pleasant girl who participates in class activities and does most, though not all, of her assigned work. She cannot seem to refrain from talking to classmates, however. Her teacher, Mr. Gonzales, has to speak to her repeatedly during lessons, to the point that he often becomes exasperated and loses his temper.

What suggestions would Curwin and Mendler give Mr. Gonzales to help with Sara's misbehavior?

Case 3: Joshua Clowns and Intimidates

Joshua, larger and louder than his classmates, always wants to be the center of attention, which he accomplishes through a combination of clowning and intimidation. He makes wise remarks, talks back (smilingly) to the teacher, utters a variety of sound-effect noises such as automobile crashes and gunshots, and makes limitless sarcastic comments and put-downs of his classmates. Other students will not stand up to him, apparently fearing his verbal and physical aggression. His teacher, Miss Pearl, has come to her wit's end.

What do you find in Curwin and Mendler's work that might help Miss Pearl deal with Joshua?

Case 4: Tom Is Hostile and Defiant

Tom has appeared to be in his usual foul mood ever since arriving in class. On his way to sharpen his pencil, he bumps into Frank, who complains. Tom tells him loudly to shut up. Miss Baines, the teacher, says, "Tom, go back to your seat." Tom wheels around and says heatedly, "I'll go when I'm damned good and ready!"

How would Curwin and Mendler have Miss Baines deal with Tom?

QUESTIONS AND ACTIVITIES

1. In small groups, conduct practice situations in which classmates act as students who make hurtful comments to you, the teacher. Begin with the examples given here and explore new ones you have seen or think might occur. Take turns being the teacher and responding to the comments in some of the ways Curwin and Mendler suggest.

   Example 1
   TEACHER: Jonathan, I'd like to see that work finished before the period ends today.
   JONATHAN: [*Sourly*] Fine. Why don't you take it and finish it yourself if that's what you want?
   TEACHER:

   Example 2
   TEACHER: Desirée, that's the second time you've broken our rule about profanity. I'd like to speak with you after class.
   DESIRÉE: No thanks. I've seen enough of your scrawny butt for one day.
   TEACHER:

   Example 3
   TEACHER: Marshall, I'd like for you to get back to work, please.
   MARSHALL: [*Says nothing but nonchalantly makes a finger signal at the teacher. Other students see it and snicker.*]
   TEACHER:

   Compose additional occurrences. Practice de-escalating the confrontations without becoming defensive, fighting back, or withdrawing your request.

2. Explore Scenario 1 or 2 in Appendix I. Discuss how Curwin and Mendler would have Mrs. Miller or Mr. Platt respond to the situation encountered.

3. One of the suggestions given for motivating students who are difficult to motivate was "Make your class activities events that students look forward to. Make them wonder what might happen next." For a selected grade level, brainstorm ways of complying with this suggestion.

REFERENCES AND RECOMMENDED READINGS

Curwin, R. (1980). Are your students addicted to praise? *Instructor, 90*, 61–62.

———. (1992). *Rediscovering hope: Our greatest teaching strategy*. Bloomington, IN: National Educational Service.

———. (1993). The healing power of altruism. *Educational Leadership, 51*(3), 36–39.

Curwin, R., & Mendler, A. (1980). *The discipline book: A complete guide to school and classroom management*. Reston, VA: Reston Publishing.

———. (1984). High standards for effective discipline. *Educational Leadership, 41*(8), 75–76.

———. (1988a). *Discipline with dignity*. Alexandria, VA: Association for Supervision and Curriculum Development.

———. (1988b). Packaged discipline programs: Let the buyer beware. *Educational Leadership, 46*(2), 68–71.

———. (1992). *Discipline with dignity* [Workshop participants handout]. Rochester, NY: Discipline Associates.

Mendler, A., & Curwin, R. (1983). *Taking charge in the classroom*. Reston, VA: Reston Publishing.

Toward Building a Personal System of Discipline

The culminating purpose of this book is to help users develop personal systems of discipline that meet the needs of their students while remaining consonant with each teacher's personality, philosophy, and preferred style of teaching. To help achieve that purpose, Part III includes the following chapters:

CHAPTER 11

Classrooms That Encourage Good Behavior

As we move now toward building unique systems of discipline attuned to student and teacher realities, it is well to remember that in classroom discipline an ounce of prevention is worth considerably more than a pound of cure. Once misbehavior has occurred, even the best corrective techniques will disrupt teaching and erode feelings and relationships. Of course, misbehavior cannot be eliminated entirely; it occurs even in the best classes. But it can be kept to a minimum when teachers organize their classrooms to promote good behavior. The goal therefore is to establish classrooms that are warm and nuturing while they are also efficient and marked by high levels of achievement. A number of tactics for establishing such classrooms are examined in this chapter, within three broad categories referred to as the *person component*, the *management component*, and the *teacher component*.

THE PERSON COMPONENT

The *person component* has to do with students and how they are treated. Students who feel secure seldom cause much trouble, except for talking and laughing when they shouldn't. But as William Glasser (Chapter 8) and Richard Curwin and Allen Mendler (Chapter 10) noted in their models, a great many of today's students have low self-image and little interest in school. Their behavior—all too frequently misbehavior—reflects their attempts to protect or bolster their sense of self.

Strengthening Student Self-Concept

Teachers can do much to strengthen student self-concept, generally by routinely (1) giving each student regular personal attention, (2) making sure that each student experiences success in learning, and (3) helping students receive recognition for their accomplishments. At the same time teachers must make sure that failure, rejection, and humiliation have no place in their classrooms. As teachers enhance student self-concept, they simultaneously facilitate learning and reduce student misbehavior.

Personal Attention from the Teacher.   Most of us, when thinking back on the teachers we liked best, recall that those teachers gave us much personal attention. They acknowledged us, spoke with us, encouraged us, sometimes pushed us, and enjoyed the improvements we made. One result of their efforts was to make us see ourselves as worthwhile. We felt we belonged, were capable, and that someone important cared about us. As a result, we came to believe more strongly in ourselves.

What those fine teachers did was not especially difficult. They merely treated us as all students want to be treated—with attention, encouragement, and support. At the same time, those teachers managed to get across the message that it was not acceptable for us to be second-rate. They somehow encouraged us to excel.

Ensuring Genuine Success.   People can often be made to think they are successful when honestly they are not. Students can be told they are "really learning" or "behaving great" when the opposite is true. Teachers sometimes say such things to try to keep students motivated. But any sense of success that results from inaccurate praise is short-lived, for sooner or later experience will bring out the truth.

That is why *genuine success* is necessary for students—success based on true accomplishment, significant improvement, and efforts fully given. One of the most important tasks of teachers is to teach so that students experience genuine success regularly. That can be accomplished by (1) setting realistic goals and using them as clear targets; (2) employing a curriculum that builds competence; (3) providing good direction, urging, and help; (4) using effective instructional materials; and (5) teaching students how they are expected to behave.

Clear Goals as Targets.   In order to facilitate success, goals must be clearly understood, attainable, and seen as worthwhile by the students. Discussions should be held to make sure these criteria are met; if they are not, the goals should be changed accordingly. Time lines and checkpoints can be established to monitor progress toward goals that take time to reach. These milestones show students that they are improving, and this helps keep them motivated.

Curriculum for Competence.   A good curriculum leads to attainment of worthwhile goals—that is, competence in important matters—as opposed to hit-and-miss activities that fill time but lead nowhere. A sound curriculum often builds new learnings atop old ones, which helps students see that they are becoming steadily more competent. Students should note their progress frequently and should be acknowledged for improvements they make.

Direction, Urging, and Help. Many students are neither self-directed nor self-controlled and will not work well on their own even in the best activities. In such cases teachers must monitor, guide, urge, help, and otherwise encourage quality work. This helping role is very important and should not be overlooked. Reality teaches us that many students need a considerate and positive taskmaster to help them learn well in school.

Effective Instructional Materials. Good instructional materials enliven learning by making the subject interesting and understandable. They provide extensions, examples, illustrations, problems, and entertainment. They allow students to explore far afield and help them apply new learnings. There is no way most students can visit the Amazon jungle, the Pyramids, Antarctica, or the Laplanders of Finland. They cannot see molecules, solar systems, or the inner workings of nuclear reactors. Yet they deal with such topics regularly. Instructional materials help them do so with understanding and success.

Teaching Students How to Behave. Teachers usually take for granted that students know how to behave properly, and indeed that may be true in most cases. Nevertheless, it has become increasingly evident that student behavior is improved when teachers demonstrate exactly how they expect students to behave in the classroom—academically and socially—and when students are given practice demonstrating those behaviors through guided activities and role playing.

Building Esprit de Corps. Esprit de corps, or group spirit, strengthens the learning environment through stimulation, direction, sense of purpose, enjoyment, and desire to work for the benefit of the group.

Regrettably, no precise formula exists for building esprit de corps, though it is known to be affected by the teacher's enthusiasm, personal attention to students, Golden Rule concern, enjoyability of the curriculum, and a sense of group purpose. Often, classes with esprit de corps have a major goal to accomplish, such as a contest to win or a performance to stage. But such is not always the case. Sometimes personalities simply mesh so that the class members take genuine delight in group accomplishment. This is not to say, however, that esprit de corps occurs entirely spontaneously. Teachers can do several things to encourage it, as the following paragraphs indicate.

A Sense of Togetherness. A first step is to work toward an understanding that the class is a unit that lives and works together, that all members are striving toward a common goal, that all face similar obstacles, that all benefit from helping each other, that all lose something when any member is unsuccessful, and that all can take justifiable pride in the accomplishments of the group.

Contrast that group view with an individualistic view, in which the successful student is prized and rewarded while the unsuccessful is slighted and disparaged. The unsuccessful soon begins to give up and stop participating, which produces an uncomfortable sense of failure for the teacher, or else becomes actively disruptive, which hinders class learning and makes the teacher miserable.

To foster a sense of togetherness, the teacher should continually talk with the class about what they can accomplish as a group, how they will deal with the problems they encounter as a group, and how they will work together to get the best achievement possible for every individual. In order to bring this about, responsibilities are given and shared, students are encouraged to speak of their concerns while the class attempts to find solutions, and the teacher draws students into the ongoing work of the class.

Purpose in Class Activities.   Sense of purpose grows with student understanding of what is to be accomplished and how it is to be done. Specific short-range goals are helpful, such as completing a class mural by Friday, having every student get at least 90 percent correct on the vocabulary test, or even getting the six math problems completed correctly by the end of the class period. Short-term specific goals are vastly preferable to vague, long-range goals such as enjoying life more, passing the final test at the end of the year, or making a better living later in life.

It should be noted that sense of purpose is not dependent simply on the enjoyability of activities. It is dependent—at least for those students beyond primary grades—on students' having a fairly good understanding of the importance of the new learnings in their immediate lives. Students resent busy work unless it is made very interesting. Even then, they know it does not serve an educational purpose.

Public Recognition.   Group spirit is greatly enhanced through anticipation of public exposition. The kindergarten class puts on its annual Thanksgiving feast, to which parents are invited. The children work eagerly to make paper costumes to wear, complete artwork for decorations, and learn songs about Thanksgiving to sing to their parents. The general science class holds its semiannual science fair. Students work enthusiastically on projects, all of which will be displayed. The physical education department presents its recreational sports night for the public. Students take pride in performing for the audience rhythmic exercises, collaborative games, and tumbling. Events such as these are often reported in the local newspapers and occasionally on television. As students anticipate public recognition, their behavior becomes more purposeful and responsible. Sense of success grows and, along with it, self-concept.

Of course, only a small portion of a semester's or year's work can be shown in exhibitions, but recognition can also be furnished in the classroom. The following show how some teachers provide recognition for their students.

Chart Group Gains.   Gains and other improvements shown by the class as a whole can be depicted graphically. Many elementary classes demonstrate progress through time lines made of string or paper and placed high along the walls. Some make murals that illustrate activities and accomplishments. Elementary and secondary classes can keep class diaries with entries decided on by the class. This provides a documented history of class activities and accomplishments, which students very much enjoy reading later in the year.

Chart Personal Gains.   Charts showing individual progress also motivate student effort. These charts are not to be displayed in the classroom if they show any student in a derogatory light, but all students may keep them in personal folders to be seen by teacher and parents. Such charts can indicate attainment of objectives, amount of work attempted and completed, percentage of correct responses, and the like. Parents react well to such documentation, which demonstrates the teacher's plans and efforts on behalf of their child.

Inform Parents.   Student motivation usually rises when the teacher informs parents regularly about their child's success, not just the lack thereof. This information can be provided through student communication with parents, teacher communication with parents, and other materials that show student progress. In order to help students better report to parents, at the end of the day for elementary students and the end of the week for secondary students, teachers should take a few minutes to review what the class has accomplished. Students can then relay this information to their parents.

Systematic communication from teacher to parents is also excellent for publicizing group and individual success. Communication takes time but pays good dividends. Teachers can send notes home with students, prepare occasional newsletters, and make very brief telephone calls. In all cases, the purpose is to convey accomplishment and success, not to speak of problems. Of course, problems must be dealt with, too, but in separate communications.

Parents are always eager to see samples of their child's work, including worksheets, written assignments, and test results. But teachers are well advised to carefully check any work they send home. Teacher errors or omissions are almost certain to be noticed by parents, and one small mistake may erode respect.

Share in the Classroom.   Students are motivated by having peers recognize their efforts and accomplishments. Attention for every student can come from oral presentations, demonstrations, and displays of work. Some students are hesitant at first to participate, but with gentle encouragement most overcome their reticence.

Produce a Class Newsletter.   Many classes enjoy producing a monthly or quarterly newsletter that explains projects, contains creative student work, and presents announcements of displays and performances. The tone of the newsletter is best when it is kept businesslike. Issues should include all students' names in one place or another. The newsletters can be sent to administrators, parents, other community members, and even at times to organizations and businesses. Local newspapers usually show interest in them. The positive attention that results does much for everyone concerned.

THE MANAGEMENT COMPONENT

The *management component* involves the treatment of students and the organization, delivery, and monitoring of instructional programs. In well-managed classrooms students work as intended without being cajoled by the teacher. Disruptions are minimal, and little conflict occurs. Students learn, and teachers feel successful, even rewarded. Poorly managed classrooms, on the other hand, are often in turmoil. Unproductive noise abounds. Students are dissatisfied, and they misbehave. Teachers labor under stress and continual frustration. Since good management increases efficiency, purpose, and proper behavior, teachers are well advised to give attention to the following elements of management.

Managing the Classroom Climate

Climate refers to the *feeling tone* that prevails in the classroom. This feeling tone is a composite of attitudes, emotions, values, and relationships. All teachers are aware of its existence and, when visiting a classroom, can almost always tell whether the climate is good or bad.

A poor classroom climate tends to be chaotic and disorganized or else cold, unfriendly, and threatening. Humor is likely to be absent and is often replaced by sarcasm and animosity. Such climates depress learning. Although a threatening environment may cause students to work under duress, such an atmosphere may also make them dislike both teacher and school. When coldly and rigidly controlled, students fear making errors. They obey the rules only to prevent teachers' taking reprisal against them.

In contrast, a good classroom climate is warm, supportive, and pleasant. It is friendly and filled with good nature and acceptance. It is encouraging, helpful, and nonthreatening. Such a climate encourages productive work and promotes a sense of enjoyment and accomplishment. Cynthia, a second-grade teacher, describes how she attempts to set the tone in her classroom.

> "I begin the year with a discussion about my expectations for the year. I tell the children that I consider them my 'school family.' I explain that just as in any family we might not always agree on everything, nonetheless I will always care about them. I say that each and every one of them is very special and important to me and that I want them to have the best possible school year.
>
> "Because they are so important to me, I will not tolerate any cruelty or unkindness to each other. I expect them to be the best behaved and well-mannered class in the entire school, both in the classroom and on the playground. I tell them that good behavior is really just good manners, because it shows respect for others, whether children or adults. I also go over the Golden Rule, and I make a bulletin board on that theme. I refer to the Golden Rule as our class motto. That is the only rule we have in the class, and I discuss with them how it covers everything. If you don't want to be called names, then don't call other people names. If you

want people to listen to you, then be sure to listen to others. And most important, if you want to have friends, then be a friend.

"The children seem to understand and accept all of this very well. They see it as a fair and sensible way to do things, and I think it helps them know they have a teacher who cares about them."

Human Relations Skills and Classroom Climate

Human relations skills improve the quality of classroom interactions, thereby contributing to a positive atmosphere. In particular, three groups of human relations skills merit understanding and implementation: (1) general human relations skills, (2) human relations skills with students, and (3) human relations skills with parents.

General Human Relations Skills.   Four general human relations skills serve well in almost all situations. They are (1) friendliness, (2) positive attitude, (3) ability to listen, and (4) ability to compliment genuinely.

Friendliness.   Friendliness is a trait everyone admires, yet many of us have difficulty displaying it, especially when we are threatened or in the company of people we dislike. Yet with small effort we can show friendliness even toward people who displease us—by smiling, speaking gently, addressing them by name, asking how they are, asking about their family and work, and so on. When we behave in this way, we find that others begin to respond similarly.

Positive Attitude.   A *positive attitude* means that we focus on the brighter side of things. When dealing with problems, we look for solutions rather than lamenting obstacles or finding fault in others. We refrain from complaining, backbiting, and gossiping. When we speak positively, others begin to do so as well.

Ability to Listen.   The *ability to listen* is a trait we admire in others but often find lacking in ourselves. Most of us would rather talk than listen. Yet listening produces so many desirable outcomes that all teachers should cultivate the habit. Listening communicates genuine interest in the other person. This essential first step in establishing good relationships shows that we value the other person's opinions, and it improves the quality of communication by permitting a true exchange of ideas.

Ability to Compliment Genuinely.   The *ability to compliment genuinely* is a behavior that receives relatively little attention in human relations. It nevertheless has considerable power. Many of us, having seen compliments used falsely to curry favor, are reluctant to compliment others. Still, it is obvious that we all like to receive compliments. Weigh your attitude toward people who compliment you against those who do not (or who give you unsolicited "constructive criticism"). With which of the two would you rather work and socialize?

As you learn to give compliments, however, you must make sure they are genuine. It helps if you make your compliment explicit. Rather than say, "Your ideas are brilliant," you might say, "Your explanation of the Mesopotamian lifestyle was very clear." On a more personal level, rather than saying, "Hey, looking great today!" you might say, "That color surely suits you."

Human Relations Skills with Students.   The general skills of human relations apply to everyone in all situations. When working with students, however, there are three additional human relations skills that teachers should employ: (1) giving regular attention, (2) showing continual willingness to help, and (3) modeling courtesy and good manners.

Giving Regular Attention.   Giving *regular attention* to students does much to build trust and enlist cooperation. Attention should be given to all students equally, not just to favorites and those who misbehave.

Showing Continual Willingness to Help.   *Continual willingness to help* is a trait much appreciated in teachers. Students gravitate to helpful teachers, tend to admire them, and usually remember them with respect years later. You hear students say, "Yeah, Miss Smith expected a lot, but she really tried to help every one of us."

Modeling Courtesy and Good Manners.   You should make a point to exemplify in your own behavior the *courtesy and good manners* that you hope to see in your students. You should be genteel, even when they are boorish. You should always remember your manners, especially when they forget theirs. If you want students to live by the Golden Rule, your behavior must illustrate the Golden Rule in practice.

Human Relations Skills with Parents.   Teachers have a responsibility to communicate with parents. Many teachers use this responsibility to advantage while others avoid it, believing either that parents don't care or that it's not worth the effort. Yet good communication usually brings increased parental support. For building stronger relationships with parents, teachers should employ the general skills of human relations described earlier as well as four others: (1) communicating regularly, (2) communicating clearly, (3) describing expectations, and (4) emphasizing the child's progress while downplaying the child's shortcomings.

Communicating Regularly.   *Communicating regularly* with parents is accomplished through notes, telephone calls, and newsletters. It shows respect for parents and interest in their child, and it causes parents to hold teachers in high regard.

Communicating Clearly.   *Communicating clearly* is accomplished by bearing in mind that most parents do not understand educational jargon such as "critical thinking" or "cognitive levels," nor do they recognize acronyms such as SAT, IEP, or GATE. It is also wise to avoid involved sentence structure and the use of big words where little ones suffice. In short, make sure your messages to parents are clear, simple, and to the point.

Describing Expectations. *Describing expectations* is accomplished by outlining for the parent what your program is and explaining what their child is involved in and supposed to do, how you will evaluate, what you require concerning homework, and what their role at home is to be. Most parents like to know this information.

Emphasizing Progress. Always remember one thing: Parents don't like to hear their child criticized. Criticism is a sure way to alienate parents at once. *Emphasizing progress* is a better approach. Where shortcomings exist, call them new learnings that you and the child are working on.

Conferencing with Parents. All teachers must conference with parents, routinely or when difficulties arise. Such conferences produce anxiety on both sides. Teachers fear criticism of their program, judgment, ways of teaching, or means of dealing with students. Parents don't want to hear about faults in their children, which they internalize as faults in themselves.

However, the purpose of parent conferencing is to improve the overall success of the child. If you keep that essential point in mind, and if you prepare adequately for the conference, you will find that most meetings with parents are pleasant and productive.

Preparing for the Parent Conference. Careful preparation is important to the success of the conference. Remember to do these things:

1. Have the student's strengths and needs clearly in mind.
2. Prepare an attractive folder with the student's name on it.
3. Include in the folder a summary of your program, showing work completed and work yet to be done.
4. Include samples of the student's work.
5. Have available grades and tests that back up your evaluation.
6. Anticipate questions parents are most likely to ask.
   How does my child get along with others?
   Does my child cause problems?
   Is my child progressing as well as expected?
   What are my child's specific needs?
   Is there anything you want me to do to help?

Once you have made your preparation, free your mind to concentrate on conducting the conference professionally.

1. Put yourself in the parent's place. Be tactful and polite.
2. Greet the parent in a friendly, relaxed manner.
3. Sit side by side with the parent at a table rather than on opposite sides of a desk.

4. Begin by chatting about the student as a worthwhile person. Reassure the parent by mentioning good traits.

5. Guide the parent through the student's file, commenting on samples of work included. Refer to tests and grades if appropriate.

6. Encourage the parent to talk. Listen carefully and be accepting. Do not argue or criticize; this causes resentment. Parents cannot be objective about their child.

7. Throughout the conference, make sure the parent sees that you want the best education for the child.

8. End the conference by describing your plans for the student's future progress. Earnestly request the parent's support. Thank the parent for meeting with you to talk about the child.

On Giving Advice to Parents.   Be careful about giving parents advice on matters in which you have no expertise. Limit advice to academics and normal behaviors that affect learning. If parents ask you about matters outside of what you are trained to do, refer them to the school nurse, psychologist, or other expert. If they ask you about study time at home, suggest that they stipulate a specific place for doing homework with no distractions and that they talk with the child about schoolwork. If they ask about how to control misbehavior at home, tell them only what you insist on in school—sticking to a few important rules, invoking reasonable consequences when the rules are followed and broken, maintaining open communication, and showing that the child is wanted, loved, and respected.

Managing Classroom Routines

Generally speaking, effective teachers have learned to put into place classroom routines that minimize disruption while maximizing productive work. Keith, a secondary math teacher, describes an opening routine he uses to good advantage and shares some related views.

> "It is important to me for things to run smoothly. I begin the period with a one-minute timed exercise. The students know I will quickly say 'Go,' and if they don't have their pencils, scratch paper, and test sheet ready they are out of luck—they can try again the next day.
>
> "The subject matter is very important to me. Assignments are to be completed. If they are not, a note goes home, filled out by the student, stating what was not completed and why. The work must be made up on their own time. I go over all the assignments ahead of time so students know exactly what is expected. They know the schedule of tests and what they have to do to earn their grades. This makes them responsible for their own grades.
>
> "Occasionally, I receive a call from a parent whose child has received a failing grade for the first time ever. Their anger quickly subsides when I remind them

that the child knew exactly what work was required for a good grade, and I explain how little the child did.

"This may sound harsh, but I treat the students with great respect and courtesy. I always say, "Please" and "Thank you" and "Excuse me." I admit my mistakes and tell the students I am sorry. They reflect my example. We are courteous, we are considerate, we have an enjoyable time, and best of all, we get our work done."

Routines, the commonplace procedures and chores inherent in day-to-day activities, are far more important to discipline than is generally recognized. Well-managed routines permit students to know exactly what they are supposed to do and thus reduce dead time that fosters misbehavior. Teachers should establish routines for (1) opening and ending class activities, (2) using materials, (3) handling completed work, (4) using student assistants, and (5) providing assistance to students at work.

Opening and Closing Activities. In many classrooms students waste several minutes before starting work. They come into the classroom talking, are slow to take their seats, continue talking once seated, and do not stop until the teacher's insistent voice is heard above the noise. This condition is corrected by establishing routine procedures to follow upon entering the room. Generally, it is best to have students begin work immediately. This can be established as one of the class rules. Secondary teachers may write an assignment on the board. Students enter, sit down, and begin work within one minute after the bell. Elementary teachers may have students write in journals, read silently from library books, or do math or vocabulary exercises while roll is taken. Very young children may begin by playing with instructional toys or sitting quietly while the teacher or aide reads a story. In all cases, students are helped to begin schoolwork at once rather than talk and fool around.

It is equally important to establish routine procedures for ending class activities. In classes such as art, shop, and physical education, a cleanup time is required. In practically all classes, materials are to be re-stored, completed work is to be filed, and everything is to be readied for dismissal. Students should be taught to follow established routines on cue.

Using Materials. Inefficient classrooms permit wasted time while students obtain materials and replace them after use. Procedures should be established for quickly obtaining needed materials. If materials are distributed, several students should help, each distributing materials to five or six other students. If students are to get their own materials, they should be able to go to convenient shelves or cupboards without crowding or waiting in line. Pencil sharpening can be especially distracting. Many teachers permit pencil sharpening only before class begins. Others keep containers of sharpened pencils at hand; students can exchange their dull pencils for sharp ones when necessary.

At the end of the period, materials should be replaced as efficiently as they were obtained. Students are taught exactly what to do and are allowed a minimum of time to replace the materials.

Handling Completed Work.   Clear procedures should spell out what students are to do with completed work. If students are allowed to come individually to the teacher and hand in their work, there is likelihood of noise, wasted time, and disturbance to students still working. For that reason, many teachers use more efficient procedures such as having students place completed work on the corner of their desks or tables or in conveniently located baskets. The work is then collected by a teacher, aide, or student assistant.

Using Student Assistants.   It is strongly recommended that class members be assigned duties to help with routine procedures. Not only does this assist teachers, but it also improves student attitude. At the secondary level, student assistants are most useful for distributing and collecting materials and for replenishing and taking care of supplies. They are frequently used as well for simple checking of papers, keeping records, typing, and duplicating. At the elementary level, teachers often assign tasks to every student in the class—president, flag salute leader, lights monitor, window monitor, news and weather reporter, messenger, line monitor, group or table leader, plant and pet caretaker, materials monitor, audiovisual assistant, visitor greeter, and so on. There are plenty of jobs for all students, and all should participate.

Providing Assistance to Students at Work.   As you recall from the Jones model (Chapter 7), teachers tend to be inefficient in providing help to students doing seatwork. In particular, they spend too much time with each student who raises a hand, thus allowing other students to sit for several minutes doing nothing or getting into trouble. Jones provided excellent advice on how to give help efficiently. As you may remember, his suggestions included the following:

1. Make sure students know what they are supposed to do and how they are supposed to do it.
2. Provide a written model to which students can refer.
3. Circulate among students to check for progress and errors.
4. When students raise their hands, give them direct help and then move away quickly, preferably in 20 seconds or less. Do not let students become psychologically dependent on your presence before they will do their work.
5. Do not succumb to the temptation to reteach individual students or take them through question-and-answer tutorials. If several students are having the same difficulty, reteach the concept or process to the entire class.

THE TEACHER COMPONENT

While all teachers can ultimately develop good discipline techniques, some do so only through considerable effort. Others seem to give discipline little attention, yet their classes run smoothly with few difficulties. Such teachers are often called "naturals," though they may vary considerably in the way they teach. One thing they have in common is that they seem to anticipate problems and take steps to prevent them.

The *teacher component* of classroom management focuses on these teachers with good preventive discipline. They seem to be of three rather distinct types, which we will call (1) well-liked teachers, (2) efficient teachers, and (3) expert teachers. The three types are certainly not exclusive. Not only is there overlap, but some teachers vacillate between types from day to day, especially with regard to efficiency.

Well-liked teachers are sought out by students because they provide individual attention, interesting activities, a relaxed atmosphere, and an abiding sense of humor. Good academic learning can occur in their classes, but learning can also be mediocre or poor. Students behave well because they want to please the teacher and because they want the teacher to like them in return.

Efficient teachers plan, organize, instruct, and manage well, leaving nothing to chance. Achievement tends to be high in their classes, but those teachers are not necessarily well liked, especially when efficiency takes precedence over stimulation and caring. As students are often uncomfortable in classrooms that contain little personal warmth, they do not enjoy their educational experience. They usually behave well because there is little opportunity to do otherwise in tightly structured programs backed by strong rules and consequences.

Expert teachers display the best qualities of the other two types. These teachers are efficient yet flexible. They show that they care about students. They do what they can to make learning interesting, exciting, and satisfying. Their students learn well, admire and respect them, and usually like them personally. Good behavior occurs because of the teacher's reasonable standards and personal concern for the students, which makes students want to please the teacher in return.

How to Become an Expert Teacher

If you see yourself as well-liked but feel you need to be more efficient, work on procedures that keep students on task. Add more structure to your lessons, concentrate on helpful feedback, and keep your teaching as free from disruptions as possible. But remember that while expert teachers organize well, they are not slaves to efficiency. They remain flexible in accord with circumstances.

As much as anything else, expert teachers provide stimulating lessons. They add mystery, suspense, and drama to their teaching. They provide active involvement. While doing so, they use communication skills to build human relations, which contribute to that most desirable of all classroom qualities, esprit de corps.

APPLICATION EXERCISES

1. Examine this contribution from teacher Colleen Meagher, and identify management that has to do with physical environment, classroom climate, and routines.

"I arrange things so that the daily schedule flows more smoothly and I don't have to give unnecessary directions. Transitions are timed with a kitchen timer, and the class is challenged to see if they can quietly clean up and prepare for the next activity before it rings. I allow the students to work in cooperative groups and at times allow them to talk quietly and move about the room. Traffic patterns are clearly defined. Desks are arranged in a U-shape facing the chalkboard, so I have eye contact and easy access to all students."

2. Mr. Tales has prepared the following note to send to parents describing his goals for the class:

We will be working to maximize self-image through both traditional and newer affective approaches. Intended learnings will be stated in terms of experiences rather than behaviorally. Assessment of progress will be accomplished observationally. Your input into this process will be valued.

Mr. Tales asks you to look over the note and make suggestions before he sends it out. What do you suggest to him?

3. For a grade, subject, and topic you select, describe how you would manage materials distribution and collection, work routines, and assistance for students during independent or group work.

4. For a grade or subject you select, describe what you would want to communicate to parents at the beginning of school and how you would communicate with them. Be realistic in terms of time and effort required.

5. You are preparing for a conference with the father of James, a delightfully humorous and well-intentioned boy who is barely passing his course work. His study habits are poor in school and, you suspect, nonexistent at home. The principal has informed you that James's father requires that James work in their upholstery shop after school hours. How will you approach the father? What will you say?

6. Examine Scenario 1 or 2 in Appendix I. From what you can see in the scenario you select, what changes would you make so that better behavior might be encouraged, as opposed to enforced?

REFERENCES AND RECOMMENDED READINGS

Angell, A. (1991). Democratic climates in elementary classrooms: A review of theory and research. *Theory and Research in Social Education, 19*, 241–266.

Augustine, D., Gruber, K., & Hanson, L. (1990). Cooperation works! *Educational Leadership, 47*, 4–7.

Banbury, M., & Hebert, C. (1992). Do you see what I mean? language in classroom interactions. *Teaching Exceptional Children, 24*, 24–28.

Bartell, J. (1992). Starting from scratch. *Principal, 72*, 13–14.

Brophy, J. (1987). Synthesis on strategies for motivating students to learn. *Educational Leadership, 45*, 40–48.

Brophy, J., & Putnam, J. (1979). Classroom management in the elementary school. In D. L. Duke (Ed.), *Classroom management: The seventy-eighth yearbook of the National Society for the Study of Education* (pp. 182–216). Chicago: University of Chicago Press.

Cangelosi, J. (1993). *Classroom management strategies: Gaining and maintaining students' cooperation* (2nd ed.). White Plains, NY: Longman.

Canter, L., & Canter, M. (1992). *Assertive Discipline: Positive behavior management for today's classroom.* (2nd ed.). Santa Monica, CA: Canter & Associates.

Cawthorne, B. (1981). *Instant success for classroom teachers, new and substitute teachers in grades K through 8.* Scottsdale, AZ: Greenfield.

Charles, C., & Senter, G. (1995). *Elementary classroom management* (2nd ed.). White Plains, NY: Longman.

Corno, L. (1992). Encouraging students to take responsibility for learning and performance. *Elementary School Journal, 93*, 69–83.

Emmer, E., Evertson, C., & Anderson, L. (1980). Effective classroom management at the beginning of the school year. *Elementary School Journal, 80*, 219–231.

Evertson, C. (1989a). Classroom organization and management. In M. Reynolds (Ed.), *Knowledge base for the beginning teacher.* Oxford: Pergamon Press.

———. (1989b). Improving elementary classroom management: A school-based training program for beginning the year. *Journal of Educational Research, 83*, 82–90.

Evertson, C., Emmer, E., Clements, B., Sanford, J., & Worsham, M. (1989). *Classroom management for elementary teachers.* Englewood Cliffs, NJ: Prentice-Hall.

Evertson, C., & Harris, A. (1992). What we know about managing classrooms. *Educational Leadership, 49*(7), 74–78.

Fraser, B., & O'Brien, P. (1985). Student and teacher perceptions of the environment of elementary school classrooms. *Elementary School Journal, 85*(5), 567–580.

Jones, V., & Jones, L. (1990). *Comprehensive classroom management: Motivating and managing students.* Needham Heights, MA: Allyn & Bacon.

Kramer, P. (1992). Fostering self-esteem can keep kids safe and sound. *PTA Today, 17*(6), 10–11.

Latham, G. (1993). *Managing the classroom environment to facilitate effective instruction* [Six-part videotape in-service training program]. Logan, UT: P & T Ink.

Markoff, A. (1992). *Within reach: Academic achievement through parent-teacher communication.* Novato, CA: Academic Therapy Publications.

Novelli, J. (1990). Design a classroom that works. *Instructor, 100* (1), 24–27.

Schell, L., & Burden, P. (1992). *Countdown to the first day of school: A 60-day get-ready checklist for first-time teachers, teacher transfers, student teachers, teacher mentors, induction-program administrators, teacher educators* (NEA Checklist series). Washington, DC: National Education Association.

Sidman, M. (1989). *Coercion and its fallout.* Boston: Authors Cooperative.

Slavin, R. (1991). Synthesis of research on cooperative learning. *Educational Leadership, 48*, 71–82.

Weade, R., & Evertson, C. (1988). The construction of lessons in effective and less effective classrooms. *Teaching and Teacher Education, 4*(3), 189–213.

Weinstein, C. (1992). Designing the instructional environment: Focus on seating. In *Proceedings of selected research and development presentations at the Convention of the Association for Educational Communications and Technology.* ERIC Document Reproduction Service.

Wong, H., & Wong, R. (1991). *The first days of school: How to be an effective teacher.* Sunnyvale, CA: Harry K. Wong.

CHAPTER 12

Building a Personal System of Discipline

The culminating purpose of this book is to help you build an effective system of discipline that attends to the traits and needs of your students while remaining consonant with your own personality. In the past, teachers and students typically faced each other somewhat adversarially rather than cooperatively, but that condition no longer need pertain. Preceding chapters have shown how acceptable classroom behavior can be secured through noncoercive means so that energy and instructional time are conserved, personal relationships enhanced, and good morale maintained.

Thus, the primary question for teachers today is not whether they can bring about acceptable classroom behavior but rather how they might do so while meeting everyone's predominant needs. One might think the best approach would be to analyze the models presented in this book and select that which serves best. But as many teachers have discovered, prepackaged systems seldom serve as expected. For example, they find that behavior modification works well with the very young and certain behaviorally challenged students but not so well with older or rowdier students. Too, teachers grow tired of forever dispensing reinforcers and begin suspecting that their students work only for tangible rewards. Similarly, many teachers feel uneasy about Assertive Discipline. Most agree it is wonderfully organized and effective in controlling misbehavior, but some find it too harsh for young children, and teachers at all levels have questioned whether it is effective in helping students develop self-control and responsibility. And so it goes for all the established models: despite their marvelous attributes, they do not interface well with all groups and situations. Student backgrounds differ, as do language patterns, values, experiences, and support from home. Teachers differ, too. Any five at random are likely to have five distinct personalities, philosophies, sets of preferences, styles of communication, and ways of teaching. Given such a range of differences among environments, schools, students, and teachers, it is understandable that preorganized discipline programs seldom accomplish all that a teacher might hope.

For that reason, teachers do best to build personal systems of discipline tailored to their students, situations, and preferences. Preparing personal systems is not difficult. The various models contain a wealth of workable strategies and appealing techniques from which teachers can select to form a system that meets their particular needs.

BACKGROUND FOR BUILDING YOUR PERSONAL SYSTEM OF DISCIPLINE

Judith Schulman (1989) reports a teaching experience related by Michael, a new inner-city teacher with a master's degree in marine biology.

> My descent from innocence was swift and brutal. I was faced with classes populated by unruly students, gang members, and other children with only rudimentary scholastic skills. Convinced that with kindness and patience I could help them all if only the students saw my concern for them, and eager to disseminate my knowledge to the masses, I launched into my lessons. I typed up lab sheets [on a metric unit] explaining in detail what should be measured and in what units I wanted the measurements. The students were then assigned lab tables, paired off, and provided with metric sticks. What next ensued can only be described as pandemonium.
>
> My intention had been to visit with each group of students and answer any questions they might have. I also figured this would provide an excellent opportunity for me to get to know some of the students. Unfortunately, as I have found to occur with alarming frequency, intentions and reality often have nothing whatsoever to do with one another. (p. 4)

What Teachers Want

Teachers dread situations like that of Michael. They want students to be well behaved and keenly interested in learning. But since they rarely encounter such ideal groups, teachers search for a discipline system that accomplishes the following:

1. Prevents most misbehavior
2. Redirects misbehavior positively
3. Promotes trusting relationships between teacher and students
4. Is accepted as fair by students
5. Engenders parental support and assistance
6. Is efficient and easy to use

See if this list describes what you want in your system of discipline. If you need to modify the list, do so. You can use it to check quality while building your system.

What Teachers Know, and Don't Know, about Students

In order to serve as intended, a system of discipline must take student traits into account. Many of those traits are genetically controlled and are fairly well understood. But others are culturally determined and elusive. This is a time of rapid social change. Drug use has devastated a significant portion of the population. Poverty is increasing—it now affects one child in every four. The homeless are seen in almost every city. Tens of thousands of children live in single-parent homes, often with no parental supervision during the day. Inadequate nutrition and lack of health care are common. Grant and Sleeter (1989) report the following characteristics of students now entering public schools in the United States:

> 25% are from families living in poverty.
>
> 14% are children of teenage mothers.
>
> 15% are non-English-speaking immigrants.
>
> almost 30% are of color.
>
> 40% will live in a single-parent home before age 18.
>
> 25%–30% are latchkey children. (pp. 1–2)

Trends indicate that by the year 2020 one person of every three in the United States will be what we now call a minority (Sobol, 1990). Most of those people will exhibit cultural, social, and linguistic traits associated with lower school achievement, possibly exacerbating the so-called "achievement gap" that exists between certain groups (Hernandez, 1989). Poverty, which also depresses school achievement, exists in differing degrees. In 1987 it was reported that 48 percent of African Americans lived in poverty, compared to 42 percent for Latinos, 29 percent for other nonwhite groups, and 13 percent for whites (Slavin, Karweit, & Madden, 1989). On a numerical basis, twice as many white children live in poverty as all nonwhite groups combined (Hernandez, 1989, p. 15).

Accompanying the changes in social conditions is the disquieting fact that Americans no longer place as much value on education as they once did. Community support for schools has declined, as has parental insistence that children do well in school. Students now drop out in alarming numbers, while many of those who remain make little effort to learn.

This is not to say that teachers know nothing about their students. To the contrary, they know a great deal, especially about human traits that cut across social and economic groups, as indicated in the following paragraphs.

Primary Grades (Ages 4 to 9).   Kindergarten children come to school at the age of 4 or 5—still babies in many ways. They parallel play, talk to themselves, tire easily, get fussy, cry, and require frequent rest. They fall, sprawl, and crawl about the floor. They make little distinction between work and play, and they require close supervision. Some play well together; others are spoiled and expect to have their own way.

Teachers at this level usually establish two or three rules for behavior, knowing that those rules will be broken regularly. They spend much time reminding students of rules and proper behavior. This pattern continues into grades 1 and 2, with students gradually becoming socialized to school, learning to raise hands, stand in lines, and wait patiently.

At the primary level, students accept adult authority without question though they often try to circumvent it. They respond well to praise, affection, and personal attention.

Intermediate Grades (Ages 9 to 12).   As students move into grade 4 they are becoming much more independent, though they still want attention and affection from their teachers. Hugging may no longer be eagerly sought; holding hands with the teacher may take its place.

These students now recognize the need for rules and rule enforcement. They accept reasonable consequences for breaking rules, especially when others break them. They can help establish rules and consequences and are usually eager to discuss procedures of enforcement.

No longer is teacher authority blindly accepted. Students may argue, talk back, and drag their heels. But they are sure to complain if rules and consequences are not administered consistently and impartially.

Middle School Grades (Ages 12 to 14).   Behaving properly is difficult for students at the middle school level, and their teachers must have exceptional skill if they are to maintain control, teach well, build supportive relationships, and retain their own sanity.

Teaching these students is difficult for many reasons. Their bodily changes worry, perplex, excite, and dismay. New realities of an opposite sex stir and baffle. Psychological weaning from parents leaves them feeling lost and cut off. If that were not enough to contend with, they are required to adjust to new school organization, curriculum, and styles of teaching.

These factors provide devastating distractions to learning. Meanwhile, students are becoming increasingly rebellious and disposed to probing at outer boundaries of rules and customs. Their awe of the teacher has waned, but awe can be replaced with respect and affection for those who provide encouragement and support.

High School Grades (Ages 15 to 18).   The high school years mark a time of settling down, as most students begin to find themselves and reach a truce with their bodies and emotions. Some develop ideas of what they hope to do in the future. Others, lamentably, become further alienated from the educational mainstream.

A new level of relationship with adults becomes evident. For most students, the love-hate attitude of earlier years fades, while respect for adults grows as students recognize their own interdependence with the larger community.

Teachers should now deal with students on an adult-to-adult basis. This does not imply equal authority. The teacher is still in charge, but students assume greater responsibility for their own learning and behavior while looking upon teachers as guides and role models.

Persistent Annoyances

Teachers know they must contend with a cluster of persistent problems that sometimes drive them to distraction, such as the following:

1. *Tattling.* This is the elementary teacher's great exasperation. It makes teachers want to scold, but they do better to say, "We have a rule against tattling" or "Would you tell me about it at recess please?" or "Would you write it out for me so I can read it later?"
2. *The "cool" syndrome.* An extremely annoying means of seeking attention, this behavior emerges in preadolescence and blossoms during adolescence. It breaches limits without overt confrontation. It is shown in slight tardiness to class, a bit of back talk with a pleasant face, facial signals to other students, clothing of borderline acceptance, and intentionally misspoken answers to teacher questions. All this is reinforced by other students who admire the cool behavior but are not daring enough to try it themselves. Wise teachers, instead of getting drawn into controversy (from which the cool student backs off smilingly), deal with this problem through class discussions, personal talks with offending students, and requests for parental assistance.
3. *Cliques.* Endemic though certainly not limited to preadolescent girls, student cliques can be harmful to class morale. They exclude and demean, and they produce anger and jealousy. Cliques are most popular during years when emotions are fragile; their effects are therefore doubly damaging. Teachers should hold class discussions about this matter and solicit student input concerning its avoidance. They should also organize work groups so that the members of cliques are separated.
4. *Refusal to do or complete work.* This is seen at all grade levels but becomes chronic in middle school and high school. It may be part of the cool syndrome or may represent disengagement from school. Teachers have tried to improve the situation through punishments such as bad grades, only to conclude that adolescents can't be forced to do schoolwork. A more promising approach involves providing interesting topics and cooperative work groups that motivate students.

Reminders

Keep these thoughts in mind as you begin building your system of discipline: Students do misbehave. They do require discipline for positive social development and educational progress. You are the most important figure in establishing class discipline, but you need to involve students in its development and implementation. You will want to communicate your plan to parents and administrators. You may not enjoy all this, but it is one of the most important things you can do for your students and yourself.

As you implement your plan, remember that the best way to teach good behavior is through example. The personal standards you exhibit will be imitated to a surprising degree. If you are kind and respectful, students will tend to follow your lead; if you are negative and sarcastic, they will almost certainly behave that way, too. For professional satisfaction, you must have the opportunity to teach students who are attentive, cooperative, and appreciative. Your system of discipline will provide you with that opportunity. Follow Lee Canter's insistence on two basic rights in the classroom: (1) the students' right to learn in a caring atmosphere and (2) your right to teach without disruption.

BUILDING YOUR SYSTEM OF DISCIPLINE

Three Faces of Discipline

It is helpful to think of discipline as having three faces: (1) preventive, (2) supportive, and (3) corrective. The labels suggest the different but equally important aspects of classroom discipline to which you must give attention.

Preventive Discipline.   Preventing misbehavior is greatly preferable to having to deal with it after it has occurred. People once said that the best way to prevent classroom misbehavior is to provide a very interesting curriculum that involves students so deeply that they never think of misbehaving. Those same people, knowing that a curriculum of that sort can only occasionally be provided, simultaneously advised teachers to get their bluff in early so students wouldn't defy them. That advice may have been good in the past, but more is required for discipline today. Consider the following suggestions for *preventive discipline*:

- *Make your curriculum as worthwhile and enjoyable as possible.* Focus on valuable learnings, and provide enjoyable activities. Remember that students crave fun, belonging, freedom, power, and dignity.
- *Remain the ultimate authority in your classroom.* Be pleasant and helpful. Ask for student input and help. But the final decisions are yours, and you must accept responsibility for them.
- *With your students, make good rules for class conduct.* Keep the rules short, clear, and few in number. Discuss each rule thoroughly with students, then post the list in the room for reference and review.
- *Continually emphasize good manners and abidance by the Golden Rule.* Make plain from the outset that you care enough about your students to expect them to behave properly, show good manners, and never be cruel. Be

the best model you can by showing concern, etiquette, courtesy, and helpfulness. Discuss manners frequently and call attention to student improvements.

Supportive Discipline. All students at times become restive and subject to temptation. When signs of incipient misbehavior appear, bring *supportive discipline* into play. This facet of discipline assists students with self-control by helping them get back on task. Often only the student involved knows it has been used. The following tactics are suggested for supportive discipline:

- *Use signals directed to a student needing support.* Learn to catch students' eyes and use head shakes, frowns, and hand signals to guide them.

- *Use physical proximity when signals are ineffective.* Simply moving nearer students is usually more than enough to return their attention to work.

- *Show interest in student work.* Move alongside those who appear restless. Look at their work and ask cheerful questions or make favorable comments. Sometimes provide a light challenge: "You have done a great deal of this already. I bet you can't get five more done before we stop."

- *Restructure difficult work or provide help.* Watch for students who seem to be having difficulty. Give a hint, clue, or suggestion that gets them going. At times you may need to restructure an activity: change it in midstream, add excitement, or reduce the level of difficulty.

- *Inject humor into lessons that have become tiring.* Students place high value on humor; they enjoy its lift and respite from tension. A momentary break is all that is needed. You must be careful, though, that humor does not provoke horseplay that ruins the lesson.

- *Remove seductive objects.* A great variety of objects appears in the classroom—toys, comics, rubber bands, stuffed animals, notes, and various unmentionables. They intrigue students and subvert learning. If students do not put them away when asked, calmly take possession of the objects. Return them along with a few pointed comments at the end of the period or day.

- *Acknowledge good behavior in appropriate ways at appropriate times.* This should be done informally with nods, smiles, and words such as "Thanks," "Good," or "Keep it up." Compliment students when they show good effort, but be cautious about lauding them in front of their peers. Direct your compliments to the group when they are deserved.

- *Request good behavior.* Use suggestions, hints, and I-messages as students begin to drift toward misbehavior. Show that you recognize their discomfort: "You have worked so hard, and we are all getting tired. Please give me five more minutes of your best attention and we will complete this work."

Corrective Discipline.   Even the best efforts in preventive and supportive discipline cannot eliminate all misbehavior. When students violate rules, you must deal with the misbehavior expeditiously. *Corrective discipline* should neither intimidate students nor engage them in power struggles but rather should proceed as follows:

- *Stop the misbehavior.* It is best to put an immediate end to misbehavior rather than ignore it and hope it will go away. If the behavior is a gross violation of rules or decorum—fighting or loud swearing, for example—it should be squelched immediately: "Johnny, there is no swearing in this class!" or "Boys, sit down at once!"

- *Invoke a consequence appropriate to the misbehavior.* Since you have thoroughly discussed class rules and consequences, your students understand this procedure. You should remain calm and simply say, "Susan, you are not living up to our agreement, so you must sit at that table and complete your work by yourself."

- *Follow through consistently.* Make sure you invoke consequences the same way time after time. Being stern one day and lax the next leaves students confused and encourages them to test your rules. Don't let students talk you out of the consequence you have selected; if you do, they will certainly test you at every opportunity.

- *Redirect misbehavior in positive directions.* Ask offending students to return to work as agreed. If they resist, allow them to select from among optional work tasks that you suggest. Talk with them when you can about their behavior. Ask how you can help them get the most out of school yet not interfere with others.

- *Be ready to invoke an insubordination rule.* Students who refuse to comply with a reasonable consequence should go to in-school suspension until they are willing to fulfill the consequence.

Eight Steps to Personalized Discipline

Your preventive, supportive, and corrective techniques can provide a balanced approach that serves everyone comfortably. What remains is to tailor the system so it allows you to function naturally. You can accomplish this final task through eight steps.

1. *Clarify needs and tentatively set limits.* Make a list of your students' predominant traits and needs, then make a list of your own traits and needs. Envision behavior limits (what students should and/or should not do) that allow both sets of needs to be met. Consider matters such as talk, movement, noise, manners, self-control, effort, and beginning and completing work. If you have an especially strong need, such as for quiet or order, be up front about it and willing to ask for cooperation.

2. *On the first day, discuss with students behavior that will serve the class best.* Ask older students how they would prefer to work so that they can learn well under pleasant circumstances. Share your needs and explore procedures students find comfortable. Show that you are flexible and willing to compromise, but retain the right to veto suggestions that are not in the students' best interest.

3. *Together with students, write out rules and consequences for governing behavior in the classroom.* Make sure students understand the agreements and consider them fair.

4. *Establish a support system.* Inform your principal about your discipline plan and ask for support. Ask one or more fellow teachers if you can turn to them for assistance, should it be needed. Write out a description of your system and send it to parents. Tell them that the system is intended to provide the best learning opportunity for their children. Request their support. Ask that they sign a copy to indicate they understand and support your system.

5. *Decide what you will do regarding preventive and supportive discipline.* List ideas for building a positive classroom climate that will help students maintain self-control as they learn. Select activities that students consider interesting and valuable. Include topics about which you are excited and knowledgeable. Establish procedures for smooth flow between activities so that dead spots and confusion do not occur.

6. *Be the best possible model for your students.* Act as you would like them to act. Speak as you would like them to speak. Talk with them and show interest not only in their work but in them personally.

7. *When students have difficulty, misbehave, or refuse to work, invoke established consequences and/or discuss the matter with them.* Ask if they would like to talk privately. Ask how you might help them learn better and enjoy school more. Keep trying to provide a quality learning opportunity, even when students don't seem to appreciate your efforts.

8. *Evaluate and modify your system.* Continually assess your system in terms of its contribution to a positive, enjoyable climate, its ease of implementation, and its effectiveness in controlling misbehavior. If you teach third grade or higher, discuss your observations with students and ask for their input. Remain open to modifying your system when necessary.

One Teacher's System

How might a system look when prepared according to these guidelines? Each person's approach would be unique because of different needs, philosophies, personalities, and situations, but there would be similarities as well. Figure 12.1 shows a model prepared by Deborah Sund for use in her third-grade class; it is presented here with her permission. (Additional discipline plans of actual teachers at other levels and subjects are presented in Chapter 13.)

FIGURE 12.1 The Sund model, third grade

My Needs, Likes, and Dislikes

My Needs

1. *Orderly classroom appearance*: good room arrangement; materials neatly stored; interesting, well-thought-out displays.
2. *Structure and routines*: a set schedule that is flexibile and allows for improvisation when needed.
3. *Transitions*: smooth transitions between activities, with no wasted time.
4. *Attention*: student attention given for directions and to all speakers and instructional activities.
5. *Situationally appropriate behaviors*: quiet attention during instruction, considerate interaction during group activities, and so forth.

My Likes

1. *Enthusiasm* from me and my students.
2. *Warmth* as reflected in mutual regard among all individuals in the class.
3. *Positive, relaxed classroom environment* reflecting self-control, mutual helpfulness, and assumption of responsibility.

My Dislikes

1. *Inattention* to speaker, teacher, other adult, or class member.
2. *Excessive noise*: loud voices, inappropriate talking, and laughing.
3. *Distractions*: toys, unnecessary movement, poking, teasing, and so on.
4. *Abuse of property*: misusing, wasting, or destroying instructional materials.
5. *Unkind behavior*: verbal or physical abuse of others in the classroom.
6. *Rude conduct*: ridicule, sarcasm, and bad manners.
7. *Tattling.*

My Classroom Rules

The following are classroom rules I try to get my students to agree to:

1. *Be considerate of others at all times.* (Speak kindly. Be helpful. Don't bother others.)
2. *Do your best work.* (Get as much done as you can. Do your work neatly so that you can be proud of it. Don't waste time.)
3. *Use quiet voices in the classroom.* (Use regular speaking voices during class discussions. Speak quietly during cooperative work groups. Whisper at other times if you need help.)
4. *Use signals to request permission or receive help.* (I explain the signal systems for assistance, movement, restroom pass.)

I discuss these topics at length with students on the first day of school. I ask for their thoughts and suggestions. In the days after we have agreed to the rules and routines, I continue to give students prompts, cues, hints, and other assistance to help them internalize the rules.

Positive Consequences

As students follow the rules, they know they will routinely receive the following positive consequences:

1. Positive verbal feedback.
2. Positive nonverbal feedback (smiles, winks, nods, and pats).
3. Occasional tangible and privilege awards (stickers, marks, and favorite activities).
4. Positive reports to parents (notes and phone calls).

Negative Consequences

When students do not abide by the rules, they know they will routinely receive the following negative consequences:

1. "Pirate eyes": a stern glance, accompanied by a disappointed and puzzled expression.
2. Unapproving general comments: "I hear noise." "Some people are not listening."
3. Direct negative verbal feedback: "Gordon, you did not use the signal. Please use the signal."
4. Unfavorable reports to parents: note, call, or school conference.
5. In-class isolation: student separated from group but still in sight of teacher.
6. Student sent to principal or counselor or removed from the class.

My Discipline Measures

My Preventive Discipline Measures

I take the following steps to minimize the occurrence of behavior problems in my classroom:

1. Involve students in establishing class rules and assuming responsibility. In discussions I ask questions such as "What do you think happens when everyone tries to talk at the same time?" and "How do you like other people to speak to you?"
2. Make contact with parents as follows:
   Send letters outlining expectations and discipline system.
   Make short, positive phone calls to parents.
   Send home with children notes concerning good work and behavior.
3. Organize a classroom environment for best temperature, light, and comfort and with traffic patterns for efficient movement within the room.
4. Emphasize, model, and hold practice sessions on good manners, courtesy, and responsibility.
5. Provide a varied, active curriculum with opportunities for physical movement, singing, interaction, and times of quiet.
6. Provide a sense of consistency, familiarity, and security through structure and routines.

My Supportive Discipline Measures

In order to help my students support their own self-control, I use the following supportive measures:

1. Eye contact; facial expressions.
2. Physical proximity.
3. Reference to classroom rules.
4. Interest in individual students' work.
5. Modification of the lesson or routine if needed to increase interest or reduce anxiety.

My Corrective Discipline Measures

When my students misbehave, I use the following corrective measures:

1. Comment on misbehavior: "I hear talking. I don't like it. Everyone should be listening."
2. Emphatic imperative: "Stop that now!"
3. Isolation of the student from the group.
4. Removal of the student to the principal or counselor's office.
5. Parental contacts by telephone.

My Way of Maintaining a Positive Classroom Climate

I have found that a positive climate results in better feelings, more enjoyment, and ultimately better self-control for both the students and myself. The following are some of the things I do to maintain such a climate:

(continued)

FIGURE 12.1   *(continued)*

1. Respect each child as an individual who is entitled to a good education.
2. Look for the good or likable qualities in each child.
3. Acknowledge appropriate behavior, good work, effort, and improvement.
4. Take time to get to know students better.
5. Give out as many nonverbal positive responses as possible—winks, nods, and smiles.
6. Take time each day to assess student feelings.
7. Talk with students in ways that imply their own competence, such as "Okay, you know what to do next."
8. Provide interesting and fun activities that are challenging but in which students can succeed.
9. End each day on a positive note, with a fond good-bye and hope for a happy and productive tomorrow.

SCHOOLWIDE SYSTEMS OF DISCIPLINE

Today many schools have established schoolwide discipline programs in which all teachers use the same system of discipline. This movement, intended to make discipline more consistent and effective, emerged in the middle 1980s, prompted in part by the nationwide push for schools that provided

- a safe and orderly environment for learning,
- high standards and expectations,
- opportunities for student involvement and responsibility, and
- emphasis on positive behavior and preventive discipline.

If you teach where a schoolwide discipline plan is used, you are expected to follow it. While it is impossible to list all the discipline systems that various schools have developed, they can be categorized into three general types: (1) power systems, (2) combination systems, and (3) noncoercive systems.

Power Systems

Power systems contain procedures for firmly stopping misbehavior and consistently invoking consequences. Assertive Discipline (Chapter 6) is an example of a power system. These systems may be differentiated from softer noncoercive systems, such as behavior modification (Chapter 2) and Cooperative Discipline (Chapter 5), that influence behavior mainly through modeling, discussion, persuasion, and assignment of responsibility.

Secondary Level.   Most schoolwide systems in secondary school are power systems that involve not only teachers but other personnel in the school. Such systems typically have three main components: (1) a policy concerning discipline that is established by the school board and then disseminated to the school and community, (2) rules for student conduct, and (3) enforcement procedures, consequences, and follow-through.

Component one, the *school board policy,* might explain (1) the district's philosophy concerning the relationship of discipline to education; (2) the students' responsibilities at school and in the educational program; (3) the teachers' responsibilities for communicating clear standards and consequences and consistently implementing them; (4) the administrators' responsibilities in communicating and enforcing discipline; (5) a list of prohibited behaviors, such as use of drugs and alcohol, destruction of property, fighting, and so forth; and (6) the consequences that will be invoked for violations of rules.

Component two in the power system is *rules of student conduct.* For secondary schools, schoolwide rules are usually similar to the following:

1. Always be on time and ready to work.
2. Treat all people and property with respect.
3. Cooperate with those in positions of authority.
4. Leave nuisance objects at home.
5. Do not disrupt the teaching-learning process.

In some schools, all school personnel, including librarians, secretaries, bus drivers, cafeteria workers, custodians, and others are empowered to enforce the rules.

Component three, *enforcement, consequences, and follow-through,* might include measures similar to the following:

1. All students are carefully made aware of the rules, consequences, and enforcement procedures. Charts displaying the rules are posted in classrooms and elsewhere in the school.
2. When a student violates a rule, a verbal warning is given. This warning carries no penalty. If the student misbehaves again, the person in authority makes a notation on a special form in triplicate—one copy goes to the student, a second to the office, and the third is kept by the person writing the complaint.
3. School counselors keep a conduct card for all students assigned to them. When the counselor receives a note indicating misbehavior, that infraction is entered on the student's conduct card.
4. Consequences are imposed on the student. They begin with making restitution and progress to detention, conferences with the teacher, referral to the counselor, calls to the parent, referral to the vice principal, and loss of normal privileges such as off-campus passes, attendance at dances, inclusion in a class trip, or participation in athletic events. Always in effect is a *severe* clause, which allows immediate referral to the principal and suspension from school for such acts as fighting and using drugs.

Elementary Level. Power systems are also used at the elementary level. Again, a popular example is Lee Canter's Assertive Discipline (Chapter 6). Many primary teachers do not approve of power systems, however, considering them harsh and overly focused on punishing misbehavior rather than on teaching proper behavior. Teachers who disagree with that view insist that power systems are best for controlling misbehavior while providing much-needed consistency. They add that nothing prevents teachers from teaching good behavior as part of the system.

Rules at the elementary level tend to be more specific than at the secondary level. They usually name behaviors such as staying in one's seat, raising one's hand before speaking, and using no bad language. In the earlier grades, strong emphasis remains on positive acknowledgment of good behavior. Parents are often asked to assist at home in reinforcing good behavior and work and study habits. Enforcement procedures for misbehavior are carried out mainly by the classroom teacher. Counselors or administrators are rarely used.

Combination Systems

Many schools favor systems that incorporate both power and persuasive techniques. Fredric Jones's Positive Classroom Discipline (Chapter 7), for example, emphasizes supportive, persuasive, and redirective techniques. The teacher, firmly in charge, provides incentives for good behavior and enforces class rules but at the same time supports and redirects students gently.

In elementary schools, many teachers use rules that they enforce through behavior modification. By second grade, students have become fully aware of the difference between acceptable and unacceptable school behavior. At the same time, they begin to fall progressively under greater influence of peers. Therefore, many teachers at fourth grade and higher move toward more powerful means of enforcing behavior. While retaining persuasive and supportive techniques, they add into their systems some of Lee Canter's, Rudolf Dreikurs's, or William Glasser's pre-1985 techniques for establishing and invoking consequences (discussed in Chapters 6, 5, and 8, respectively).

Noncoercive Systems

While power and combination systems remain very popular, systems that rely more on persuasion than power are gaining support. William Glasser's urgings that teachers serve as leaders rather than bosses are used in schools that employ his concepts of quality schools and learning. Rudolf Dreikurs's approach for building student self-control and responsibility are being expanded into many schools through Cooperative Discipline, popularized by Linda Albert, one of Dreikurs's students. Thomas Gordon's views on helping students become self-reliant, self-controlled, and responsible (described in Chapter 9) are also finding their way increasingly into schools.

Appraisal of Schoolwide Systems

While most teachers acknowledge the benefits of schoolwide systems, many, especially those who have been successful in discipline, don't support a routinized approach for everyone. They claim that overall student behavior is no better than when teachers take care of problems in their own way. They resent giving up effective approaches in favor of systems they can't wholeheartedly support.

Teachers also strongly resist anything that carries the stigma of "still more extra work." Teachers already suffer from high levels of stress, much of it attributable to too much to do and too little time. They equate new plans with more work and automatically reject them unless benefits are clear. Despite their built-in reluctance, teachers do adopt new approaches that clearly benefit students or themselves. When persuaded that schoolwide systems of discipline can be effective without requiring burdensome extra work, teachers consider them willingly.

It is fair to say that while schoolwide systems do not improve class control for stronger teachers, they do benefit teachers who have difficulty with control. They seem to improve behavior in school areas such as library, shops, cafeteria, grounds, and buses. Community and parents, appreciating the school's attempt to encourage responsible behavior in students, also support schoolwide systems.

APPLICATION EXERCISES

1. Clarify what you as a teacher consider acceptable with regard to noise, talk, movement, and courtesy. Formulate your ideas into questions or topics that you could discuss with your class.
2. Outline your personal system of discipline to include as many of the eight steps to personalized discipline as possible.
3. Select, from classroom scenarios presented in Appendix I, one that is most similar to the grade, subject, or type of students that interests you. Test your system against the scenario. Ask yourself whether your system will

   stop the misbehavior
   keep students working productively,
   reduce the cause(s) of misbehavior,
   preserve student dignity and build positive relationships, and
   engender support from parents and administrators.

REFERENCES AND RECOMMENDED READINGS

Albert, L. (1989). *Cooperative discipline: How to manage your classroom and promote self-esteem*. Circle Pines, MN: American Guidance Service.

Gaustad, J. (1992). *Schoool discipline* (ERIC Digest No. 78). Eugene, OR: ERIC Clearinghouse on Educational Management.

Grant, C., & Sleeter, C. (1989). *Turning on learning: Five approaches for multicultural teaching plans for race, class, gender, and disability*. Columbus, OH: Merrill.

Hernandez, H. (1989). *Multicultural education: A teacher's guide to content and process.* Columbus, OH: Merrill.

Knapp, M., Turnbull, B., & Shields, P. (1990). New directions for educating the children of poverty. *Educational Leadership, 48*(4), 1–8.

Schaps, E., & Solomon, D. (1990). Schools and classrooms as caring communities. *Educational Leadership, 48*(3), 38–42.

Schulman, J. (1989). Blue freeways: Traveling the alternate route with big-city teacher trainees. *Journal of Teacher Education, 40*(5), 2–8.

Slavin, R., Karweit, N., & Madden, N. (1989). *Effective programs for students at risk.* Needham Heights, MA: Allyn & Bacon.

Sobol, T. (1990). Understanding diversity. *Educational Leadership, 48*(3), 27–30.

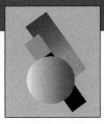

CHAPTER 13

Exemplars: Personal Systems of Discipline

This chapter presents 13 discipline systems that reflect in varying degrees the guidelines given in Chapter 12. These systems come from real teachers who have graciously allowed their work to be included here. Presented are 2 primary-grades systems, 2 intermediate-grades systems, 2 middle school systems, 3 high school systems, 3 specialty systems, and a schoolwide system of discipline used in a middle school.

TWO PRIMARY-GRADES DISCIPLINE SYSTEMS

Primary-Grades System 1

Teacher: Thomas F. Bolz, Grade K-1

Two years ago I moved from teaching a fifth grade to a kindergarten-first grade combination. I soon learned that a far different approach to discipline was required. Primary children get more excited about praise and correction—in fact, they get more excited about almost everything. At my school, we have a discipline plan that everyone uses, but into that plan I weave much of my own philosophy and personality. The rules we all use are the following:

1. I will listen and follow directions.
2. I will respect and use kind words toward others. (Profanity is prohibited.)
3. I will keep hands, feet, and objects to myself. (Fighting is prohibited.)

4. I will complete all assigned work on time.

5. I will respect school property and the property of others.

These rules apply to the playground as well as to the classroom and school environment.

We have a hierarchy of consequences set up for students who break the rules. They are:

- *Step 1.* Verbal warning. Additional consequence if apology is necessary or if there is damage to property.
- *Step 2.* Conference with teacher, with one or more of the following results: repair of damage, time out, loss of recess, loss of a privilege.
- *Step 3.* Child remains after school and calls to notify parents of reason.
- *Step 4.* Teacher contacts parents to inform them of behavior and discuss consequences for the child. Teacher may set up a conference with parents.
- *Step 5.* If all else fails and the child's behavior has not improved, teacher contacts principal, who decides on further consequences and sets up a conference with parents.

Personally, I invest much time and energy into preventive and supportive discipline. When I want students to get in their seats, sitting up with hands folded, I give the direction and then start a nursery rhyme: "One, two, buckle my shoe . . ." Soon the whole class is reciting the rhyme, and by the time we get to "a big fat hen"—usually about 10 seconds—the whole class is attentive with their eyes on me.

Another preventive technique I use is Good Walker tickets. Whenever we are walking down the hallway I hand out two or three tickets to students who are walking nicely. In class they put them in an oatmeal container, and when we line up to go outside, I draw a ticket out. That person gets to be first in line.

The major breakthrough for the year has been the Happy Face Chart. Our day usually begins like this: "Elsie, Josh, and Aaron, boom! Sign the Happy Face. Notice how they came in quietly and sat up straight and tall." A tide of good behavior ripples out from that. At the end of the week, I read off the names for each day. The names are put on slips of paper for a drawing. Whoever wins gets a coupon for a bag of french fries.

When it comes to corrective discipline, I want it to be short, simple, clearly understood, and unpleasant for the child. When individual children are noisy or not doing their work, I have them put their head down at their desk. Children know that they then have to count to 100 by ones, think about what they were doing wrong, and then get back to work. If I have to speak to them again during the day, they go to the time-out chair, where I have a three-minute egg timer. They have to sit for that length of time. They understand that this is a severe warning. The third time I have to talk with them, I put their name on the board with a check and call their parent. This corrects the behavior most of the time.

I am able to enforce these rules most of the time without getting upset. I make sure the children know I expect them to behave better. One parent commented to me that her daughter liked my room because I was "fair and treated everyone alike."

Primary-Grades System 2

Teacher: Virginia Villalpando, Grade 3

The adage about an ounce of prevention being worth a pound of cure serves as the foundation for my discipline program. I create an environment that discourages misbehavior by arranging tables and chairs to allow easy access to instructional areas and to provide clear lines of vision to all parts of the room.

Supplies are placed in conveniently accessible locations. Special interest areas are separated from work areas so as not to distract students. I do not seat students close together, and I make sure the seating allows me to reach every student in the room quickly when necessary.

I make my expectations known clearly on the first day. I emphasize that I want my students to have a learning environment that is free from disruptions and that I will expect the students' help in keeping it friendly and pleasant. I let them know that I want to know their feelings so that we can make many decisions together. We immediately begin developing rules to make our classroom run well. We discuss what the rules mean and explain the consequences for following and breaking them. I continually emphasize that they choose to behave the way they do and also that they choose the consequences that come with following or breaking rules. When the rules are completed, I go over them carefully, explain them with examples, and describe the consequences.

I post the basic rules (but not the explanations and consequences) on a chart at the front of the room (see Figure 13.1, p. 240). When students break the rules, I invoke the consequences and often refer to the rules chart. If the infractions are minor or infrequent, I merely use eye contact or head shakes to get students back on track. I make a point of thanking them when they behave well. I smile and say, "Good. Keep it up. That's the way." I want them to feel good about behaving well.

TWO INTERMEDIATE-GRADES DISCIPLINE SYSTEMS

Intermediate-Grades System 1

Teacher: Nancy Natale, Grade 4

I believe a positive atmosphere is most conducive to learning, so I set up my discipline system to be fun and rewarding for my students. My system is based on points; the points have value that can later be used to buy items such as toys, games, and books.

Earning Points. Each student is able to earn points all during the week. I assign points for a number of different behaviors. For example, when I begin an activity, I give points to those students who begin work immediately. First, I give them verbal praise:

Rule	Explanation	Consequences
Respect others.	No hitting, tattling, name-calling. Let others work. Speak quietly. Be kind.	Negative: time out, isolation, note to parents, stay in at recess. Positive: rewards.
Raise hand.	Do this before speaking, getting a drink, asking for help, or requesting permission.	Negative: ignore, deny request, frown. Positive: rewards.
Work quietly.	No loud noise. Don't disturb others.	Negative: move to other area. Positive: stars, smiley faces, thank-yous.
Be orderly.	Don't run. Enter the room quietly. Stay in line.	Negative: frown, checkmark by name. Positive: smile, praise.
Respect property.	Take care of things. Keep them clean.	Negative: note sent home. Positive: note sent home, thank-you.

FIGURE 13.1

"Thank you, Jennifer. Good going, Shawn." As I do this I give them each a point on a master chart I keep near my desk. This provides immediate reinforcement and also influences other students positively, reminding them that they, too, can earn points.

As an extra work incentive, I assign points to students who bring into class something that is pertinent to what we are studying. For example, one day I was teaching about diagrams. The next day a girl brought in a diagram of a house her parents were building and a boy brought in a diagram of a model airplane he was putting together.

I use discretion in offering numbers of points. For example, my class was writing autobiographies to be bound and displayed at open house, but they just weren't using their time well. I decided to offer five points to each student who completed his or her work to my satisfaction by noon of the day of the open house. This motivated students to high work output.

I also give out points at unexpected times. In a recent geometry lesson, we were discussing the number of faces, edges, and vertices that various shapes have. After we had examined about 10 different shapes, a girl pointed out to me that on every pyramid the number of faces was always equal to the number of vertices, regardless of whether the pyramid had a triangular-, square-, hexagonal-, or other-shaped base. We tested her observation and found it to be true. I gave her a point for an excellent observation.

Class Rules. I use only four class rules, as follows:

1. Pay attention during class.
2. Keep hands and feet to yourself.
3. Do not prevent others from learning.
4. Follow directions and complete your work.

Misbehavior. Even with all the attention I give to keeping a positive atmosphere, my students still misbehave sometimes. When they do, I have them fill out a See Me card. On this card, the student must answer these four questions:

1. What was I doing?
2. Why was I doing it?
3. What should I have been doing?
4. What class rule was broken?

After the card is filled out, the student must bring it to me so that we can have a discussion about it. If any student accumulates three See Me cards in one week, that student has to write a letter to his or her parents stating why they received the cards. This procedure helps me document misbehaviors in my classroom, but, better yet, it makes the student own the misbehavior. If a student receives even one See Me card in a week, he or she may not participate in the week's spending of earned points but must do homework instead.

Intermediate-Grades System 2

Teacher: Micheal Brus, Grade 5

I base my discipline system on the Golden Rule and find I need to spell out only three rules, which I prepare calligraphically in gold, Gothic lettering and display prominently in the room. My rules read as follows:

- Teachers have a right to teach!
- Students have a right to learn!

Therefore:

1. We agree to treat fellow students and teachers as we ourselves would like to be treated.
2. We agree to be on time, to be prepared to work, and to stay on task.
3. We agree to have no unauthorized food, gum, or drink.

I believe in treating my students very much like adults, letting them know they are responsible for how they behave. I define the behavior boundaries within my three rules and discuss gray areas around them. I invite my students to add a fourth rule, if there is one in which they believe strongly.

I use much positive reinforcement. Whenever I see a student behaving especially well, I ask him or her to go to the master list of student names (displayed on a wall chart) and make a vertical stroke beside the name with my gold marker. The student receiving the most marks in a month is named citizen of the month. Having been a professional portrait artist, I honor the student by drawing a color pastel portrait of him or her.

The points accumulated by other students may be used at an end-of-the-month auction to bid for prizes I furnish, such as inexpensive toys, books, erasers, pieces of chalk, and stickers. In order to emphasize good group behavior, I keep a separate tally of points earned by the class as a whole for being quiet and orderly at lunch, library, auditorium, and especially for helping us all have an unusually pleasant day at school. These points accumulate toward free minutes on Fridays, extra physical education, or time for playing with computers and games.

By my own demeanor in the classroom, I try to show my sincere belief that there is much good in every person. I try to find in all my students something they do especially well and help instill in them a sense of pride and achievement.

When my students break class rules, I have them go to the master chart and make a black tally mark beneath their name. The consequences associated with the black marks are as follows:

> First mark: I verbally reinforce the opposite behavior in another student.
>
> Second mark: I give a short verbal desist, referring to the rule that is broken.
>
> Third mark: I send the student to a fellow teacher's room with an assignment to complete. (This is arranged in advance, reciprocally, with the other teacher.)
>
> Fourth mark: The student is sent to the principal's office. The principal knows and supports my system and takes further appropriate action.

When the consequences for more serious misbehavior are invoked, I follow up with the student, insisting that a plan for proper behavior be made that is acceptable to both the student and me. At appropriately private times, I talk openly and honestly with the student about his or her success in living up to the plan and what must be done next when the plan does not work.

TWO MIDDLE SCHOOL DISCIPLINE SYSTEMS

Middle School System 1

Teacher: Gail Charles, Grade 8
Subject: English

I have been teaching for 17 years. Most of that time I tried to control student misbehavior with scowls, reprimands, lectures, threats, and detentions. My students grudgingly behaved well enough and they learned, but I'm sure they felt under siege. I know I did, and the effort left me continually frustrated and exhausted.

In recent years I have begun to understand that I am more effective and enjoy my work more when I organize the curriculum to accommodate, even embrace, the needs of my adolescent students. While I still provide a strong and challenging curriculum, I have switched from a coercive to a collaborative way of teaching. I now try to guide, encourage, and support my students' efforts rather than push and prod. The result has been fewer power struggles, more success, and happier students and teacher.

Winning My Students Over. My students want to feel part of the group. They want to feel accepted and valued by each other and especially by me. They want to feel safe, so I forbid all ridicule and sarcasm. I've never ridiculed a student, but sorry to say, I have spoken sarcastically many times when struggling against students who defied my rules. I no longer use sarcasm nor allow students to belittle each other in any way.

I give my students a voice in classroom matters and listen to them sincerely. I allow them to make decisions about where they sit and with whom they wish to work. I do this as part of trying to make learning enjoyable. They like to work with each other, participate, talk, and cooperate.

Meeting My Needs. We discuss the importance of making classwork enjoyable, and I tell my students that the class needs to be enjoyable for me, too. I tell them up front what I need in order to feel good about the class—that I want the tone to be positive, with everyone showing patience, tolerance, good manners, and mutual respect. I tell them that I want them to show enthusiasm and do the best work they can. I say I need their attention and that I want them to help care for materials and keep the room clean. I promise to treat them with respect, and they usually want to reciprocate.

Rules and Student Input. My new style of discipline has required me to make changes in my curriculum and ways of establishing rules. I have learned to request and make use of student input concerning expectations, operating procedures, and codes of conduct. Formerly, I greeted new students with a printed set of rules and consequences, but they always saw them as impositions rather than as cooperative agreements they wanted to support. Now when I meet a new class, I discuss their needs and mine and focus on how we can meet those needs and make our class productive. I give students power to make many decisions and show that I respect what they say.

Together we write a plan for how we will work and behave in the class. Because I want them to make thoughtful suggestions, I ask them, for their first homework assignment, to think back on previous years in school and write brief responses to the following:

1. When have you felt most successful in school?
2. What did the teacher do to help you feel successful?
3. What kinds of class activities have you found most helpful and enjoyable?
4. What suggestions do you have for creating a classroom in which all can work, learn, and do their best?

The next day, I organize students into small groups to share and discuss what they have written. Volunteers present each group's responses, which I list on the overhead. Occasionally I may add a suggestion of my own. We then streamline, combine, reword, and sometimes negotiate until we reach a set of agreements we think best. Before the next class, I type up the agreements and ask each student and his or her parent to sign, indicating their support. I do this for each of my five classes. The agreements turn out to be quite similar from class to class.

Enforcement.   With the collaborative plan in place, I have few discipline problems and little difficulty dealing with those that occur. Most often, a simple reminder is all that is needed to get students back on track. For the occasional student who repeatedly misbehaves despite our agreement, I ask the counselor to set up a meeting with the student's parents and, sometimes, other teachers. We discuss the problem and how it can be resolved. Very occasionally, a student may behave in a dangerous manner or prevent my teaching. When that happens, I call on the vice-principal for immediate intervention.

Prevention.   In classes of 35 adolescents, there exists an endless supply of distractions. It is up to me to keep students engaged successfully in activities they enjoy and find rewarding. I have had considerable success using reading and writing activities in which students choose books to read and respond to them in writing. I present minilessons that address common needs I see in the class. Students evaluate their own work and make it the best possible for inclusion in their Showcase Portfolios, which are displayed for parents, teachers, administrators, and others at a Writers' Tea. In addition, students complete at least one project per quarter. They have choices on what they will pursue in their projects and how they will show what they have learned. Always there is a high emphasis on quality.

During these efforts, I try to interact personally with every student. It is not easy to forge relationships with 160+ students, but I do so in order to show them I "see" and like them. At the beginning of the year I write a letter to my students introducing myself and telling a bit about my family, hobbies, interests, and goals. I ask them to do the same so I can know them better. I keep a birthday calendar to remember student birthdays. I try to comment on new hairstyles, new outfits, or how great a now brace-free set of teeth looks. I chaperon field trips and dances, supervise the computer writing lab after school, and make myself available for conversation before and after school. These little things mean a lot to students.

For their part, many students like to involve themselves in the workings of the classroom. I assign them tasks such as classroom librarian, bulletin board designer, plant caregiver, and class secretary. Their involvement makes them feel important and useful.

More than anything else, I have found that if I want respect from my students, I must show them respect. I want writers, so I write along with them. I want them involved, so I get involved with them. I want them to show good manners, humor, and kindness, so I exemplify those qualities the best I can. I make mistakes in these efforts and lots of them, but the more sincerely I try, the more forgiving my students become.

Middle School System 2

Teacher: Deborah Trivoli, Grade 7
Subject: Humanities Core

When school begins, I use a four-day sequence to establish rules of behavior for the class, as follows:

Day 1: Students' Needs, My Needs, and Rules

Students' Needs.   When I first meet the students, I spend as much time as necessary—usually about an hour—discussing how we would like our class to function. I tell them I want the class to be worthwhile and enjoyable, for them as well as for me, and that if we work together we can make it so. I then ask them to tell me, without mentioning any names, some of the things they have *not* liked about school in the past, things we would like to avoid. Their comments usually include the following:

- Stupid (irrelevant, meaningless, boring) work
- Mean (inconsiderate, demanding, unreasonable, unfriendly) teachers
- Put-downs (sarcasm, remarks) by teachers and other students
- Not being listened to by teachers
- Not being allowed to discuss or express their own opinions

I list their comments on the board and assure them I don't want those things in our class. But, I say, we will need to work together if we are to keep them out.

My Needs.   I move on to say that sometimes there are things in classes that I don't like either and that just as I will try to make the class good for the students, I need them to help make it good for me. I don't list my concerns as dissatisfactions; rather, I list them as my needs, which I write on the board alongside their concerns:

- Considerate behavior (students and teacher being kind and helpful)
- High-quality work (work to be proud of)
- Student responsibility in learning (attention, participation, completing assignments)
- Low level of noise (just one of my personal needs, I explain)
- Clean, orderly classroom

For each of my needs, I give a positive and negative example to help explain what I mean.

Rules.   I ask them if they can help come up with some rules for the class that will meet their needs as well as mine. We compare the lists and before long decide that one rule could have to do with respectful behavior for everyone, teacher and students alike. Another rule could have to do with important learnings done well. The students express other rules, but after discussion usually decide that only two rules are needed.

1. Every person in the class—teacher and student alike—shows consideration and respect for everyone else.
2. Every person in the class—teacher and student alike—shows responsibility for doing high quality work on important learnings.

We discuss these two rules. I relate example scenarios and ask the class whether in those scenarios our rules are being followed or violated.

I end the first day's session by thanking them for their excellent thinking and by asking this question: "Do you ever see drivers speeding—driving well over the speed limit?" They all say they do. I then say, "The speed limits are rules that most people consider wise and important. And yet those rules are sometimes broken. In our class, I know you consider our rules wise and important, yet there may be times when they are broken. For your homework tonight, I'd like you to write out four suggestions concerning how we can remember to follow our rules."

Day 2: Suggestions for Rules Enforcement

Next day, students make many suggestions for enforcing our rules. Most of their suggestions are unrealistic or counterproductive, such as the following:

- Make them (rule breakers) stay in after school.
- Send them to the principal's office.
- Make them do extra work.
- Make them sit in the back of the room.
- Make them apologize.

I remind the students of our rule 1, showing consideration and respect for everyone. I ask what we might do, or what I might do, that would be helpful and respectful to students who violate our rules. This question really causes students to think. It is hard for them to come up with much besides the following:

- You could warn us that we are breaking a rule and need to stop.
- You could talk with students who break rules.
- Maybe you could tell the parents and get them to help.
- Maybe we could remind each other.

I end the second day's session by saying, "I need to think about your suggestions. You think some more about them, too. Tomorrow let's see what we come up with."

Day 3: Enforcement

On the third day I tell students I have thought a good deal about their excellent suggestions for helping us follow rules. I ask them if they have had new thoughts. I lead them into a discussion in which I give them credit for guiding us to the following:

1. Post the two rules on a chart on the front wall.
   Rule 1: Be considerate of everyone.
   Rule 2: Do our best work.
2. Have some sessions in which we practice showing consideration and working responsibly.
3. Refer to the rules occasionally, evaluate how well we are abiding by them, and compliment ourselves when we deserve it.
4. For students who continue to break rules, the teacher talks with them privately and tries to find ways to help them follow the rules.
5. For students who continue to break rules after private conferences with the teacher, a discussion meeting will be set up that involves student, teacher, parent, and principal, who together will try to decide how best to help.

We discuss these ideas and sometimes modify them a bit. When finished with the third day's session, I say that by tomorrow I will have the rules and agreements printed for them to sign and have their parent sign to show agreement and support.

Day 4: Forward

I have students take agreements home for parents to read and sign. They bring them back and I keep them on file. We continue to refer to our rules regularly. When I see minor violations, I take the opportunity to explore with the class whether the rules are working. I conduct occasional practice activities in which we role-play abiding by or violating the rules. In some of these, I have the teacher violate a rule and ask students what they think should be done. These practices clarify and serve as reminders to do the following:

1. Use considerate behavior.
2. Take responsibility for learning.
3. Keep the classroom pleasant and orderly.
4. Resolve difficulties without causing hurt feelings.

The activities also help me remember to do the following:

1. Treat all students with dignity and respect.
2. Provide worthwhile learnings through interesting activities.
3. Use verbal and physical cues to help students follow rules.
4. Maintain positive interactions with all my students.
5. Have fun and pat myself on the back at the end of each day.

THREE HIGH SCHOOL DISCIPLINE SYSTEMS

High School System 1

Teacher: Linda Blacklock
Subject: English Language Development

Over the years, I have developed my discipline style by incorporating good ideas from many different sources. I have learned the importance of laying groundwork before school begins, which helps bring about a low-stress, successful, and fun year for my students and me. I never leave the discipline structure to chance, because I know I will pay for it if I do. My discipline system always precedes my instructional program.

My discipline plan emphasizes four areas, all of which allow me to approach discipline in a positive way: (1) classroom environment and seating, to facilitate learning and physical proximity to students, (2) limit setting, to ensure that students understand how we are to conduct ourselves in the classroom; (3) responding to misbehavior by disciplining with body movements instead of my mouth, and (4) training for responsibility through preferred activity time.

Classroom Environment and Seating.   In this area of discipline, I try to arrange every aspect of the classroom environment so that learning is more likely to occur and student fooling around is less likely to happen. I arrange student seating close to the board with rows moving across the room instead of front to back. I put my desk at the side and leave two aisles from front to back. This arrangement allows me to circulate easily within the group. I call it the *interior loop*.

Limit Setting.   We do not have rules, as such, for the class. Instead, we have what I call *understandings*. We understand that our purpose is to get our work done in a responsible manner, that I will try to make the work interesting so students will enjoy it, and that none of us will interfere with student learning in any way. This requires essentially that we treat others the way we wish to be treated. We discuss these ideas at length to ensure understanding and acceptance.

Responding to Misbehavior.   When it is necessary to react to student misbehavior, I have trained myself to remain cool, calm, and collected so that I can rely on understanding and experience rather than act on the heat of the moment. I remind myself that I cannot control students if I cannot first control myself.

My Body Language.   I emphasize body language and timing, as follows:

1. I turn in a slow, regal fashion to face the disruptive student(s).
2. I point my toes toward the student, thus committing myself to discipline. I give no mixed messages.
3. I focus on the student's face and look only at that student.
4. I keep my hands down so that I won't appear agitated.

5. I show no expression on my face. I do not smile, which would give ambivalent messages and appear submissive.

6. I keep my breathing slow and deep, remain relaxed, and move slowly.

Students' Body Language.   All the while, I am reading the students' body language as well. I look under the desk at their knees and feet. If they are talking and don't come all the way around with their bodies turned to work, I know they are likely to begin talking again. I have learned that students use their upper bodies for faking and their lower bodies for commitment.

Dealing with Back Talk.   I have learned that when students talk back, it triggers a strong reaction in me. But I have also learned that I'm better off ignoring it. When a student talks back, I stay calm and relaxed and keep my mouth shut, which causes the student's show to fizzle out.

Training for Responsibility   I use preferred activity time (PAT) as an incentive to encourage students to behave responsibly. I include discussions of PAT on the first day of school, and I implement it beginning on the second day. Students enjoy PAT, which leads to good relations and good behavior. I use it as follows:

1. I explain the meaning of preferred activity time, what it can consist of, what students can do to earn it, and what they can do to lose it.

2. I use a wall chart for each class and a stopwatch.

3. I award bonuses (minutes of time) to the class for being in the right place at the right time, for smooth class transitions, and for contests between classes.

4. When students misbehave or waste time, I record the amount of lost time on the chart with a minus sign and continue class instruction. I never have to do any nagging.

5. When students have earned enough minutes to fill a complete class period, I let them decide which day they prefer to use it and what they prefer doing that day. They may select from test reviews, skill drills, homework, team games, or enrichment activities.

I have found that this system of discipline gives me a variety of nonadversarial procedures for encouraging good behavior and intervening when necessary to stop misbehavior.

High School System 2

Teacher: Leslie Hays
Subject: Physical Science

My personal belief is that every one of my students can behave appropriately in my classroom every day. My personal goal is to be an effective teacher for them. I try to accomplish this through clarity, firmness, and a human touch. It is very important to me to establish a sense of class belonging and unity marked by shared objectives and goals. Toward that end I try to inject humor and fun, and I find that student participation follows naturally.

At the same time I concentrate on preventive and supportive discipline by doing extensive planning and by constantly monitoring each of my students. This frees me

FIGURE 13.2 Class behavior contract

Dear Student and Parent:

In order to guarantee all the students in my classroom the excellent learning climate they deserve, I use the following discipline plan.

Attendance: Attendance is essential to the learning process. You cannot expect to succeed if you do not participate in the daily activity of the classroom. Therefore, after a student's fourth absence, the parent will be notified. After 15 absences, the student will be subject to failure in the class.

Tardies: Students are expected to be in their assigned seat and ready to begin work when the final bell rings. A warning is issued after two tardies, and the parent will be informed. Citizenship grades will be lowered one grade for every two tardies. After four tardies a letter will be sent home describing the situation. Following the seventh tardy, the student is subject to being dropped from the class with an F.

Class Behavior: I believe that all my students can behave appropriately in my classroom. I will not permit a student to stop me from teaching or to keep other students from learning.

Class Rules:
1. Bring your science book, notebook, and pencil every day. I don't lend anything.
2. Be attentive while the teacher, or a student who is called on, is talking.
3. Bring no food, drink, candy, gum, hats, or sunglasses to the class.
4. Handle all equipment properly.
5. Profanity and verbal abuse are not tolerated.
6. Remain in your seat at the end of the period until dismissed by the teacher.

Consequences: High citizenship and conduct grades will be awarded to those students who contribute positively to the daily activities of the classroom. If, on the other hand, a student chooses to interfere with the learning process, the following consequences will be invoked:

First time : Warning; mark on discipline card.

Second time: Notify parent of behavior problem.

Third time : Refer student to counselor.

Fourth time: Refer student to vice-principal for disciplinary action.

Students who write on desks or throw trash around the room will be assigned immediate after-school detention to clean the desktops and remove all the trash.

Note : More serious problems such as defiance, fighting, theft, abuse of equipment, or violation of laboratory safety rules will result in immediate referral to the vice-principal.

It is in the student's best interest that student, teacher, and parent work together. I will therefore be in close contact with parents regarding students' progress. Parents, please sign the tear-off signature portion of this contract and have the student return it to me tomorrow. If you have any questions or comments, please call me or write them on the tear-off.

from having to deal continually with misbehavior. I communicate with parents by note and telephone, and most of them are so thankful that I have called them to talk about their child that they become my allies in class control.

My students range from remedial (almost always considered behavior problems) to advanced. With all levels, my discipline plan works best for me with a very structured approach that communicates my standards and requirements.

My plan goes into effect within the first five minutes of class each September. Students are given a class behavior contract, which must be taken home, signed by their parents, and returned to me the next day. If they bring it back when due, I give them points; if they are a day late, they get no points; and if it doesn't come back the third day, I call the parents at home. The contract outlines my philosophy and behavior guidelines (Figure 13.2).

After reviewing the rules with the students, I have them fill out a behavior card that becomes part of my system for recording behavior problems. This is yet another way of telling the students that discipline is an important part of my classroom organization. I begin by seating students according to a seating chart, then explain procedures concerning homework, grading, and required materials. Textbooks are distributed and we go over the plans for the semester. After that, we begin the first lesson. By the end of the first class, all students have the feeling that I am in control and have a well-organized plan.

Over years of trying various discipline approaches, I have found that students react positively to my system. As the year progresses, occasional gentle reminders are usually enough to maintain good behavior. I also use eye contact, hand signals, and physical proximity to assist. When more serious disruptions do occasionally occur, students know the rules and consequences, and it thus becomes easier to invoke the consequences without emotional upheavals and confrontations that I find personally offensive.

High School System 3

Teacher: Elaine Maltz
Subject: Math Basic Skills

At my first class meeting, I distribute a copy of class rules to each student. We discuss the rules carefully, and in a spirit of fun I ask a number of oral questions to make sure students understand. I have students take their copies home to be signed by parent and student and returned to me the next day. The signed copy of the rules is kept in each student's math notebook. The rules are as follows:

1. Come to class on time and be in your seat when the bell rings.
2. Bring your textbook, math notebook with paper, and a sharpened pencil every day.
3. Work quietly at your seat unless you have permission to do otherwise.
4. Food and drink are not allowed in the classroom.

Consequences

(All will be shown in citizenship grades.)

- For tardiness:

  0–3 tardies = G (good)

  4 tardies = S (satisfactory)

  5 tardies = N (needs improvement)

  6 tardies = U (unsatisfactory)

- For truancy: Two truancies lower citizenship grade. Four truancies lower academic grade.

- Infractions of other rules:

  0–4 infractions = G

  5–6 infractions = S

  7–8 infractions = N

  9–10 infractions = U

When I present the rules, I discuss my expectations and explain the rules fully. I mention that in addition to my consequences, the school maintains a system by which students get referred to the counselor or vice-principal. If necessary, the parents are contacted for assistance.

In teaching, I feel that an essential element of classes in math is the use of humor. It combats boredom as well as "math phobia." The tone has to be set at the beginning of the class as a part of an overall atmosphere of acceptance and encouragement where each student is treated with respect. At the same time, good behavior and effort are expected of each student. I work hard to avoid sarcasm and try never to attack the students personally.

I find it also helps to provide occasional changes of pace. Reviewing homework, introducing new material, and starting corresponding homework are the nuts and bolts of my class, but I try to intersperse visual problems with abstract ones and include real problem solving at least once in each class as a respite from routine work.

To help with behavior, I also stay active while my students are working at their seats. Constantly circulating and helping not only allows me to help students with their work, but it permits me to deal subtly with incipient misbehavior without drawing the attention of other class members. I use eye contact, facial expressions, and light touches to help students control their own behavior.

I admit there are times when I use nagging, or the *broken record technique*, to remind students of standards and expectations. I do this to help my students give high priority to academics and to proper social behavior. At the same time, I remember to smile when dealing with my students. I think teenagers, more than others, need concrete proof of their teacher's feelings. Other ways I try to give this proof are to be as helpful as possible, get work corrected and back to students quickly, and provide unending encouragement, especially to reluctant students. I work hard at all this. Being a consistent disciplinarian has not come naturally to me.

THREE SPECIALTY DISCIPLINE SYSTEMS

The following are called *specialty systems* because they have special focuses or techniques that have served well for the teachers who developed and used them.

Specialty System 1: Kindergarten Conflict Resolution
Teacher: Linda Poblenz

The discipline system I use with my kindergarten children revolves around *win-win conflict resolution*. The conflicts may be between students or between a student and myself. Young children learn the process easily, and by using it they learn to solve their own problems and situations. I also help them learn how to evaluate their behavior. As they become more proficient in doing so, they become more self-directed.

Learning the Win-Win Process. To introduce the win-win process to my children, I help them understand something of how the mind works and then have them apply what they have learned to a problem situation that does not involve conflict. I begin like this:

TEACHER: Do you have a big toe?

STUDENT: Yes.

TEACHER: How do you know? We can't see it through your shoes.

STUDENT: I know because it's there.

TEACHER: Wiggle your toe. [*Pause*] Did you wiggle it?

STUDENT: Yes.

TEACHER: I couldn't see it. How do you know your toe wiggled?

STUDENT: I could feel it.

TEACHER: You know that inside your head you have a brain to think with. The brain is part of your body, just as your big toe is. You cannot see your brain inside your head, but you can make it work.

I move ahead to three special terms to describe thinking. I teach students the term *mud mind* to describe thinking that is bogged down, where there is a problem but the person can't think of a solution. I teach them the term *air mind* to describe thinking that is calm and has no problems to worry about. I teach them the term *twinkler mind* to describe thinking that helps find solutions to problems. I go on to show how twinkler minds can find answers to a number of problems that students encounter every day. I begin this process by pretending I have lost my green marker:

TEACHER: Oh me! I can't find my green marker to write on the chart. I guess I can't teach. We'll just have to stop everything. Oh dear, we can't do that during school time. Oh, what can I do? I'm really in my mud mind. I guess I can throw a tantrum. Or can somebody help me find a solution?

FIRST STUDENT: I can go look for it.

TEACHER: You used your twinkler mind for that good idea. Does anyone have a different idea?

SECOND STUDENT: You could use a different color marker.

TEACHER: Another good idea from a twinkler mind. Those are both good suggestions. Now that my mud mind is gone, I can choose. I'll try writing with a different color first. Thank you for using your twinkler mind.

Applying the Win-Win Process.   After I have modeled several such examples, I introduce children to the terms *I-messages* and *active listening*. Then, I show how the process is applied in resolving personal conflict. I use a role-playing scenario where Jonathan and Aliseah are arguing over a crayon. I walk students through the process as follows:

TEACHER: Aliseah, did you take Jonathan's crayon?

ALISEAH: I needed a red crayon to do my work.

TEACHER: Why didn't you use your own red crayon instead of taking Jonathan's?

ALISEAH: I don't have a red crayon. I had to use his.

TEACHER: I see. The problem is that you need a red crayon, but Jonathan needs his. Is there a different way we could solve the problem?

ALISEAH: I don't know.

TEACHER: I believe you. Let's take a minute to get out of our mud minds and see if a twinkler mind can find another idea. [*Pause*] Is there a place in this room where spare crayons are kept?

ALISEAH: In the crayon can on the shelf?

TEACHER: The problem is that you need a red crayon. How can you solve your problem?

ALISEAH: I can get a red crayon from the crayon can.

TEACHER: I hear you using your twinkler mind to solve this problem. Can you think of still another way to solve it?

ALISEAH: Ask Jonathan to share his red crayon?

TEACHER: Your twinkler mind is really working now. Which solution would you like to try?

ALISEAH: I'll go get a crayon from the can.

TEACHER: Okay. Try your plan. Let's talk at recess. I want to hear about how you took care of your problem.

Continual follow-up is necessary as students learn this process. It helps if they receive feedback in the form of a smile, nod, or thumb's-up signal when they resolve conflicts and personal problems.

Specialty System 2: Second-Grade Behavior Modification

Teacher: Constance Bauer

I had been teaching for five or six years before I ever understood what behavior modification was all about and what it could do for teachers. I had controlled my second graders through the usual stern-voiced admonitions and had tried to motivate them by telling them how much fun we were going to have in school that day. Neither approach ever went over well enough to suit me.

Then, our school had an in-service training session on behavior modification and its uses in the classroom. Because our principal expected us to, I halfheartedly began to try out some of the approaches in my classroom—such things as finding a student who was behaving correctly and praising that behavior, rather than scold those who were misbehaving, and setting up a Bookworm chart so that students who did their work could add another segment to their worm.

My students responded so well to those first efforts that I decided to see what more I could accomplish with positive reinforcement. I set up individual progress charts for my students so they could keep track of their improvement in reading, math, and spelling. I made little stuffed rabbits that could sit on desks where there were Good Workers. I made note forms that I sent home each day with Good Helper students so that their parents could be proud of them.

Before long I found that I was controlling and motivating the class with these devices and everything was going much more smoothly and positively than ever before. I am told that it is easier to use such programs at the primary-grades level than with older students. I don't know if that's so, but in any case behavior modification has made a believer out of me.

Specialty System 3: Middle School Token Economy

Teachers: Mike Straus and Roy Allen (Team Teachers)

For the first few years we taught, we used authority as our way of keeping discipline. We are large, can talk mean, and can order students to behave. But that was wearing us out and making the kids afraid of us. Nobody was enjoying school very much.

Then one year we decided to try a behavior control system based on fake money. We called our currency "strallens" (from our combined names), and we printed up several hundred bills of different denominations. A couple of years ago a student's mother took photographs of us and made up a batch of strallens with our pictures on them.

Anyway, we decided to pay our students strallens when they worked quietly, did their homework, finished work on time, did extra work, participated well in class, and so on. We also decided we would fine them when they didn't do their work, misbehaved, or talked back. We had been told to give kids rewards for good behavior but not to penalize them when they acted bad. That's not real life, so far as we are concerned. In society when you break the law you get fined, and that was how we wanted it in our classroom.

We usually walk around the classroom with strallens in our hand or pocket. We give them out personally. When students misbehave, like talking when they're not supposed to, we say, "Jack, that's a ten-strallen fine." Jack knows he has to put 10 of his strallens in the fine box.

As students accumulate strallens, they can use them to buy special things we provide. Every couple of weeks, for example, we rent a video movie that the kids want to see. We charge admission. Those who don't have enough strallens can't watch the movie. We have popcorn sometimes, take field trips to interesting places, and hold white elephant sales. Students can spend strallens for those things, too.

After a while some of the students don't care to spend their strallens—they want to see how many they can get. Some amass several hundred. We set up bank accounts for them that earn interest, to teach students about interest, writing checks, and balancing checkbooks.

The strallen system doesn't work for every student. We tell students at the beginning that they don't have to participate in it if they don't want to. They can have the usual praise if they behave and the usual scoldings and staying-in if they don't. An occasional student takes that option. Once in a while students on the strallen system misbehave so much that they go hopelessly in the hole. We take them off the system and use conventional controls with them.

All in all, we like our system. It works for us. It is effective and easy to operate, and the kids react to it positively. It has made our teaching easier and more enjoyable. We almost never have to scold a student. They accept the rewards and fines as reasonable, and everyone stays in a pretty good mood most of the time.

A SCHOOLWIDE DISCIPLINE SYSTEM

Dry Creek Elementary School, Rio Linda, California

Kris Halverson, Assistant Principal
(Courtesy of Kris Halverson and Linda Albert)

Dry Creek School is in the midst of a five-year restructuring project that emphasizes brain-based education. One of our most important tasks in this effort is implementing a positive learning environment in which everyone feels safe yet excited about learning.

Toward this end, we have put into schoolwide practice Cooperative Discipline, which has helped us build quality relationships between students and staff. The strategies in Cooperative Discipline are made specific to individual students' needs through five steps.

1. Pinpoint and describe the student's behavior.
2. Identify the goal of the misbehavior.

3. Select and apply appropriate intervention techniques.
4. Apply encouragement strategies to build self-esteem.
5. Involve the parents as partners in the process.

Prior to using Cooperative Discipline, our staff had made use of a more forceful type of class discipline. As we have moved into Cooperative Discipline, we have been challenged to rethink, redefine, and rework our former ways of dealing with children.

The Critter Code. In order to provide uniformity and continuity in behavior management, our staff developed what we call the Dry Creek Critter Code. This code of behavior, used by everyone in the school, aims at Cooperative Discipline's Three C's: Capable, Connect, and Contribute. We have designed a logo in the form of an umbrella with CAPABLE, CONNECT, CONTRIBUTE written on the umbrella. Just beneath the umbrella are these four statements:

I will respect myself, others, and property.
I will be responsible for my behavior.
I will be punctual and prepared.
I will be safe.

We make a constant effort to help everyone live by these code statements.

Life Skills. In connection with the Critter Code and Cooperative Discipline, we provide our students systematic instruction in life skills of teamwork, perseverance, responsibility, caring, and cooperation. This is aimed at helping our students become more effective citizens. In this effort we make use of Dorothy Rich's *Megaskills* and Susan Lovalik's *Integrated Thematic Instruction Model*. We devote a month to each of the major skills; at the end of each month, we hold a ceremony to recognize students who have demonstrated the skill in exemplary fashion.

The Citation Program. When students misbehave seriously, they are given citations. But rather than carry a punitive connotation, the citations provide a positive opportunity for us to help students understand why they are misbehaving, to assist them with problem-solving skills, and to support them as they learn to connect effectively with school. The following are some of the key elements of our citation program:

1. Manners and Safety Class. Any student receiving a citation must attend manners and safety class during the last recess to make a problem-solving map with a teacher. This allows the child to connect with a caring adult and to learn problem-solving skills that support better behavior choices.

2. Action Plan Meetings. These meetings are held once a week. Student referrals are made by classroom teachers on the basis of accumulated citations or social, emotional, or academic needs. These meetings are attended by teacher, student, parent, principal, and action plan coordinator, and their purpose is to develop a plan to positively reconnect the student to the school.

3. Critter Activities. On Friday afternoons, we provide Critter Activities for students who have lived by our code. These activities, used as incentives for good behavior, tap into the seven intelligences. [H. Gardner's (*Frames of mind: The theory of multiple intelligences*, New York: Basic Books, 1983) seven intelligences are: (1) logical-mathematical, (2) linguistic-verbal, (3) musical, (4) spatial, (5) bodily-kinesthetic, (6) interpersonal, and (7) intrapersonal.] They are characterized by meaningful content, student choice, multiage groupings, and adequate time for goal accomplishment. Activity groups include landscape architects, dance troupes, newsletter editors, culinary academicians, artists in residence, clay masters, musicians, athletes, jewelers, math masters, and technologists.

4. Citation Clinic. This is a weekly counterpart of Critter Activities. The clinic is conducted by the Student Success Team, comprised of sixth-grade students who have been trained to work, under adult supervision, with peers and younger students who have received serious citations, such as those for fighting or repeated use of profanity. Problems are discussed and worked out, strategies that lead to good behavior are reviewed, and supportive connections are established between students. The Success Team also helps in other leadership roles, such as schoolwide decision making. As school leaders, their self-esteem grows and they become models of responsibility.

5. The Newcomer Club. This club of sixth-grade students creates and extends a warm, welcoming environment for new students. Each new student at Dry Creek School is invited to a luncheon to meet club members and other new students. At the luncheon, they receive folders with supplies and special correspondence welcoming them.

All of these programs at Dry Creek School focus on making students feel that they are capable, connected, and contributing members of our school. We believe these programs are helping greatly to cultivate good citizenship, enhance self-esteem, and raise academic achievement.

Classroom Scenarios for Analysis and Practice

Presented here are descriptions of 10 classrooms exhibiting misbehaviors teachers are likely to encounter. The scenarios can be used for behavior analysis, application of concepts and strategies, and testing of personal systems of discipline.

Each scenario consists of a general description of the class followed by one or more typical occurrences. As you read the scenarios, ask yourself the following: (1) What is the problem behavior, if any, and why is it a problem? (2) What seems to be causing the problem? (3) What should the teacher do to stop the misbehavior(s)? (4) What can the teacher do to give positive redirection to the misbehavior(s)? (5) What tactics should be included in the correction so as to maintain student self-respect and good personal relations?

SCENARIO 1: FIFTH GRADE

The Class

Mrs. Miller's fifth grade enrolls students from a small, stable community. Since the transiency rate is low, many of her students have been together since first grade, and during those years they have developed certain patterns of interacting and role playing. Unfortunately, many of those behaviors interfere with teaching and learning.

During the first week of school Mrs. Miller noticed that four or five students enjoyed making smart-aleck remarks about most things she wanted them to do. When such remarks were made, the other students laughed and sometimes joined in.

Even when Mrs. Miller attempts to hold class discussions about serious issues, many of the students make light of the problems and refuse to enter genuinely into a search for solutions. Instead of obtaining the productive discussion she had hoped for, Mrs. Miller finds the class degenerating into flippancy and horseplay.

Typical Occurrences

Mrs. Miller has begun a history lesson that contains a reference to Julius Caesar. She asks if anyone has ever heard of Julius Caesar. Ben shouts out, "Yeah, they named a salad after him!"

The class laughs and calls out encouraging remarks such as "Good one, Ben!"

Mrs. Miller tells Ben she does not appreciate such contributions. She waits for some semblance of order, then says, "Let us go on."

"Lettuce, continue!" cries Jeremy from the back of the room. The class falls into a chaos of laughter and talk.

After waiting a while, Mrs. Miller slams a book down on the desk and yells for quiet. "Any more such comments and you will go straight to the office!" she asserts.

For the remainder of the lesson, no more students call out remarks, but most continue to smirk and whisper comments about Caesar salad. A great deal of giggling goes on. Mrs. Miller tries to ignore the display of disrespect, but because of the disruptions she is not able to complete the lesson on time or to get the results she hoped for.

SCENARIO 2: HIGH SCHOOL BIOLOGY

The Class

Mr. Platt teaches advanced placement classes in biology to students from middle- to upper-income families. Most of the students have already made plans for going to college. When the students enter the classroom, they know they are to go to their assigned seats and write out answers to the questions of the day that Mr. Platt has written on the board. After that, Mr. Platt lectures on text material that he assigned students to read before coming to class. During the lecture, he calls randomly on students to answer questions and requires that they support their answers with reference to the assigned reading. Following the lecture, students engage in lab activity for the remainder of the period.

Typical Occurrences

Mr. Platt has begun his lecture on the process of photosynthesis. He asks Arlene what the word *photosynthesis* means. She pushes her long hair aside and replies, "I don't get it." This is a comment Mr. Platt hears frequently from Arlene.

"What is it you don't understand?"

"None of it."

Mr. Platt snaps, "Be more specific! I've only asked for the definition!"

Arlene is not intimidated. "I mean, I don't get any of it. I don't understand why plants are green. Why aren't they blue or some other color? Why don't they grow on Mercury? The book says plants make food. How? Do they make Twinkies? That's ridiculous. I don't understand the point of photosynthesis."

Mr. Platt stares at Arlene for a while, and she back at him. He asks, "Are you finished?"

Arlene shrugs. "I guess so." She hears some of the boys whistle under their breath; she enjoys their obvious admiration.

Mr. Platt says to her, "Arlene, I hope some day you will understand that this is not a place for you to show off."

"I hope so, too," Arlene says. "I know I should be more serious." She stares out the window.

For the remainder of the lecture, delivered in an icy tone of voice, Mr. Platt calls only on students he knows will give correct answers.

His lecture completed, Mr. Platt begins to give instructions for lab activity. He notices that Nick is turning the valve of the gas jet on and off. He says to Nick, "Mr. Turner, would you please repeat the rule about the use of lab equipment?"

Nick drops his head and mumbles something about waiting for directions. Arlene says calmly, "Knock it off, Nick. This is serious business." She smiles at Mr. Platt.

Mr. Platt stares at the class for a moment, then completes his directions and tells them to begin. He walks around the room, monitoring their work. He stands behind lab partners Sherry and Dawn, who are having a difficult time. He does not offer them help, believing that advanced placement students should be able to work things out for themselves. But as they blunder through the activity, he shakes his head in disbelief, leaving the strong impression that he hopes the two girls will drop the class.

SCENARIO 3: MIDDLE SCHOOL LIBRARY

Setting and Students

Mrs. Daniels is a media specialist in charge of the middle school library. She sees her job as serving as resource person to students who are seeking information and is always eager to give help to those who request it. The students in her school are characterized as lower middle class. About half are white, the remainder African American, Latino, and Southeast Asian. Each period of the day differs as to the number and type of students who come under Mrs. Daniels's direction. Usually, small groups have been sent there to do cooperative research. Always some unexpected students appear who have been excused from physical education for medical reasons but who hate to be sent to the library, or else they bear special passes from their teachers for a variety of purposes.

Typical Occurrences

Mrs. Daniels has succeeded in getting students settled and working when Tara appears at her side, needing a book to read as makeup work for missing class. Mrs. Daniels asks Tara what kinds of books interest her. Tara sullenly shrugs her shoulders. Mrs. Daniels takes her to a shelf of newly published books. "I read this one last night," she says. "I think you might like it. It's a good story and fast reading."

Tara only glances at it. "That looks stupid," she says. "Don't you have any good books?" She glances down the shelf. "These are all stupid!"

Another student, James, is tugging at Mrs. Daniels's elbow, with a note from his history teacher, who wants the source of a particular quotation. Mrs. Daniels asks Tara to look at the books for a moment while she takes James to the reference books.

As Mrs. Daniels passes a table of students supposedly doing research, she notices that the group is watching Walter and Tim have a friendly pencil fight, hitting pencils together until one of them breaks. She admonishes Walter, who appears to be the more willing participant. Walter answers hotly, "Tim started it! It wasn't me!"

"Well," Mrs. Daniels replies, "if you can't behave yourself, just go back to your class." The other students laugh at Walter, who feels he has been treated unjustly. He sits down and pouts.

Meanwhile, Tara has gone to the large globe and is twirling it. Mrs. Daniels starts to speak to her but realizes that James is still waiting at her shoulder with the request for his teacher.

Somehow, before the period ends, Tara leaves with a book she doesn't want and James takes a citation back to his teacher. The research groups have been too noisy. Mrs. Daniels knows they have done little work and wonders if she should speak to their teacher about the students' manners and courtesy. After the period finally ends, Mrs. Daniels notices that profane remarks have been written on the table where Walter was sitting.

SCENARIO 4: SECOND GRADE

The Class

Mrs. Desmond teaches second graders in a highly transient neighborhood. She receives an average of one new student each week, and those students typically remain in her class for fairly short lengths of time before moving elsewhere. Most are from single-parent, dysfunctional homes, and their poor behavior, including aggression, boisterousness, and crying, seems to reflect many emotional problems.

Typical Occurrences

The morning bell rings, and students who have been lined up outside by an aide enter the classroom noisily. Mrs. Desmond is speaking with a parent who is complaining that her son is being picked on by others in the class. When finally able to give attention to the class, Mrs. Desmond sees that Ricky and Raymond have crawled underneath the reading table, while a group of excited children is clustered around Shawon who has brought his new hamster to share with the class. Two girls are pulling at Mrs. Desmond's sleeves, trying to give her a note and lunch money. Mrs. Desmond has to shout above the din before she can finally get everyone seated. Several minutes have passed since the bell rang.

Mrs. Desmond, having lost much of her composure, finally gets the reading groups started when she suddenly realizes that the assembly scheduled for that morning has slipped her mind. She suddenly stands up from her reading group and exclaims, "We have an assembly this morning! Put down your books and get lined up quickly! We are almost late!"

Thirty-one students make a burst for the door, pushing and arguing. Rachael, a big, strong girl, shoves Amy and shouts, "Hey, get out of the way, stupid!"

Amy, meek and retiring, begins to cry. Mrs. Desmond tries to comfort Amy while Rachael pushes her way to the front of the line.

During the assembly, Ricky and Raymond sit together. They have brought some baseball cards and are entertaining the students seated around them. When the first part of the assembly performance is over, they boo loudly and laugh instead of applaud. Under the school principal's disapproving eye, Mrs. Desmond separates Ricky and Raymond, but for the rest of the performance they make silly faces and gestures to each other, causing other students to laugh.

Upon returning to the classroom, Mrs. Desmond, certain that the principal will speak to her about her class's behavior, tries to talk with them about the impropriety of their actions. She attempts to elicit positive comments about the assembly, but several students say it was dumb and boring.

The discussion has made little progress before time for recess. Mrs. Desmond sighs and directs the students to line up, ordering them sternly to use their best manners. As they wait at the door, Rachael is once again shoving her way to the head of the line.

SCENARIO 5: HIGH SCHOOL SPECIAL EDUCATION

The Class

Mrs. Reed teaches special education English to high school students, all of whom have a history of poor academic performance, though some seem to her to have at least average intelligence. Some of the students have been diagnosed as learning disabled. For others, no specific learning difficulties have been identified. Several live in foster homes. About one-third are Latinos bused from a distant neighborhood. Some of the students are known to be affiliated with gangs.

Typical Occurrences

The students enter the classroom lethargically, find their seats, and as directed, most of them begin copying an assignment from the board. Something is going on between Lisa and Jill, who shoot hateful glances at each other. Neither begins work.

When the students are settled, Mrs. Reed reviews the previous day's lesson and then begins instruction on how to write a business letter. She asks the class to turn to an example in their textbooks. Five of the fourteen students do not have their books with them, though this is a requirement that is repeated almost daily. Students without books are penalized points that detract from their course grade.

Mrs. Reed sees that Lisa has her book and asks her to open it to the correct page. Lisa shakes her head and puts her head down on the desk. Mrs. Reed gives her the option of time out. Lisa leaves the room and sits by herself at a table outside the door.

Mrs. Reed goes on with the lesson. She asks the students to work in pairs to write a letter canceling a magazine subscription and requesting a refund. She lets them pick their own partners but finds after a while that several students have formed no partnerships.

Lisa's absence leaves an odd number of students. Jill asks if she can work by herself. Mrs. Reed grants her request, but Jill spends most of her time glancing back at Lisa.

Two other girls, Marcia and Connie, have taken out mirrors and are applying makeup instead of working on their assignment. Mrs. Reed informs them that she intends to call on them first to share their letter with the class.

After the allotted work time, Mrs. Reed asks for volunteers to read their letters. With prodding, a pair of boys is first to share. Mrs. Reed then calls on Marcia and Connie. They complain that they didn't understand how to do the assignment. Mrs. Reed tells them they must complete the letter for homework. They agree, but Mrs. Reed knows they will not comply and expects them to be absent the next day.

Other students read their letters. Some are good; others contain many mistakes. The students do not seem to differentiate between correct and incorrect business letter forms. Mrs. Reed tries to point out strengths and weaknesses in the work, but the class applauds and makes smart-aleck remarks impartially.

At the end of the period, Mrs. Reed, intending that the students refine their work the next day, asks the students to turn in their letters. She finds that two papers are missing and that Juan and Marco have written on theirs numerous A+ symbols and gang-related graffiti.

SCENARIO 6: CONTINUATION HIGH SCHOOL PHOTOGRAPHY LAB

The Class

Mr. Carnett teaches photography lab, an elective class, in a continuation high school attended by students who have been unsuccessful for behavioral reasons in regular high school settings. Many of the students want to attend this particular school, as it is located in what they consider their turf. Some of the students are chemically dependent and/or come from dysfunctional homes. The photography lab class enrolls 18 students, all of whom are on individual study contracts.

Typical Occurrences

As students begin work, Mr. Carnett busies himself with a number of different tasks: setting out needed materials, giving advice on procedures, handing out quizzes for students who have completed contracts, examining photographs, and so forth. He sees Tony sitting and staring into space. He asks Tony if he needs help. Tony shrugs. Mr. Carnett asks if Tony has brought his materials to work on. Tony shakes his head. Mr. Carnett tells Tony he can start on a new part of his contract. Tony doesn't answer. Mr. Carnett asks what's the matter. When Tony doesn't respond, Mike mutters, "He's blasted out of his head, man."

At that moment, Mr. Carnett hears heated words coming from the darkroom. He enters and finds two students squaring off, trying to stare each other down. He asks what the problem is but gets no reply. He tells the boys to leave the darkroom and go back to their seats. They ignore him. As tension grows, another student intervenes and says, "Come on, we can settle it later. Be cool." Mr. Carnett calls the office and informs the counselor of the incident. The boys involved hear him do so and gaze at him insolently.

The class settles back to work, and for the remainder of the period Mr. Carnett circulates among them, providing assistance, stifling horseplay, urging that they move ahead in their contracts, and reminding everyone that they only have a limited amount of time in which to get their work done. From time to time he glances at Tony, who does no work during the period. He asks Tony if something is bothering him. Tony shakes his head. Mr. Carnett asks Tony if he wants to transfer out of the class, since it is elective. Tony says, "No, man, I like it here."

"That's fine," Mr. Carnett says. "But this is not dream time. You do your work, or else we will find you another class. You understand?"

"Sure, man. I understand."

Mr. Carnett turns away, but from the corner of his eye he is sure that he sees Tony's middle finger aimed in his direction.

SCENARIO 7: SHELTERED ENGLISH KINDERGARTEN

The Class

Mrs. Bates teaches a sheltered English kindergarten class comprised of 30 students, only 7 of whom speak English at home. The ethnic/racial makeup of the class is a mixture of Vietnamese, Laotian, Chinese, Samoan, Iranian, Latino, Filipino, African American, and Caucasian. The emphasis of the class is rapid English language development. For the most part, the students work in small groups, each of which is directed by a teacher, aide, or parent volunteer. The groups rotate every half hour so as to have a variety of experiences.

Typical Occurrences

Shortly before school begins, a new girl, Mei, is brought into the class. She speaks very little English and is crying. She tries to run out of the classroom but is stopped by the aide. When Mrs. Bates rings her bell, the students know they are to sit on the rug, but those already at the play area do not want to do so. Mrs. Bates calls them three or four times, but finally she has to get up and physically bring two of them to the rug.

As the opening activities proceed, Mrs. Bates repeatedly asks students to sit up. (They have begun rolling around on the floor.) Kinney is pestering the girl seated next to him. Twice Mrs. Bates asks him to stop. Finally, she sends him to sit in a chair outside the group. He has to sit there until the opening activities are finished, then he can rejoin his group for the first rotation at the art table.

As soon as the groups get under way, Mrs. Bates hears a ruckus at the art table, which is under the guidance of Mrs. García, a parent volunteer. She sees that Kinney has scooped up finger paint and is making motions as if to paint one of the girls, who runs away from him. Mrs. García tells him to put the paint down.

Kinney, who speaks English, replies, "Shut up, you big fat rat's ass!"

Mrs. Bates leaves her group and goes to Kinney. She tells him, "You need time out in Mrs. Sayres' room (a first-grade next door to Mrs. Bates's kindergarten)."

Kinney, his hand covered with blue paint, drops to the floor and refuses to move. He calls Mrs. Bates foul names. Mrs. Bates leaves him there, goes to the phone, and calls the office for assistance. Kinney gets up, wipes his hand first on a desk and then on himself, and runs out the door. He stops beside the entrance to Mrs. Sayres's room, and when Mrs. Bates follows he goes inside and sits at a designated table without further resistance.

Mrs. Bates returns to her group, comprised mostly of Asian students. They sit quietly and attentively but do not speak. Mrs. Bates is using a Big Book on an easel, trying to get the students to repeat the words she says, but she has little success.

When it is time for the next rotation, Mrs. Bates goes quickly to Mrs. Sayres's room and brings Kinney back to the class. He rejoins his group. As Mrs. Bates begins work with her new group, she sees Ryan and Duy at the measuring table pouring birdseed on each other's heads. Meanwhile, the new girl, Mei, continues sobbing audibly.

SCENARIO 8: JUNIOR HIGH WORLD HISTORY

The Class

Mr. Jaramillo's third-period world history class is attended by students whose achievement levels are average to below average. He paces his work slowly and keeps it simple. For the most part he enjoys the class, finding the students interesting and energetic.

Mr. Jaramillo's lessons follow a consistent pattern. For the first part of the period, students take turns reading aloud from the textbook. Mr. Jaramillo selects the student readers at random from cards with students' names on them. If a student who is called on has lost the place in the textbook or is unable to answer a question about material read by the previous reader, the student loses a point, which affects the final grade.

For the second part of the period, the class is divided into work groups. Each group selects a portion from the text reading and uses the information it contains as the basis for making something creative, such as group posters, to be shared at the end of the class if time allows.

Typical Occurrences

During oral reading, Mr. Jaramillo calls on Hillary to read. Although she has been following along, she shakes her head. This has happened several times before. Mr. Jaramillo, not wanting to hurt Hillary's feelings, simply says, "That costs you a point, Hillary," and he calls on someone else.

Unfortunately, Hillary's reluctance carries over into group work as well, in which she refuses to participate. The other students ignore her and complete the work without her involvement. Occasionally, Clarisse refuses to involve herself in group work as well. When Mr. Jaramillo speaks to her about it, she replies, "You don't make Hillary do it."

Mr. Jaramillo answers, "Look, we are talking about you, not about Hillary." However, he lets the matter lie there and says no more if Clarisse doesn't participate.

On this particular day, Deonne has come into the classroom looking very angry. He slams his pack down on his desk and sits without opening his textbook for reading. Although Mr. Jaramillo picks Deonne's card from the deck, he recognizes Deonne's mood and decides not to call on him.

Will is in an opposite mood. Throughout the oral reading portion of the class, he continually giggles at every mispronounced word and at every reply students give to Mr. Jaramillo's questions. Will sits in the front row and turns around to laugh, seeing if he can get anyone else to laugh with him. Although most students either ignore him or give him disgusted looks, he keeps laughing. Mr. Jaramillo finally asks him what is so funny. Will replies, "Nothing," and looks back at the class and laughs.

At the end of the period, there is time for sharing three posters. Will makes comments and giggles about each of them. Clarisse, who has not participated, says, "Will, how about shutting up!"

As the students leave the room, Mr. Jaramillo takes Deonne aside. "What's the matter with you, Deonne?" he asks.

"Nothing," Deonne replies with clenched jaw as he strides past Mr. Jaramillo.

SCENARIO 9: HIGH SCHOOL AMERICAN LITERATURE

The Class

Mr. Wong teaches an 11th-grade one-semester course in American literature. The course is required for graduation. Among Mr. Wong's 33 students are 8 seniors who failed the course previously and are retaking it. The students at Mr. Wong's school are from middle-class affluent families, and many of them are highly motivated academically. At the same time, there is also a significant number who have little interest in school aside from the opportunity to be with their friends.

Mr. Wong's teaching routine proceeds as follows: First, he begins the period with a three-question quiz over assigned reading. The quiz items focus on facts such as names, places, and description of plot. Second, when the quiz papers are collected, Mr. Wong conducts a question-and-discussion session about the assigned reading. He calls on individual students, many of whom answer, "I don't know." Third, Mr. Wong has the class begin reading a new chapter in the work under study. They take turns reading orally until the end of the period. The remainder of the assignment not read orally is to be completed as homework.

A Typical Occurrence

The students enter Mr. Wong's classroom lethargically and begin taking the quiz from questions written on the board. Mr. Wong notices that many of the answers are obvious guesses. He notices Brian in particular, who has already failed the class and must pass it now in order to graduate. Mr. Wong says, "Didn't any of you read your assignment?"

When oral reading begins, Mr. Wong notices that Brian does not have his copy of *Huckleberry Finn*, the work being studied. This is nothing new. Mr. Wong lends Brian a copy. Brian follows along in the reading for a while, then begins doodling on a sheet of paper. Mr. Wong calls on Brian to read. Brian cannot find the place.

Mr. Wong says, "Brian, this is simply unacceptable. You have failed the class once; fail it again now and you know you don't graduate."

Brian does not look up but says, "Want to make a bet on that?"

"What?"

"I guarantee you I'll graduate."

"Not without summer school, you won't!"

"That's okay by me. That will be better. This class is too boring, and the assignments are too long. I've got other things to do besides read this stupid story. Who cares about this anyway? Why can't we read something that has to do with real life?"

Mr. Wong, offended, replies, "You couldn't be more wrong! Other students enjoy this work, and it is one of the greatest books in American literature! There is nothing wrong with the book! What's wrong, Brian, is your attitude!"

Brian's eyes are hot, but he says nothing further. His book remains closed. Mr. Wong struggles through the final 10 minutes of class. Brian is first out of the room when the bell rings.

SCENARIO 10: SIXTH GRADE, STUDENT TEACHER

The Class

Denise Thorpe is a student teacher in an inner-city magnet school that emphasizes academics. Half of her students are African American, and the other half, of various ethnic groups, have been bused in to take advantage of the instructional program and rich resources. All are academically talented, and none has what would be called a bad attitude toward school.

Mrs. Warde, the regular teacher of the class, does not seem to rely on any particular scheme of management or discipline, at least none obvious to Miss Thorpe. Mrs. Warde simply tells the students what to do and they comply.

For the first few lessons that Miss Thorpe teaches, Mrs. Warde remains in the room, acting the role of aide to Miss Thorpe. The students work well as always, and Miss Thorpe feels happy and successful.

When Mrs. Warde Leaves the Room

Mrs. Warde tells Miss Thorpe that she will leave the room during the math lesson so that Miss Thorpe can begin getting the feel of directing the class on her own. Mrs. Warde warns her that the class might test her with a bit of naughtiness, though nothing serious is likely to occur. Just be in charge, Mrs. Warde counsels.

The math lesson begins well, without incident. The lesson has to do with beginning algebra concepts, which Miss Thorpe approaches through a discovery mode. She tells the class, "I want you to work independently on this. Think your way through the following equations and decide if they are true for all numbers."

$$a + 0 = a$$
$$a + b = b + a$$
$$a(b + c) = ab + c$$
$$a + 1 = 1$$
$$a \times 0 = a$$

The students begin work, but within two minutes hands are shooting up. Miss Thorpe goes to help Alicia, who is stuck on the third equation. "What's the matter?" Miss Thorpe whispers.

"I don't understand what this means."

"It was like what I showed you on the board. The same."

"Those were numbers. I don't understand these letters."

"They are the same as the numbers. They take the place of the numbers. I showed you how they were interchangeable, remember? Go ahead, let me see. Tell me what you are doing, step-by-step."

Miss Thorpe does not realize it, but she has spent almost five minutes with Alicia. Meanwhile, a few of the students have finished and are waiting, but most are holding tired arms limply in the air. Miss Thorpe rushes to the next student and repeats her questioning tutorial.

Meanwhile, Matt and Alonzo have dropped their hands and are looking at each other's papers. They begin to talk, then laugh. Others follow, and soon all work has stopped and the classroom has become quite noisy.

Miss Thorpe repeatedly says, "Shhh, shhh!" but with little effect. At last she goes to the front of the room, demands attention, and tells the class how disappointed she is in their rude behavior.

Comprehensive List
of Concepts
in Classroom Discipline

ability to choose

ability to compliment genuinely

ability to listen

acceptance and acknowledgment

accountability

acknowledgment responses

action

active listening

activity movement

activity reinforcers

administrative support

advising

agreement with put-downs

alerting

alternatives to punishment

analyzing

antecedents

appreciative praise

assertive response style

assertive teacher

authority

authority C

authority E

authority J

authority P

autocratic teacher

aversive discipline

aversive stimulus

backup systems

behaviorally at risk

behavior contracts

behavior modification

behavior shaping

behavior window

belonging

body carriage

body language

boss teacher

caretakers

catch 'em being good

challenge arousal

change of valence

choosing

clarity

Bibliography

Albert, L. (1989). *Cooperative discipline: How to manage your classroom and promote self-esteem.* Circle Pines, MN: American Guidance Service.

———. (1996). *A teacher's guide to cooperative discipline* (rev. ed.). Circle Pines, MN: American Guidance Service. (Original work published 1989)

Angell, A. (1991). Democratic climates in elementary classrooms: A review of theory and research. *Theory and Research in Social Education, 19,* 241–266.

Augustine, D., Gruber, K., & Hanson, L. (1990). Cooperation works! *Educational Leadership, 47,* 4–7.

Banbury, M., & Hebert, C. (1992). Do you see what I mean? Body language in classroom interactions. *Teaching Exceptional Children, 24,* 24–28.

Bartell, J. (1992). Starting from scratch. *Principal, 72,* 13–14.

Blendinger, J., et al. (1993). *Win-win discipline.* Bloomington, IN: Phi Delta Kappa Educational Foundation.

Boothe, J., et al. (1993). The violence at your door. *Executive Educator, 15* (1), 16–22.

Brophy, J. (1987). Synthesis on strategies for motivating students to learn. *Educational Leadership, 45,* 40–48.

Brophy, J., & Putnam, J. (1979). Classroom management in the elementary school. In D. L. Duke (Ed.), *Classroom management: The seventy-eighth yearbook of the National Society for the Study of Education* (pp. 182–216). Chicago: University of Chicago Press.

Burke, K. (1992). *What to do with the kid who. . . : Developing cooperation, self-discipline, and responsibility in the classroom.* Palatine, IL: IRI/Skylight.

Cangelosi, J. (1993). *Classroom management strategies: Gaining and maintaining students' cooperation* (2nd ed.). White Plains, NY: Longman.

Canter, L. (1976). *Assertive Discipline: A take-charge approach for today's educator.* Seal Beach, CA: Canter & Associates.

———. (1978). Be an assertive teacher. *Instructor, 88*(1), 60.

———. (1988). Let the educator beware: A response to Curwin and Mendler. *Educational Leadership, 46*(2), 71–73.

Canter, L., & Canter, M. (1986). *Assertive Discipline Phase 2 in-service media package* [Videotapes and manuals]. Santa Monica, CA: Canter & Associates.

———. (1989). *Assertive Discipline for secondary school educators: In-service video package and leader's manual.* Santa Monica, CA: Canter & Associates.

———. (1992). *Assertive Discipline: Positive behavior management for today's classroom* (2nd ed.). Santa Monica, CA: Canter & Associates.

———. (1993). *Succeeding with difficult students: New strategies for reaching your most challenging students.* Santa Monica, CA: Canter & Associates.

Cawthorne, B. (1981). *Instant success for classroom teachers, new and substitute teachers in grades K through 8.* Scottsdale, AZ: Greenfield.

Charles, C., & Senter, G. (1995). *Elementary classroom management* (2nd ed.). White Plains, NY: Longman.

Corno, L. (1992). Encouraging students to take responsibility for learning and performance. *Elementary School Journal, 93*, 69–83.

Curwin, R. (1980). Are your students addicted to praise? *Instructor, 90*, 61–62.

———. (1992). *Rediscovering hope: Our greatest teaching strategy.* Bloomington, IN: National Educational Service.

———. (1993). The healing power of altruism. *Educational Leadership, 51*(3), 36–39.

Curwin, R., & Mendler, A. (1980). *The discipline book: A complete guide to school and classroom management.* Reston, VA: Reston Publishing.

———. (1984). High standards for effective discipline. *Educational Leadership, 41*(8), 75–76.

———. (1988a). *Discipline with dignity.* Alexandria, VA: Association for Supervision and Curriculum Development.

———. (1988b). Packaged discipline programs: Let the buyer beware. *Educational Leadership, 46*(2), 68–71.

———. (1989). We repeat, let the buyer beware: A response to Canter. *Educational Leadership, 46*(6), 83.

———. (1992). *Discipline with dignity* [Workshop participants handout]. Rochester, NY: Discipline Associates.

Dewey, J. (1938). *Logic: The theory of inquiry.* New York: Holt, Rinehart & Winston.

Dreikurs, R. (1968). *Psychology in the classroom* (2nd ed.). New York: Harper & Row.

Dreikurs, R., & Cassel, P. (1972). *Discipline without tears.* New York: Hawthorn.

Dreikurs, R., Grunwald, B., & Pepper, F. (1982). *Maintaining sanity in the classroom.* New York: Harper & Row.

Elam, S. (1989). The second Gallup/Phi Delta Kappa poll of teachers' attitudes toward the public schools. *Phi Delta Kappan, 70*(10), 785–798.

Elam, S., Rose, L., & Gallup, A. (1994). The 26th annual Phi Delta Kappa/Gallup Poll of the public's attitudes toward the public schools. *Phi Delta Kappan, 76* (1), 41–56.

Emmer, E., Evertson, C., & Anderson, L. (1980). Effective classroom management at the beginning of the school year. *Elementary School Journal, 80*, 219–231.

Evertson, C. (1989a). Classroom organization and management. In M. Reynolds (Ed.), *Knowledge base for the beginning teacher.* Oxford: Pergamon Press.

———. (1989b). Improving elementary classroom management: A school-based training program for beginning the year. *Journal of Educational Research, 83*, 82–90.

Evertson, C., Emmer, E., Clements, B., Sanford, J., & Worsham, M. (1989). *Classroom management for elementary teachers*. Englewood Cliffs, NJ: Prentice-Hall.

Evertson, C., & Harris, A. (1992). What we know about managing classrooms. *Educational Leadership, 49*(7), 74–78.

Firth, G. (1985). *Behavior management in the schools: A primer for parents*. New York: Charles C. Thomas.

Fraser, B., & O'Brien, P. (1985). Student and teacher perceptions of the environment of elementary school classrooms. *Elementary School Journal, 85*(5), 567–580.

Gaustad, J. (1992). *School discipline* (ERIC Digest No. 78). Eugene, OR: ERIC Clearinghouse on Educational Management.

Ginott, H. (1965). *Between parent and child*. New York: Avon.

———. (1969). *Between parent and teenager*. New York: Macmillan.

———. (1971). *Teacher and child*. New York: Macmillan.

———. (1972). I am angry! I am appalled! I am furious! *Today's Education, 61*, 23–24.

———. (1973). Driving children sane. *Today's Education, 62*, 20–25.

Glasser, W. (1965). *Reality therapy: A new approach to psychiatry*. New York: Harper & Row.

———. (1969). *Schools without failure*. New York: Harper & Row.

———. (1977). 10 steps to good discipline. *Today's Education, 66*, 60–63.

———. (1978). Disorders in our schools: Causes and remedies. *Phi Delta Kappan, 59*, 331–333.

———. (1985). *Control theory: A new explanation of how we control our lives*. New York: Perennial Library.

———. (1986). *Control theory in the classroom*. New York: Harper & Row.

———. (1990). *The quality school: Managing students without coercion*. New York: Harper & Row. (Reissued with additional material in 1992)

———. (1992). The quality school curriculum. *Phi Delta Kappan, 73*(9), 690–694.

———. (1993). *The quality school teacher*. New York: Harper Perennial.

Gordon, T. (1970). *Parent Effectiveness Training: A tested new way to raise responsible children*. New York: New American Library.

———. (1974). *T.E.T.: Teacher Effectiveness Training*. David McKay.

———. (1976). *P.E.T. in action*. New York: Bantam Books.

———. (1989). *Discipline that works: Promoting self-discipline in children*. New York: Random House.

Grant, C., & Sleeter, C. (1989). *Turning on learning: Five approaches for multicultural teaching plans for race, class, gender, and disability*. Columbus, OH: Merrill.

Hakim, L. (1993). *Conflict resolution in the schools*. San Rafael, CA: Human Rights Resource Center.

Hartzell, G., & Petrie, T. (1992). The principal and discipline: Working with school structures, teachers, and students. *Clearing House, 65*(6), 376–380.

Hernandez, H. (1989). *Multicultural education: A teacher's guide to content and process*. Columbus, OH: Merrill.

Hill, D. (1990). Order in the classroom. *Teacher Magazine, 1*(7), 70–77.

Hughes, H. (1994, February). *From fistfights to gunfights: Preparing teachers and administrators to cope with violence in school*. Paper presented at the annual meeting of the American Association of Colleges for Teacher Education, Chicago.

Jones, F. (1979). The gentle art of classroom discipline. *National Elementary Principal, 58*, 26–32.

———. (1987a). *Positive classroom discipline*. New York: McGraw-Hill.

————. (1987b). *Positive classroom instruction*. New York: McGraw-Hill.

Jones, J. (1993a). *Instructor's guide: Positive classroom discipline—a video course of study*. Santa Cruz, CA: Fredric H. Jones & Associates.

————. (1993b). *Instructor's guide: Positive classroom instruction—a video course of study*. Santa Cruz, CA: Fredric H. Jones & Associates.

Jones, V., & Jones, L. (1990). *Comprehensive classroom management: Motivating and managing students*. Needham Heights, MA: Allyn & Bacon.

Knapp, M., Turnbull, B., & Shields, P. (1990). New directions for educating the children of poverty. *Educational Leadership, 48*(4), 1–8.

Kohn, A. (1993). *Punished by rewards: The trouble with gold stars, incentive plans, A's, praise, and other bribes*. Boston: Houghton Mifflin.

Kounin, J. (1977). *Discipline and group management in classrooms* (rev. ed.). New York: Holt, Rinehart & Winston. (Original work published 1971)

Kramer, P. (1992). Fostering self-esteem can keep kids safe and sound. *PTA Today, 17*(6), 10–11.

Ladoucer, R., & Armstrong, J. (1983). Evaluation of a behavioral program for the improvement of grades among high school students. *Journal of Counseling Psychology, 30*, 100–103.

Landen, W. (1992). Violence and our schools: What can we do? *Updating School Board Policies, 23*, 1–5.

Latham, G. (1993). *Managing the classroom environment to facilitate effective instruction* [Six-part videotape in-service training program]. Logan, UT: P & T Ink.

Macht, J. (1989). *Managing classroom behavior: An ecological approach to academic and social learning*. White Plains, NY: Longman.

Mahoney, M., & Thoresen, C. (1972). Behavioral self-control—Power to the person. *Educational Researcher, 1*, 5–7.

Markoff, A. (1992). *Within reach: Academic achievement through parent-teacher communication*. Novato, CA: Academic Therapy Publications.

McCormack, S. (1989). Response to Render, Padilla, and Krank: But practitioners say it works! *Educational Leadership, 46*(6), 77–79.

McIntyre, T. (1989). *The behavior management handbook: Setting up effective behavior management systems*. Boston: Allyn & Bacon.

Mendler, A., & Curwin, R. (1983). *Taking charge in the classroom*. Reston, VA: Reston Publishing.

Morrison, J., Olivos, K., Dominguez, G., Gomez, D., & Lena, D. (1993). The application of family systems approaches to school behavior problems on a school-level discipline board: An outcome study. *Elementary School Guidance and Counseling, 27*(4), 258–272.

Novelli, J. (1990). Design a classroom that works. *Instructor, 100*(1), 24–27.

Office of Educational Research and Improvement. (1993). *Reducing school violence: Schools teaching peace. A joint study* (Report No. RP-91002002). Washington, DC: Author.

Precision teaching in perspective: An interview with Ogden R. Lindsley. (1971). *Teaching Exceptional Children, 3*, 114–119.

Rardin, R. (1978, September). Classroom management made easy. *Virginia Journal of Education*, 14–17.

Redl, F. (1972). *When we deal with children*. New York: Free Press.

Redl, F., & Wattenberg, W. (1959). *Mental hygiene in teaching* (rev. ed.). New York: Harcourt, Brace & World. (Original work published 1951)

Redl, F., & Wineman, D. (1952). *Controls from within*. Glencoe, IL: Free Press.

Render, G., Padilla, J., & Krank, H. (1989). What research really shows about Assertive Discipline. *Educational Leadership, 46*(6), 72–75.

Rich, J. (1992). Predicting and controlling school violence. *Contemporary Education, 64*(1), 35–39.

Rosen, L. (1992). *School discipline practices: A manual for school administrators*. Perrysburg, OH: School Justice Institute.

Schaps, E., & Solomon, D. (1990). Schools and classrooms as caring communities. *Educational Leadership, 48*(3), 38–42.

Schell, L., & Burden, P. (1992). *Countdown to the first day of school: A 60-day get-ready checklist for first-time teachers, teacher transfers, student teachers, teacher mentors, induction-program administrators, teacher educators* (NEA Checklist series). Washington, DC: National Education Association.

Schulman, J. (1989). Blue freeways: Traveling the alternate route with big-city teacher trainees. *Journal of Teacher Education, 40* (5), 2–8.

Schwartz, F. (1981). Supporting or subverting learning: Peer group patterns in four tracked schools. *Anthropology and Education Quarterly, 12*(2), 99–120.

Sharpley, C. (1985). Implicit rewards in the classroom. *Contemporary Educational Psychology, 10,* 349–368.

Sheviakov, G., & Redl, F. (1956). *Discipline for today's children*. Washington, DC: Association for Supervision and Curriculum Development.

Sidman, M. (1989). *Coercion and its fallout*. Boston: Authors Cooperative.

Skinner, B. F. (1948). *Walden two*. New York: Macmillan.

———. (1953). *Science and human behavior*. New York: Macmillan.

———. (1971). *Beyond freedom and dignity*. New York: Knopf.

Slavin, R. (1991). Synthesis of research on cooperative learning. *Educational Leadership, 48,* 71–82.

Slavin, R., Karweit, N., & Madden, N. (1989). *Effective programs for students at risk*. Needham Heights, MA: Allyn & Bacon.

Smith, M. (1993). Some school-based violence prevention strategies. *NASSP Bulletin, 77* (557) 70–75.

Sobol, T. (1990). Understanding diversity. *Educational Leadership, 48*(3), 27–30.

Study backs induction schools to help new teachers stay teachers. (1987). *ASCD Update, 29*(4), 1.

Tauber, R. (1982). Negative reinforcement: A positive strategy in classroom management. *Clearing House, 56,* 64–67.

Wattenberg, W. (1955). *The adolescent years*. New York: Harcourt Brace.

———. (1967). *All men are created equal*. Detroit: Wayne State University Press.

Weade, R., & Evertson, C. (1988). The construction of lessons in effective and less effective classrooms. *Teaching and Teacher Education, 4*(3), 189–213.

Weinstein, C. (1992). Designing the instructional environment: Focus on seating. In *Proceedings of selected research and development presentations at the Convention of the Association for Educational Communications and Technology* (p. 7). *Resources in Education*, Phoenix, AZ: Oryx Press. (ERIC Document Reproduction Service No. IR 015 706).

Williams, S. (1991). We can work it out. *Teacher Magazine, 3*(2), 22–23.

Wong, H., & Wong, R. (1991). *The first days of school: How to be an effective teacher*. Sunnyvale, CA: Harry K. Wong.

Index